AN ABSOLUTE
SECRET

BY

NICHOLAS KINSEY

Printed on acid-free paper
First Printing, October 2017
ISBN 978-0-9952921-2-3

Cinegrafica Films & Publishing
820 Rougemont
Quebec, QC G1X 2M5
Canada
Tel. 418-652-3345

In memory of my mother
Winifred Mary Pryce

FOREWORD

I am a Canadian and British writer and director of film and television drama and this novel started as a television mini-series project in six episodes. Hopefully it will one day become a successful television drama and will be seen around the world, but in the meantime readers can enjoy this great spy thriller in book form. It takes the reader on an exciting ride through wartime intelligence operations when Stockholm was a bourse for foreign intelligence and German war booty.

Solid historical research went into writing this novel, which was inspired by W. Hugh Thomas' investigative work entitled *The Strange Death of Heinrich Himmler*, the 'White Buses' operation organized by Count Folke Bernardotte to save the Scandinavian prisoners of German concentration camps, the secret negotiations between *SS-Brigadeführer* Walter Schellenberg and the Swedish, British and American governments at the end of the war and numerous books on SOE and MI6 operations in Sweden. This novel is based on a lot of well-known facts and, of course, when the facts are not available the writer's job is to invent. This book remains a work of historical fiction.

MAIN CHARACTERS

The British:
Peter Faye, MI6 agent and Consular Services officer
Bridget Potter, Consular Services officer
Bernie Dixon, Legation documents officer
Ewan Butler, SOE officer and press attaché
Joanna Dunn, SOE officer and assistant to Butler
Michael Tennant, SOE officer and press attaché
Sir Victor Mallet, Chief of the British Legation
Anthony Blunt, MI5 officer
Major Keith Linwood, MI6 officer
Jane Archer, Soviet counterintelligence expert
Dorothy Furse, SOE Head of Personnel in London
Mary Butler, Ewan's wife

The Swedes:
Anders Berger, journalist, Stockholms-Tidningen newspaper
Britta, Anders' wife, secretary at the Enskilda Bank
Count Folke Bernadotte, Swedish Red Cross executive
Gustav Lundquist, Stockholms-Tidningen newspaper
Sabrina, Bernie's wife
Aksell, Sabrina's father and music composer
Stefan, photographer, Stockholms-Tidningen newspaper
Vincent Ansell, Swedish trade officer at the British Legation
Magnus, Sabrina's brother and jeweller
Rolf Lagerman, Britta's brother, prisoner in Germany
Ahlman, senior accountant at the Enskilda bank
Ekstrom, freight manager at the Bromma airfield
Akerson, art dealer and businessman
Felix Kersten, physical therapist to Himmler
Colonel Gottfrid Björck, Swedish military man

The Germans & Austrians:
Dr Karl-Heinz Kramer, *Abwehr* spy and press officer
Eva Kramer, Karl-Heinz's wife

Kriminaldirektor Golcher, *Abwehr* station head
Hanne, Austrian Jew and cleaning woman
Nadja, secretary at the German press office
Elsa Ansell, Vincent Ansell's Austrian wife
SS-Brigadeführer Walter Schellenberg, head of *SD Ausland*
'Der Grosse' Federmann, German nightclub owner
Wilhelma, nanny to young Heidi in the Kramer household
Oberleutnant Kemper, informant to Golcher
Gestapo chief Heinrich Müller
Abwehr chief and Admiral Wilhelm Canaris
Obergefreiter Hoffmann, German *Wehrmacht* officer
Hauptman Schultz, Gestapo man
Kriminalinspektor Bauer, Gestapo officer in Stockholm
SS-Reichsführer Heinrich Himmler, head of the RSHA
Hans and Fritz, two young German soldiers

The Soviets:
Soviet Ambassador Alexandra Kollontai
Major Vladimir Petrov, NKVD officer
Evdokia Petrov, NKVD officer and wife to Vladimir
Sasha, NKVD hitman

The Others:
Wanda Hjort, Norwegian social worker
Dr Bjorn Heger, Norwegian medical doctor
Colonel Reino Hallamaa, head of Finnish Radio Intelligence
Wilho Tikander, American OSS station chief in Stockholm
Mads, Finnish adjutant to Colonel Hallamaa
Hendrik, Finnish adjutant to Colonel Hallamaa
Colonel Saarson, Estonian military attaché
General Makoto Onodera, Japanese intelligence officer
GRU, the Soviet military foreign-intelligence service
NKVD, the Soviet secret police service
RTK, the Finnish Intelligence service
Säpo, the Swedish Security service

One

Stockholm, August 1943

A tall, blond intelligence officer with the German *Abwehr* left a reception at the Stockholm Grand Hotel on the arm of an elegant woman, accompanied by a small entourage of thoroughly inebriated German Legation press officers. Together they marched down the hallway towards the exit, singing lewd German songs and brandishing bottles of champagne.

It was a hot summer night as the party left the hotel with its view of the waterfront and the Royal Palace across the strait. A white DKW F8 Cabrio convertible pulled up and a hotel car jockey stepped out, handing the keys to the intelligence officer.

"Gute Nacht, Herr Kramer."

Dr Karl-Heinz Kramer thrust some krona coins into the young man's hand.

"Tack, tack (Thanks).*"*

In different circumstances Karl-Heinz, in a smart double-breasted suit, and Nadja, in a fashionable red evening gown with her hair in waves and curls, would have made a striking couple, but tonight they were as drunk and dishevelled as the others. Nadja slipped into the front seat next to Karl-Heinz

1

while his colleagues piled into the back seat.

A man with a Brownie Hawkeye camera and flashbulb stepped into the road to snap a picture as the DKW convertible took off, but Karl-Heinz just gave him a cheerful wave as he floored the gas pedal and drove away. The photographer swore in frustration and ran towards a waiting car.

Anders Berger tossed his cigarette away and got in behind the wheel as Stefan jumped into the passenger seat. They took off after the Germans. Near the hotel entrance an elegantly-dressed man in a grey fedora watched the journalists leave. He walked to a car parked across the street.

Anders drove at high speed through the dark streets, following the Germans in the white convertible.

"Where do you think they are going?" Anders asked his colleague.

"Who knows? Careful, Anders."

In the rear view mirror Anders noticed a car following them at a distance. The white DKW eventually turned into a park near the canal. Anders stopped his car near the entrance and observed the Germans getting out of their car on a grassy patch near the pier. They stumbled drunkenly towards the water.

Helmut, an athletic-looking young man with a shaved, undercut hairstyle, his fat partner Fritz and skinny consumptive Heinrich followed Karl-Heinz and Nadja towards the pier where several boats were tied up. Nadja struggled to walk in the grass and had to stop to remove her high heels. Karl-Heinz was holding two champagne bottles and some glasses and, by the time Nadja caught up with him, he had managed to fill one of the glasses and was offering it to Helmut.

"Helmut, let's have a drink first."

"I'm ready, Karl-Heinz," Helmut replied.

Nadja reached out and took the glass from Karl-Heinz.

"Go, Helmut," she smiled. "I won't watch."

Karl-Heinz shrugged and filled the glasses of Fritz and Heinrich. The men yelled encouragement as young Helmut stripped naked in the moonlight. Karl-Heinz filled a glass and handed it to Helmut. This time Helmut took it without protest, downing the champagne in an instant and diving naked into the dark water.

On the pier Karl-Heinz and his friends watched for Helmut's bubbles at the surface of the water. The group became more and more nervous as they counted down the minutes.

"Karl-Heinz, some one must go in. Helmut can drown," Nadja insisted after two minutes without any sign of bubbles.

"Not possible. Helmut is a great swimmer," Karl-Heinz said confidently.

"We must do something, Karl-Heinz."

"But Nadja. I can't swim, nor can Heinrich and Fritz is too drunk and maybe a bit too fat. You are our best swimmer."

Nadja couldn't wait any longer. She hurriedly stripped off her dress and stockings revealing large breasts and a strong, muscled body.

"I will hold your bag. Go on now, save our poor Helmut," Karl-Heinz implored Nadja.

Fritz and Heinrich admired Nadja's magnificent hourglass physique in her brassiere and knickers.

Just as Nadja gathered her courage to plunge into the cold water, Helmut emerged silently from the other side of the pier. The men grinned at Helmut.

"Go, Nadja, go," Karl-Heinz said.

Nadja carefully placed her shoes near her clothes and started to position her body, arms and legs together, for a perfect dive into the deep when she noticed Helmut's wet tracks on the pier. She looked up to see Helmut standing naked behind her dripping water.

"Damn you, Karl-Heinz. You tricked me."

The men laughed loudly as Nadja slapped Karl-Heinz, grinning mischievously at her.

"But you are so lovely in your knickers, Nadja."

Fritz handed Helmut a dish towel from the hotel as Nadja put her clothes on. Shivering from the cold, Helmut pulled on his underpants and trousers as Heinrich passed him a flask of schnapps. He took a swig and then put on his shirt and jacket.

To make amends, Karl-Heinz tried to cradle Nadja in his arms, but still fuming from the incident, she pushed him away. Nearby, their colleagues were clowning around on the pier, drinking and singing lusty renditions of German drinking songs.

"Fritz, why don't you go for a swim?" Karl-Heinz asked.

"The only water I like is in my bath, not too cold and not too warm," Fritz said with a laugh.

Karl-Heinz was pouring a drink for Nadja and Helmut when there was a sudden squeal of brakes and they looked up in time to see a car slide to a stop on the grass near the DKW. A man jumped out of the passenger seat and took a picture, the flash bulb momentarily blinding them.

"Those damn journalists again," Fritz shouted. "Let's get their camera and teach them a lesson."

Heinrich, Helmut and Fritz stumbled towards the DKW, but the man with the camera was already getting back into the car. Heinrich pulled out his Luger pistol and took aim.

"*Nicht schießen!*" Karl-Heinz ordered Heinrich not to shoot and ran towards the car. "They are journalists, we can catch them."

Anders accelerated away as Karl-Heinz reached the DKW

and started the engine, waiting impatiently for Nadja and the others to arrive. He then backed up in a hurry and changed gears, flooring the gas pedal as the DKW shot out of the park onto the road in hot pursuit.

"Faster, Karl-Heinz," Fritz yelled.

"Maybe if I shoot at them, they'll stop," Heinrich said.

"I don't want my husband seeing a picture of me in the newspaper, Karl-Heinz," Nadja said with concern. "Offer them money for the film."

"Don't worry, Nadja, we'll get it," Karl-Heinz said.

"If your husband sees the picture, Nadja," Helmut said, "then it will be bye-bye Sweden, hello Russian front for all of us."

"Shoot the tyre," Fritz yelled. "Go on, Heinrich. Let's have some fun."

Heinrich leaned out the window as the cars headed into a curve overlooking a Stockholm canal. He fired twice and one of the tyres exploded.

In the journalist's car Anders heard the shots and the car jerked to the left and then to the right.

"Damn, those Nazi bastards are shooting at us. I think they punctured a tyre," Anders said.

Anders lost control in the curve and ran off the road into the canal with a huge splash. The car filled quickly with water and started to sink. Anders and Stefan struggled to climb clear of the car through the open windows. They paddled toward the shore. On the road they could see Karl-Heinz and his friends in the convertible slow down to watch them swimming to shore.

It had been an interesting evening, Peter Faye thought as they pulled up beside the canal in the British Legation car. In a dark suit and grey fedora, Faye got out of the car and looked down at the canal. The driver, a squat fireplug of a man with a receding hairline, laughed at the men in the water.

"Gawd blimey," Bernie Dixon said, "these blokes just love a dip in the bleedin' canal."

Faye watched the Swedish journalists coming ashore. They had been parked across the street from the hotel and had seen the Germans driving away with the journalists in hot pursuit. They'd been following them ever since.

Faye jumped down onto the rocks. There was a jauntiness about his movements as he scrambled towards the two journalists. The photographer held a camera to his chest, dripping water and looking disgruntled.

"Everybody all right?" Peter asked.

"Yes, we are fine. Thank you," Anders said, shaking the water from his hat.

"I saw you go off the road. I thought you might need some help."

"You are British, I think?"

"Yes, I am."

"Can you give us a lift back to town?"

"Of course."

Bernie arrived from the car with two woolen blankets and handed them to the wet journalists who quickly wrapped themselves in them.

On the way Peter offered the two men cigarettes as they sat shivering in the back of the car.

"We are journalists. I am Anders, this is Stefan. You are with the British Legation?"

"Yes. What happened back there?" Peter asked.

"Our fault, I'm afraid. We got into a race with a German DKW and lost."

"Which paper do you work for?" Peter asked.

"Stockholms-Tidningen."

"You are working very late."

"A special assignment. And you?" Anders asked as he looked at Peter with a curious expression.

"Coming home from a party."

"That's funny."

"What is funny?"

"I saw someone just like you about an hour ago at the Grand Hotel."

"Must have been someone else, I'm afraid."

"It's possible," Anders said with a smile.

The car pulled up near the Grand Hotel and the two Swedes got out.

"Well, thank you for the lift."

"Pleasure to be of some help. Good night."

"Good night."

As Peter's car pulled away, Stefan turned to Anders.

"Damn, what are we going to do now?" Stefan asked, looking totally discouraged. "The camera is soaked. I am sure the pictures are spoiled."

Anders took out his cigarettes and was about to light up when he noticed they were damp from the canal. He put them back in his pocket as he thought about the presence of a British diplomat arriving so suddenly on the scene of the accident.

"It is not a complete loss, Stefan. I may have another story."

Two

It was either very late at night or very early in the morning, depending on how you looked at it. Peter was leaning on the front fender of the car while Bernie napped behind the wheel. They had hidden the car in a copse of trees in the Stockholm suburb of Stora Essingen. From where he was standing, Faye could see Karl-Heinz's DKW parked in front of an elegant yellow brick house with a red tiled roof. In spite of the hour, there was a light on in the first floor window.

A German staff car arrived and pulled in behind the DKW. A messenger got out and went to the door, knocking three times. He waited silently until Karl-Heinz appeared at the door in a dressing gown. Karl-Heinz took the package from the messenger and then stepped back inside turning off the light.

Peter watched the staff car pull away. A moment later a light came on in a window on the second floor. A shadow passed in front of the light and then disappeared. It was time to go home, Peter thought as he approached the driver's window shaking Bernie awake.

"Let's go," Peter said.

"Righto," Bernie groaned.

Peter went around the car and opened the passenger door as Bernie started the engine.

The Consular Services office at the British Legation was divided into a public area with a counter where Swedish citizens and foreign tourists could fill out visa applications to visit Britain or British citizens could apply for a passport, and a private area where the applications were filed. A young man named Sigge was talking to a woman at the front desk, but otherwise there were few clients. With the war at its apogee Britain was not a particularly attractive tourist destination.

"That's my desk you are sitting at," Bridget Potter said indignantly as she entered the office.

Peter looked up, startled. The young woman standing before him was dark-haired and tanned, her colouring nicely set off by the summer dress she wore. Peter collected his wits and got to his feet.

"I'm sorry," he said, "I was typing a report."

"I can see that, but you're sitting at my desk."

"You must be Miss Potter?"

"And you must be the new bloke?"

"Miss Potter. I'm Peter Faye, the new bloke as you put it."

"So you are."

Peter found himself staring at her. She was pretty in an unconventional way, quite tall, and her belted summer dress accentuated her slim figure. She appeared to be in her late twenties. Even with little or no makeup, Peter thought she looked very glamorous for such a humdrum job.

"I still need my desk," she said with a smile.

"Oh, of course," Peter flushed with embarrassment.

He hastily gathered his files and carried them to a nearby table. Bridget took a key from her handbag and used it to open her desk drawer.

"So you started work last week, Mr Faye?"

"Yes, Mallet gave me the tour. Sigge has been helping me

with the applications."

"Good."

Peter thought that Bridget must be very special because his boss Major Keith Linwood at MI6 had recommended her. He said her service record was exceptional, which was unusual for Keith, a man of few words. Furthermore, Peter's predecessor had thought highly of her too. Maybe it was her good looks that had swayed the man, thought Peter. It wouldn't be the first time.

"How was your holiday, Miss Potter?"

"Wonderful. I went to Öland with friends. It's an island south of here with lovely beaches."

"I heard that the Swedish military mined the southern approaches of Öland," Peter said as he remembered seeing on the map the long finger of an island stretching from south to north along the east coast.

"The Swedish navy escorts merchant ships through Kalmar sound between the island and mainland on their way to Stockholm," Bridget said. "While I was on holiday, I saw a German troop transport ship going through the sound. They said it was on its way to Finland."

"That's very interesting."

"The Swedish government is still very pro-German."

"Haven't they stopped all German troop transits on Swedish railways?"

"Yes, they have," Bridget said. "It was about time. We put pressure on the government here with the help of the Americans. By the way, how are you finding Stockholm?"

"Wonderful, I love the city."

"You look tired, Mr Faye. Have they got you working long hours already?"

"I was out with Bernie Dixon last night. He was showing me around town."

"I like Bernie, he's married to a very nice Swedish woman named Sabrina and nobody knows Stockholm like Bernie. He's been here forever."

"He's a nice chap," Peter said. "It's very quiet at the moment, Miss Potter. Is it always like this?"

"Yes, it has been quiet for months. Not much to do I'm afraid."

Bridget busied herself at her desk for a moment, then looked up.

"So how is K?" she asked.

"K is out and about, Miss Potter, drinking and carousing as far as I can see."

"My instructions from the major are to provide you with support when necessary, same as Bernie. Here in the office, however, you are my assistant so we better install you at that desk in the corner, out of sight of the public."

"That would be fine, Miss Potter."

"I didn't mean to bark at you earlier."

"Of course, no offense taken."

"Would you like a real cup of coffee, Mr Faye?"

"Yes, I would."

"The Swedes get the best of everything," Bridget said. "Nothing like the coffee substitutes back in England. Did you meet with R?"

"Not yet. Bernie briefed me. I am to do my first pickup during the lunch hour."

"You will like Stockholm. It is a wonderful place in the summer with the canals and the restaurants. The Germans aren't so arrogant now that we are starting to win the war."

Bridget busied herself making coffee in the corner.

"Sugar and cream?"

"Black, please."

"Have you had the chance to meet with Michael Tennant?

He's our press attaché."

"Tennant, yes. He's very helpful and a goldmine of information."

"Well, then. I will let you get back to your work. The coffee won't be long."

Bridget went to her desk and started to organize her inbox as her thoughts went to her new employee. She knew that Peter was single from his file but she wondered why a handsome man like him wasn't married.

In a tiny office off the main floor of the *Abwehr* station on Nybrogatan street, *Kriminaldirektor* Golcher looked up to see his assistant *Oberleutnant* Kemper enter the room. *Abwehr* men wore off-the-rack suits and ties in neutral Sweden and kept a low profile. Kemper sat down quickly and whispered in a low voice to his boss.

"They are building a case, sir."

"You talked to our man?" Golcher asked.

"Yes, it comes from the very top. The Gestapo has instructions to keep an eye on Dr Kramer. The reports go directly to the boss in Berlin, Heinrich Müller."

Golcher looked worried.

"Is an arrest imminent?" Golcher asked.

"Doesn't seem to be. They are just watching him, sir."

"Well, they are also watching the masseur Felix Kersten and he is Himmler's physical therapist so it may be nothing."

"Yes, sir."

"What else did he say?"

"'Egmont', sir."

"'Egmont'? What is this 'Egmont'?"

"I don't know. I thought you might know, sir."

"Thank you Herr Kemper," Golcher said.

His assistant left the room and Golcher leaned back in his chair, puzzled. What the hell was 'Egmont' and why the surveillance on Dr Kramer?

Kramer was his star agent and Golcher owed his plum position in Stockholm to the quality of Kramer's work. He worked at the press office of the German Legation and did not associate with *Abwehr* officers. Kramer's reports to Admiral Canaris in Berlin were the thing of legend; even the Führer mentioned them from time to time.

Three

Near the statue to the Swedish chemist Jons Jacob Berzelius in the park of the same name, Peter sat on a bench under a tree eating a sandwich and reading a newspaper. The flower beds were in full bloom and the sky was blue. It was a perfect day and the park was full of office workers on their lunch hour and nannies pushing prams with young children.

A woman from the German press office appeared on the path leading from Stallgaten road. She was a low level employee, who provided her British contacts with regular updates on personnel working at the German Legation. Her code-name was 'R'. She carried a briefcase and a Swedish newspaper which she casually dropped in a rubbish bin as she walked by.

After a moment Faye stood up and stretched. He looked around trying to spot any surveillance and after brushing the crumbs from his suit, he walked past the rubbish bin to dispose of his sandwich wrap and to switch newspapers. He left the park, heading back to the British Legation.

Dr Karl-Heinz Kramer arrived late at the German Press office. He nodded at his colleagues Helmut and Fritz and then went to his desk in a glass-walled corner room. His secretary picked up the British and American newspapers and followed him into his office. She was the same woman who had been with him on his drunken foray to the canal.

"Any news from Berlin, Nadja?"

"Nothing yet, sir."

"Got any coffee?"

"Yes, it's fresh, sir."

Nadja left just as *Kriminaldirektor* Golcher sneaked into the room, removing his hat.

"How are you, Dr Kramer?" Golcher asked.

Karl-Heinz was surprised to see Golcher who was both his *Abwehr* liaison and boss. It was very unusual for him to come to the press office.

"Very well, sir."

"How is the work going here at the press office?"

"Busy as usual," Karl-Heinz said. "Do you want to go out?"

"No, I think it is better that we talk here. You know our superiors in Berlin are very happy with our operation."

"And they should be," Karl-Heinz whispered. "We maintain a steady flow of first-rate material. We get absolutely everything there is to find in Stockholm."

"Yes, I dare say we do," Golcher said, "but with our success we attract attention in certain circles."

"The Gestapo. I wouldn't worry, sir. I have too many friends in Berlin."

"My job is to worry, Dr Kramer," Golcher protested, "when the *Abwehr* is under attack and Müller is building a case against you."

Karl-Heinz was surprised by Golcher's comment and he looked a little less confident.

"You know," he admitted, "I am not that surprised. The

man has been plotting against Canaris for some time and I am in the line of fire."

"We need to be very careful. We cannot afford to ignore the threat."

Golcher wrote the word 'Egmont' on a scrap of paper on the desk and handed it to Kramer.

Do you know what this means, Dr Kramer?"

"No, I'm afraid not."

"Well, I can see you are busy. I better be going. Good day."

"Good day, sir."

Karl-Heinz watched Golcher slip silently out of the office. He looked at the scrap of paper with the word 'Egmont' again and lit a match burning the paper in the ashtray.

Peter returned to the Consular Services office after the lunch break. Bridget called to him as he came into the room.

"How did it go, Mr Faye?"

"Very well. I've got the envelope here."

"So I will tell Joanna that she can come and collect it."

Bridget picked up the phone and dialled an extension number.

"Joanna, it's Bridget...Yes, it's arrived...Good, see you soon."

Bridget hung up the phone and turned to Peter.

"Joanna cross references the names for us and reports back if necessary. That's the way we have been working."

"Of course. No reason to change anything, Miss Potter."

"Please call me Bridget and I will call you Peter. It's easier in such a small office."

"Of course, Bridget."

"Good, I may have an interesting development for you. It came up while I was away on holiday."

Peter looked up as Bridget approached. She came very close and leaned on his desk.

"Have you met Vincent Ansell who is our trade officer at the Legation?" Bridget asked.

"No, not yet."

"I had lunch with Vincent and several colleagues today. I had a chat with Vincent's Austrian wife Elsa who had quite a story to tell. Her friend works in the Kramer house in Stora Essingen."

"Not Karl-Heinz Kramer's house?" Peter asked.

"Yes, the same."

"My God, what a coincidence!"

"I thought you might be interested," Bridget said with a mischievous smile.

"This is very interesting," Peter said as Bridget stepped away from the desk aware her physical presence was disturbing him.

"I think you need to hear it from Elsa herself, I will ask Vincent when and where you can meet her."

"Excellent," Peter said, "I will be away from the office this afternoon. I have a meeting with Tennant."

Peter couldn't decide whether Bridget was flirting with him or whether she was even aware of his attraction for her. He could smell her perfume and noticed the light dusting of freckles on her arms and face. She retreated to her desk just as an older, rather plain woman in a dark suit crossed the barrier and appeared in the doorway.

"Bridget, darling," Joanna said. "You look absolutely gorgeous in that dress. So you had a lovely holiday?"

"Thank you, I had a lovely time," Bridget said. "It was wonderful to get away."

"Well, you will have to come by and tell me the whole story."

Bridget turned to Peter.

"Joanna Dunn, this is Peter Faye, our new officer in Consular Services."

"Hello, Peter. I believe I have seen you in the hallway. Welcome to Stockholm."

"Thank you. Tennant told me a few things about your operations."

Peter handed her the German press office list.

"Tennant doesn't know it all," Joanna said. "If you like, I can tell you more."

Joanna winked at Bridget, acknowledging the sexual tension in the room before leaving.

Four

At the offices of the Stockholms-Tidningen newspaper, Anders Berger was smoking a cigarette at his desk on the press floor as he typed up an article on an old Remington typewriter. He was consulting some papers when his boss Gustav Lundquist stopped by his desk.

"So young Anders, how is it going?"

"Slowly, sir. Our attempt to capture Dr Kramer and his legation friends on film was a disaster."

"Yes, I heard from Stefan. Keep at it. There seems to be no lack of arrogant Germans carousing in our fair city. You would think they had won the war already."

"Yes, sir. Stefan thinks he might be able to save some of the pictures."

"Very good. Send me your report when you have it."

Anders glanced at the newspapers littering his desk. The headlines announced the daylight precision bombing of Germany by the USAAF and the Quebec Conference between Churchill and Roosevelt. The German *Wehrmacht* was losing on all fronts as the Allies took Sicily and the Soviets stopped a massive German offensive in its tracks at Kursk on the Eastern Front. Anders thought that this was starting to look like the beginning of the end for Germany.

At the Bellmansro restaurant with its turn of the century architecture, Peter and Michael Tennant sat on the terrace overlooking the garden having a drink.

"We've noticed several changes at the German Legation," Michael said. "There has been a significant reduction in staff probably due to the worsening situation in Russia."

"They are returning to take up jobs in Berlin?"

"Some are being drafted into the military. Many of them have links to Sweden and would like nothing better than to remain here until the end of the war. Some are applying for visas."

As press attaché, Tennant worked closely with the chief of the British Legation, Sir Victor Mallet. In secret, he worked for the British Special Operations Executive (SOE), whose job was to mount operations against German interests in neutral Sweden. Tennant was a Trinity College, Cambridge educated linguist and spoke excellent Swedish and several European languages.

Although the SOE was involved in espionage, sabotage and reconnaissance in many occupied countries, they had been obliged to curtail their operations in Sweden after the Swedish security services discovered that a British naval officer at the Legation was planning a sabotage operation on German soil in August 1942. From then on, their efforts were limited to dreaming up various schemes to demoralize the enemy.

"I did notice one name on the list. A new chap Gunther who was with the Gestapo in Budapest, and is now working here. London thinks he was a *kriminalkommissar* and they want us to keep an eye on him."

"What can you tell me about K?" Peter asked.

"You know what he's calling himself now: Himmler's

special representative!" Michael said. "What an arrogant bastard he is. Golcher of the *Abwehr* allows him free rein. The Gestapo and his own colleagues absolutely detest the man and can't wait to take him down."

"He seems to be having a rollicking good time here in Stockholm, running around in that DKW convertible."

"Yes, he is. He's a real charmer. He's got rooms at the Grand Hotel for entertaining. He's got a network of informers. Let's go for a walk."

They finished their beer and stood up.

On the waterfront Michael and Peter walked in silence for a while enjoying the late summer weather.

"Kramer is very well connected, both with the Luftwaffe and with Canaris at the *Abwehr*. Anything you can find on the man might be useful."

"It may take some time," Peter said.

"Go slowly and be careful. I'm sure those were your instructions in London."

"Yes, they were."

"How do you like Stockholm?"

"I love it, life seems to be so simple here."

"Don't believe it for a minute. It's a hotbed of spying and black market trading. Gold, diamonds, and secrets. You really have to keep your wits about you in a town like this."

Peter noticed Michael checking his reflection in shop windows looking for a tail as they continued their walk.

"We have company, Peter," Michael said.

"Yes, they seem to be everywhere," Peter said, noticing the man following them on the street.

"You don't need to worry about the Säpo, Peter. We get

used to them."

They walked on, ignoring the surveillance by the Swedish Security service.

"You need to watch your step with Sir Victor," Michael warned. "He's meeting secretly with the Swedish financier Marcus Wallenberg and several high level Nazi party members."

Peter raised an eyebrow.

"London approves this?"

"Mallet doesn't care. He has connections through his wife to the merchant banker Kleinwort in London and enjoys a certain prestige in the banking community."

"Why the meetings?"

"It's all business, you know. British and Swedish bankers are eager to buy up Nazi assets at bargain prices in the neutral countries. My advice to you is to stay clear of Mallet, work your files and keep your head down."

Peter looked disturbed by this information.

"I can't believe Mallet is talking to the Nazis," he said. "We may be winning battles but the war is not over by a long shot."

"The bankers see war as opportunity, old chap," Michael said. "German companies own assets in Spain, Portugal, South America and in the US and want to insure that they remain in safe hands once the war is over."

"And there are British bankers interested in buying up the assets?"

"Of course, there are. Bankers are the same everywhere."

Anders Berger and his photographer were in the basement darkroom of the Stockholms-Tidningen newspaper. Stefan pulled up a wet print from a tray with his fingers. It was the shot of the DKW convertible leaving the Grand Hotel.

"What do you think?" Stefan asked.

"It doesn't say much, a fancy car in front of the hotel. It is what one would expect."

"Let's see what else I have."

Stefan played with the negative holder on the enlarger and the wide shot of the Germans on the pier came into focus.

"That's much better, Stefan. Go closer."

Stefan moved the lens and the blow-up showed the drunk Germans on the pier drinking champagne with a portion of the DKW in the foreground. Water damage obscured half of the car, but Nadja, Karl-Heinz and Helmut were easily visible in the foreground. Karl-Heinz was pouring a drink for Nadja and Helmut in his shirt sleeves while Fritz and Heinrich were sharing a bottle in the background.

"Damn, that's perfect, Stefan. Amazing luck to have salvaged the film."

"The water damage is not too apparent I think."

"No, it's fine, Stefan. Let's get those two prints to Lundquist."

Anders slapped Stefan on the back and left the room.

As Peter entered the Consular Services office, Bridget was putting some confidential files in the safe. In the outer office Sigge was closing up for the day.

"You may need to use the safe," Bridget said. "You don't want to leave anything classified on your desk."

Peter took off his hat and put it on the coat rack.

"Yes, of course."

"I am going to give you the combination."

Peter approached Bridget as she unlocked the safe. He could smell her perfume as he leaned over her shoulder. She started to compose a series of numbers turning the dial clockwise and counter-clockwise. She then pulled on the handle opening the door with a clicking sound and smiled at Peter.

"You got it?" Bridget asked.

"Yes, I got it."

"Good. Don't write it down."

"Of course. Have you had any problems with security in the past?"

"No, but you never can be too sure."

"By the way what is Joanna's security clearance?"

"MI6 has cleared her for low level documents like Bernie," Bridget said. "The message from on high is keep your nose clean and don't poke around in other people's business."

"Yes, that just about summarizes the philosophy of our secret services. They rail about security in London but end up doing very little about it."

Peter returned to his desk and noticed a little box with a ribbon around it.

"Don't forget that Sir Victor wants to show you off at the reception tonight," Bridget said.

"Of course. I better be there."

Peter picked up the box.

"What's this?"

"That's for you, Peter, a little present."

Bridget approached as Peter opened the box and found a red club tie inside.

"Your tie was looking a little worse for wear, so I thought something more colourful would please the chief."

"Thank you."

Bridget took the tie and held it up against Peter's suit.

"That looks very smart."

"You think I look a little shabby and need sprucing up, do you Bridget?"

"You are in the diplomatic service now, my dear," she said with a grin, handing him back the tie. "You're no longer a schoolmaster. You need to look sharp."

"Bloody hell, will I ever live it down? The eternal schoolmaster."

"You have an obligation to look smart, you're my assistant," Bridget said, returning to her desk.

"Well, thank you, boss. That's very kind of you."

Bridget beamed a smile at Peter and started to collect her things. She found Peter to be rather shy and not very outgoing compared to other intelligence officers she had known. He was a cautious, quiet man and kept to himself, which was probably an asset for a field agent but of little or no value in the diplomatic world. Behind the polished intellectual look, there was a hard edge to the man and something very private about him that she liked. She got the impression that when push came to shove, he would be in his element.

Five

Sir Victor Mallet, greying and distinguished in a tuxedo, greeted the new arrivals. Lady Mallet, dressed in a floral print dress and pearls, stood next to her husband at the front door of the Legation. Several distinguished Swedes including Count Folke Bernadotte and the banker Marcus Wallenberg, colleagues from the American Legation, British staff and Swedish employees in evening attire were among the guests. A bar was set up along one wall with local beer and hard liquor.

Peter and Bridget drew several bemused looks as they circulated together among the guests. Bridget looked very elegant in a black gown with her hair in a silk scarf while Peter wore his best pinstripe suit and sported the tie she had bought for him. Bridget introduced Peter to the British and Swedish Legation staff including Vincent Ansell and his wife Elsa who chatted briefly with them before Peter was interrupted by a young man tugging on his sleeve.

"Hello, Mr Faye. You remember me."

"Ah, the wet journalist from the lake. Bridget, this is Mr Berger from the newspaper."

"Anders Berger at your service, miss. I work for the Stockholms-Tidningen newspaper."

"The other night I happened upon Mr Berger after he drove his car into one of the many canals around the city."

"How did it happen?" Bridget asked.

"It was a stupid accident," Anders said. "I lost control of the car. Luckily, my photographer and I were not injured and Mr Faye gave us a lift back to town. So I hear that you are the new man here at the Legation?"

"Yes, I arrived recently."

Bridget left Peter to Anders and went to refresh their drinks at the bar.

"I wouldn't want to inconvenience you, Mr Faye, but I have a contact who is very interested in meeting you."

"What would be the purpose of such a meeting?" Peter asked.

"Herr Kramer lives in Stora Essingen and he also has a room at the Grand Hotel for parties. You know this because you are keeping your eye on Mr Kramer. Am I right, sir?"

Peter frowned and tried to regain his composure. If his surveillance of Kramer was already public knowledge, his cover was blown and he might as well return to London.

"I'm sorry, Mr Berger," Peter insisted. "I really don't know what you are talking about. I work in Consular Services."

"Don't worry, sir, your secret is safe with me."

Anders smiled as Peter looked around nervously.

"The Germans were welcome here early in the war, but now not as much," Anders said. "Herr Kramer and his staff are always having these big parties and Swedish people find him a bit too..."

"Showy, perhaps," Peter suggested.

"Yes, a show-off, an arrogant German. This is not his country. He is just a visitor. My newspaper has decided to do an article on the large German presence in Sweden."

"That's very interesting, Mr Berger, but didn't the Swedish

people welcome the Germans with open arms just a few years ago and now you say the relationship has soured?"

"In 1940, we did welcome them. We wanted to stay out of the war at any cost. Sweden has its own Nazis, Mr Faye. Per Engdahl of the New Swedish Movement is pro Nazi. We even have Swedes fighting for the Waffen-SS Nordland division in Russia and in the Balkans. Now things are changing. We think you British and your American friends are going to win the war."

"So Sweden wants to be on the winning side, is that it?" Peter asked with a cynical air.

"No, Mr Faye. Our aim is to remain neutral, which is not always an easy task."

Anders glanced over Peter's shoulder and spotted Bridget on her way back carrying their drinks.

"I believe the lady is coming back. I have a friend, he is Estonian and has some top secret information for you, sir."

Peter gave Anders an almost imperceptible nod.

"I will send you the contact information. My contact name will be *Herr våt* - the wet man," Anders said with a laugh.

He winked at Peter as he slipped away into the crowd. A moment later Bridget arrived with Peter's whisky.

"So where did he go, this journalist friend?" Bridget asked, looking around for Anders.

"Off looking for stories, I would imagine."

"So you pulled him out of the water?"

"Well, not really. We were driving by and noticed his car in the water. It is very easy to miss a turn here in Stockholm and you are in the water before you know it."

"That was very gallant of you, Peter."

"All part of our service to the Swedish population," Peter remarked with an amused air.

"Cheers, Peter."

Bridget and Peter clinked their glasses and looked around at the mix of staff and foreign diplomats.

"You look very nice with the new tie, Peter. I think it is time for you to meet Sir Victor."

"You think so?"

"Of course I do."

Bridget took Peter's hand and led him through the crowd. They were several feet away when Sir Victor noticed their approach.

"Bridget!" he boomed. "How are you? Hello, Mr Faye. I hope Bridget is looking after you."

"She is, sir. What a lovely reception!" Peter said.

"We have many friends here in Sweden, Mr Faye. I hope you are enjoying the warm weather. Don't you think Stockholm is magnificent in the summer? We are spared the bombing and the blackouts."

"It is quite amazing how quiet the nights are here away from the war."

"Oh, but the war is here, Mr Faye. There is a hidden war going on in neutral Sweden, mark my words. You look very lovely in that dress, Bridget."

"Thank you, sir."

Six

"Hanne works for Frau Kramer, Mr Faye," Elsa said in her German-accented English. "She cleans twice a week and does some cooking. She is my very best friend from Vienna."

As the reception began to wind down, Vincent Ansell and his wife Elsa sat at a table with Peter and Bridget in the garden of the British Legation. There was dance music and loud voices coming from the reception room nearby.

"We went to the same school in Hietzing. She knows my parents," Elsa said.

"How long has she been in Sweden?" Peter asked.

"Since 1940, same as me. I met Vincent in '39."

"When did she start working for the Kramers?" Peter asked.

"About three months ago," Elsa said. "It went well at the beginning, but now Hanne is furious with Frau Kramer. She's very bossy and treats Hanne as an *Untermensch*. Hanne comes from a very good Viennese family, you know."

Vincent leaned forward to get Peter's attention.

"I am going to the bar. Can I refresh your drinks?"

"No thanks, Vincent. I have had enough," Peter said.

"Ladies?"

Elsa and Bridget shook their heads and Vincent was off.

"Dr Kramer works a lot out of his study at home," Elsa said. "It's on the second floor. He has a desk drawer which he keeps locked."

"This is very interesting, Elsa, but do you think your friend Hanne would be willing to work for us?" Bridget asked.

"Hanne is Jewish, Bridget," Elsa said, "but with her blond hair you wouldn't know it. She's lost so many friends. She hates the Nazis. I think she's interested in helping the British."

Bridget put down her glass and turned to Peter.

"What do you think, Peter?"

"It cannot hurt to talk to her."

"I could meet your friend for tea somewhere after shopping perhaps," Bridget said. "What do you think, Elsa?"

"Yes, good idea. Just us women going shopping together."

Peter nodded his benediction.

"Open up, Nils. Here it comes, open the gate."

Anders held a spoon to his two-year old son. Little Nils grinned at his dad from his high chair and took a big mouthful of porridge.

Anders was in his pyjamas and dressing gown in the kitchen as his wife Britta rushed around the flat preparing to go to work. She popped into the kitchen dressed smartly in a white blouse and skirt with her blond hair pinned up in a victory roll. Nils reached out to his mother for a kiss and a hug.

"Remember to pick up Nils at grandma's," Britta said. "I won't be back until after 4 o'clock."

Britta kissed her son and drank her tea standing at the counter.

"Have you heard anything from your mother?" Anders asked.

"*Mamma* is worried. She hasn't had any news for weeks about Rolf. The priest Arne Berge thinks they may have moved him from Neuengammen."

"The Neuengammen camp is bad, but there are worse camps in Germany."

"Berge goes there every week," Britta said. "He brings clothes and food that he collects in Hamburg. He checked the list of prisoners and Rolf's name is no longer on it."

"That's not good news."

"Berge thinks he has been moved to another labour camp. It is outrageous for the Germans to hold my brother. He has done nothing."

"The Germans don't care, Britta. They arrest whoever they like."

"*Mamma* has heard that the Germans put prisoners in *Nacht und Nebel* camps where they are worked to death."

Anders helped Nils off the high chair.

"Poor Rolf, maybe it is not so bad," Anders said. "We must not lose hope. You better go, you will be late."

Britta kissed Anders and hurried out of the flat.

Seven

At the Kramer house Eva Kramer was in the master bedroom combing her hair and getting dressed. She was a short woman with a dark complexion and had her brown hair rolled and curled.

Downstairs in the kitchen, Hanne was busy collecting her things and preparing to leave the house. The nanny Wilhelma was feeding five-year old Heidi in the kitchen. Hanne left the kitchen and went to the foot of the stairs.

"Frau Kramer, I am off. See you Thursday."

Eva appeared at the top of the stairs.

"*Sehr gut, Hanne.* Don't forget to pick up the caraway seeds at the market for Karl-Heinz's sauerkraut."

"Yes, madam. Bye now."

Hanne left the house and hurried down the road to the bus stop. A gardener was weeding a rose bush near the road. He looked up and waved at her.

"Guess what my code-name is going to be?" Elsa asked.

"I really wouldn't know," Hanne said.

"Frau E. Isn't that right, Bridget?"

Bridget nodded.

They were sitting on the sunny terrace of a restaurant in the old town with their shopping bags. The restaurant was nearly empty. With war raging across Europe, there were fewer and fewer customers.

"Frau E?" Hanne asked Bridget with a laugh.

A waiter approached with another round of drinks for the women. Elsa and Hanne were drinking white Mosel wine while Bridget was having a gin and tonic.

"What would be my code-name, Bridget?" Hanne asked.

"Mata Hanne," Elsa said with a smile.

The women burst out laughing as Hanne started to wiggle about on her chair snapping her fingers to an exotic Eastern musical theme.

"Mata Hanne! I love it, I will show my navel in public and seduce all the men in the room," Hanne said as she stood up and started dancing to an exotic air.

"MATA HANNE, THAT'S ME."

As Elsa and Hanne carried on, Bridget looked around warily, finishing her drink. She leaned forward and whispered to Hanne.

"I must get back. Will you think about it?"

"I am ready, Bridget," Hanne said. "I hate the Kramers, they are Nazi pigs."

"The important thing is access, Hanne," Bridget said. "The question is how would you do it and what are your chances of success?"

"Please, I have thought about it for some time now. I know their daily routine and Frau Kramer trusts me."

"I am not sure that I understand your feelings about Frau Kramer. If she trusts you, she can't be all that bad," Bridget inquired, well aware that Peter would want an answer to this question.

"Yes, Hanne, tell Bridget what you told me," Elsa said,

looking at her friend.

"Eva is Jewish, Bridget. She even looks Jewish with her dark hair. I know her secret. I came across pictures of her parents hidden in her bedroom while I was cleaning."

"And she is married to an Aryan God with blue eyes," Elsa said impatiently.

"You have seen Karl-Heinz," Hanne said. "He is a very handsome man, so you see Eva must compensate."

"She says nasty things, does she?" Bridget asked.

"I am Jewish and I am proud of my family. At first, it didn't bother me, but now it is just too much to bear. The dust in the corner, the dirt on the carpet, the bath ring is caused by the dirty Jews. It is crazy how she carries on sometimes."

"Tell her your plan," Elsa demanded.

Hanne smiled as she talked in a low voice to Bridget.

"Herr Kramer takes a bath every day at 6:45 p.m., always the same time. He spends thirty minutes in the bath before getting dressed for dinner. It is the same routine every day like clockwork. The other day I was dusting in the hallway and entered the bedroom briefly. The keys for the desk drawer were on the dresser."

Elsa and Bridget looked at each other, excited by the prospects of Hanne's plan.

At the Consular Services office Peter crossed the barrier and found Bridget typing a document at her desk.

"Well, Bridget, how did it go?"

"Very well. I think she will do it."

"Will she?"

"'H' is very keen. Ready to start whenever you want."

Peter looked surprised.

"Would you like to meet her?"

"No, not yet. Are you sure she is ready?"

"Of course, I just said she is."

"This is a quite a mission we're undertaking and it has potentially dangerous consequences for Hanne."

"You think I don't know that, Peter."

"I know you do, but the target is not some third rate Nazi spy, he's the *Abwehr's* star performer."

"I know the danger, Peter. This is not the first time in this office we use civilians to collect information."

Peter took off his hat and was thinking about the mission when Bridget said irritably: "Well, if you're not sure, then we'll just call the bloody thing off."

She stood up and went to the window looking out at the garden.

"Look, Bridget, I don't doubt your opinion."

"Of course, you do, you doubt my opinion," she said in an angry tone. "I'm just the bloody secretary in this office. I don't know a damn thing."

Peter was stunned by Bridget's sudden rebuff as he sat down at his desk. Bridget lit a cigarette and watched the Swedish gardener trimming the rose bushes in the garden below.

Bridget had always been told by the men in her life that emotions were to be hidden. Her father had taught her to hide her feelings and her English upbringing certainly did not reward expressions of exuberance and passion. Passion was something you hid behind a wall of placid indifference. A career in the diplomatic service had impressed on her the importance of being cold and rational with the facts.

Bridget looked at Peter who was going through the files that had accumulated on his desk. He was like all the men in her life. He disapproved of women who let their emotions get away from them. But it was sometimes too much for a spirited young woman like Bridget who needed to explode from time to time with a great show of elation or anger.

"I'm sorry, Bridget. I didn't mean to..."

"Yes, you did," Bridget said. "You're the man in the room, you don't need to make excuses."

Bridget put out her cigarette and came over to Peter's desk with a mischievous smile.

"I like H. She's a remarkable person, very lively and quite brilliant. I would never put her life in danger on a whim."

"So?"

"H is determined to do anything she can to compromise K. She hates the family with reason."

"You seem to be very convinced. Why are you so sure she wants to help us?"

"The wife Eva is a Jew, Peter. You've seen the husband."

"Of course, K looks like a pin-up for the Aryan race."

"So with her dark hair and looks, Eva struggles with the fact that H is a lovely blond Jewess from Vienna. So she constantly says horrible things about the Jews in front of Hanne."

"I see," Peter said, "so this is a personal vendetta for her."

"Yes and no, I think she sincerely wants to help us. She hates the Germans."

"So what's the plan?"

"She thinks that she can get the keys to the drawer in the study when K takes his bath. He leaves his keys on the dresser. It would give her a 30-minute window to make a copy of the key."

"Not a bad plan at all, Bridget."

"You'll like her. She's tough and determined."

"I will talk to Tennant's people."

"Fortune favours the bold, Peter," Bridget said smiling.

"Yes, it does. *Audentes fortuna iuvat*, that's from Virgil. I was a schoolmaster, remember."

"Yes, I know."

Bernie Dixon was busy producing travel documents in the Legation basement as Michael and Peter entered the room. A red light spilled from the nearby darkroom.

"I think you know Dixon," Michael said.

"Yes, hello Bernie," Peter said.

"Morning, sir. No more late nights?"

"No, I have given up on late nights, at least for the moment."

Bernie laughed at this.

"I talked to Bernie about the key," Michael said. "We can make any key we like with our equipment, but we need the imprint or the original."

"I doubt we can get our hands on the original for more than half an hour," Peter said.

"Then an imprint would be the way to go," Bernie said.

"What about photographing documents?"

"It can be done quickly enough with the right installation. Are you thinking of nicking some papers from that fancy house in Stora Essingen?"

"Yes, Bernie."

"Me days of smash and grab are over, Peter," Bernie said with a laugh, "so you'll have to find another dogsbody to nick the stuff from the inside."

"Bernie could park a van near the house," Michael said, "to do the copying."

"I reckon a shed or a garage nearby would be best," Bernie said. "A van would be too easy to spot on the street."

"How much time will Bernie have?" Tennant asked.

"I would think an hour or two at the most."

"It's would have to be a two-man operation," Bernie insisted. "One fella doing the pick up and another the copying. The tricky part will be getting the documents in and out of the house quickly enough."

Eight

Hanne was dusting the hallway near the master bedroom while she listened for the sounds of Dr Kramer in the bathroom. Eva was downstairs with Heidi and Wilhelma. Hanne stopped near the bedroom door, opened it very gently and quickly went to the dresser. She collected Kramer's keys and left the room. She went to the study where she tried the keys in the locked desk drawer. She quickly determined which was the right key for the drawer and pulled a small box from her pocket. She slipped the key into the box and pressed down hard on the clay. She soon realized that the clay was far too dry to give a decent imprint.

She started to panic, ran out of the room and hurried towards the master bedroom to return the keys when she had an idea. She quickly turned around and headed in the opposite direction, descending the stairs. She entered the kitchen across from the living room where Eva, Heidi and Wilhelma were busy chatting. She went to the pantry where there was a slab of butter on a plate. She used a short knife to cut off a slice of hardened butter and slipped it into a dish towel.

"Hanne, bring me a cup of coffee," ordered Eva from the living room.

Hanne froze.

"Yes, Frau Kramer."

Hanne rushed out of the kitchen heading for the stairs. She climbed silently to the second floor and entered the master bedroom with the keys as she heard Dr Kramer sloshing water around in the tub. Standing near the dresser, she pulled out the slab of butter wrapped in the dish towel and pressed both sides of the key into the surface, easily making an imprint. She folded the dish towel carefully around the butter and then dropped the key chain back onto the dresser.

As she was about to leave the room, she noticed butter grease on the dresser top. She picked up the keys again and carefully wiped the butter off the keys and dresser before leaving the room. A voice was heard from downstairs.

"Hanne, the coffee please. Where are you?"

Hanne raced down the hall towards the stairs with a triumphant look on her face.

"What is she up to? Damn that woman," the voice came from below.

Hanne ran down the stairs and crossed the hall into the kitchen. Moments later, she emerged with a tray of coffee and biscuits for Frau Kramer.

"That took you long enough," Eva said, playing with young Heidi on the couch.

"I am off now, Frau Kramer. Will you need anything special from the shops on Tuesday?"

"No, I think we will be fine."

Hanne nodded and returned to the kitchen. She changed her shoes and put on her coat. In the living room Eva poured herself a cup of coffee and added cream and sugar. Hanne hurried out the front door to catch her bus just as Eva brought the coffee cup to her lips.

"Hanne," Eva grimaced, "the coffee is cold!"

"I think she's gone, Frau Kramer," Wilhelma said.

Hanne hurried down the road to the bus stop. She passed a motorcar parked in the road. A man was sitting on the curb attempting to repair a flat tyre. Hanne nodded to the man.

"*Bra Dag*," she said, wishing him a good day.

The man ignored her and continued tightening the bolts on the tyre. He watched Hanne walking away and then looked up at the Kramer house. He stood up wiping the grease from his hands.

"What's happening?" said his colleague, taking a nap on the back seat.

"Nothing much, the cleaning lady."

Anders Berger and Gustav Lundquist walked down the hall at the Stockholms-Tidningen newspaper.

"The pictures are rather shocking for our readers, Anders," Lundquist said. "Germans getting drunk and carousing in a park in our beautiful city."

"Yes, sir."

"I would be willing to go with it but I need to check with the owners. It could upset our political masters."

"Yes, sir. I realize that, sir," Anders said.

"I was thinking we could do it another way," Lundquist said with a sly grin.

"What way, sir?"

"Turn it into a piece about tourism, you know. This is what German tourists are doing in lovely Stockholm. They are having a wonderful time in our city."

Anders quickly grasped the idea.

"You mean slip these pictures into a banal tourism piece on what attracts our German friends to Stockholm, sir?"

"Absolutely. Yes, that would be good."

"It could be a piece about the attractions of our city with a comment from the tourism office."

"Excellent, Anders. I look forward to seeing it."

Lundquist left Anders whose head was suddenly filled with new ideas for the article.

Nine

Elsa led Peter and Bridget into the garden behind the Ansell house. In the dim light they could see a woman sitting at a wooden table on the verandah, drinking tea and smoking a cigarette.

"Hanne, this is Peter. Peter, this is Hanne."

"Hello Peter, Bridget."

Bridget nodded at Hanne.

"Nice to meet you, Hanne," Peter said, "we admire your courage."

Peter pulled the duplicate key from his pocket and handed it to Hanne.

"You will need to test it in the lock to see if it works properly, but I think we got a good imprint."

"I will do that," Hanne said.

Elsa poured the tea for her guests. Peter took a cup and there was a moment of silence as they contemplated their individual roles in this new mission.

"From our pictures of the house, the best approach would be through the back garden," Peter said.

"Yes, the back gate is never locked," Hanne said.

"You do know that the house is under observation by the Gestapo?"

"The Gestapo!" Hanne and Elsa exclaimed, exchanging frightened glances.

"I noticed some men on the road," Hanne added, "they were repairing a flat tyre."

"No doubt Gestapo men," Peter concluded.

He had not been surprised when Bernie told him that the Gestapo was keeping a watch on Kramer's house. With the declining fortunes of the *Wehrmacht* in Russia and in the Italian peninsula, every German citizen working in Stockholm was under surveillance. Peter had learned through Frau R that a young German radio employee had been held incommunicado for several days by the Gestapo after they discovered that a group of dissident Germans had been planning to demand asylum in Sweden.

Peter pulled a file from his briefcase and put it on the table. He opened the file to show several glossy, black and white photographs.

"Here's the back of the house. How do you suggest we get the documents from the second floor down to the garden for the pickup?"

Hanne looked at the pictures.

"From the house, this side of the garden is not as visible so I think it would be better to come in on this side."

"Very good," Peter said.

"Usually, I don't clean the second floor bedrooms until late morning. Dr Kramer leaves for his office around nine and returns by five or six o'clock."

"What about Frau Kramer?" Bridget asked.

"She's up in her bedroom until around ten. The nanny gets up early with young Heidi."

"Dr Kramer has a gardener, I believe," Peter said.

Hanne was surprised to see how well acquainted Peter was

with the comings and goings at the Kramer house.

"Yes, but only one day a week."

"So you could simply toss the documents out the second floor window on this side," Peter suggested.

"But what if the neighbours see her?" Bridget asked. "Tossing things out of windows would look very strange."

"There is a risk," Hanne remarked, "that the neighbours on this side see me throwing something out of the window."

"Suppose you put the documents in a shoe bag, you know an ordinary cloth bag with a drawstring," Peter said, "and simply carry them downstairs."

"No, I certainly don't want to be seen carrying a shoe bag downstairs," Hanne said. "Maybe tossing them out the window is the best plan."

"We have another idea that might work," Peter said. "A wire pulley system which could be attached to the second floor window. You hook the cloth bag with the documents to the wire at the window and drop them down to the garden. The wire would be attached to the wall so it would not be very visible."

Elsa and Hanne appeared to like this idea and nodded their approval.

"How would you install the wire to the second floor window?" Bridget asked.

"It's very simple," Peter said, "it consists of a thin wire with lead weights at the end. You twist the wire around a drain pipe or window support, then let the wire drop in a straight line to the garden. Our people will fix it to the wall below. When we return the documents, you simply pull up the wire with the cloth bag attached."

"Sounds easy enough," Hanne said.

"I think we need something stronger to drink," Elsa said as she left to fetch a bottle of aquavit and glasses.

"What do you think Hanne?" Bridget asked.

"It's good. The plan is good. The cloth bag and the wire should work well."

Elsa arrived with the aquavit and poured a round for everyone. They sipped their drinks and looked at the pictures again.

"So after the documents are gone, I continue to do my housework. What time do I return to the second floor to collect the documents?" Hanne asked.

"We estimate that the transport and copy time will take up to two hours," Peter said. "You say that Dr Kramer receives packages two or three times a week?"

"Yes, I have seen them on his desk."

"So if you put the bag on the wall drop at around eleven, we would get it back to you by one o'clock at the latest. We could try for next Tuesday. Of course, if you have to cancel, that's fine. We then move it to Thursday. I suggest a signal like an open window for a go and a closed window to cancel. We will be watching the house."

"You must be very careful, Hanne." Bridget cautioned. "If for some reason you must cancel, it doesn't matter. You must not endanger yourself."

Elsa smiled at her friend.

"Don't worry, Bridget," Elsa said. "Mata Hanne has nerves of steel."

The women burst into laughter but Peter could only manage a smile. You never knew how a relatively simple operation like this could turn out. Even with the best laid plans, disaster could be waiting in the wings.

Ten

"Mail for you, Peter," Bridget dropped an envelope on his desk as she went to make coffee.

Peter opened the letter and pulled out a single card. He read: 'Hello Peter, a meeting is set for Friday at 22.00 at the Grand Hotel waterfront. I'll be expecting you. Your friend, Herr våt."

Peter laughed at the card.

"What is it?" Bridget asked.

"It's that journalist who drove into the canal. He wants me to meet someone on Friday night."

"Are you going?"

"I don't know why not."

"Don't go alone, Peter. Stockholm can be a dangerous place at night."

"Don't worry, Bridget. I'll take Bernie along with me."

Hanne looked up at the clock on the wall. It was a little after 10:30 a.m. She was on her hands and knees scrubbing the linoleum floor in the kitchen while little Heidi and Wilhelma were playing in the dining room next door.

She was just finishing when Eva Kramer came into the

48

kitchen smartly dressed for a shopping excursion in town.

"*Guten Tag, Hanne.*"

"*Guten Morgen, Frau Kramer,*" Hanne stood up, perspiring and mopping her brow with the back of her hand.

"Don't forget to wax twice," Eva said, pouring herself a cup of coffee.

"Yes, madam."

Eva went into the dining room to see Heidi and Wilhelma. Hanne picked up a bucket in the corner and went outside to dump the dirty water. She then rinsed the bucket, brush and rags from the outside faucet. She admired the flowers and green shrubs in the garden in the sunshine and sat on a bench as she lit a cigarette to calm her nerves. She looked up at the window on the second floor and followed the wall down to its base hidden by the garden shrubs. She felt confident the wire drop would work.

Ten minutes later she was back in the kitchen on her hands and knees applying the first coat of wax to the linoleum floor. She could hear Eva and the girls in the dining room. She finished applying the first coat and stood up. She looked at the clock on the wall, it was almost eleven. She washed her hands in the sink and left the kitchen. She dragged the old Hoover vacuum cleaner up the stairs to the second floor. She heard Frau Kramer slam the door on her way out of the house.

Hanne turned on the vacuum cleaner, hoping the racket it made would drown out the sound of her movements. She left it running in the hallway and went to the study. She pulled the key from her pocket and inserted it into the document drawer. It turned easily in the lock and she heaved a sigh of relief. She quickly pulled out a pile of documents. From a pocket in her apron, she removed the shoe bag and slipped the documents inside, then locked the drawer and left the study.

She went down the hall to the open window at the rear. Just as she stuck her head out the window, she thought she heard a sound from downstairs.

"Hanne, I forgot my glasses," Eva called from the front door. "Can you get them? They are on the bedside table."

Hanne stopped dead in her tracks.

"Yes, madam. Just a moment."

Hanne rushed through to the master bedroom, grabbed Frau Kramer's glasses from the bedside table and headed for the stairs. Eva was half-way up as Hanne descended to her.

"Here you go," Hanne said, sweating profusely.

"What have you got there?" Eva asked.

Hanne suddenly noticed the cloth bag sticking out from under her arm.

"My shoes, Frau Kramer. I keep my shoes in the bag."

Eva looked down momentarily at Hanne's housework shoes and then at the bag under her arm.

"Of course, bye now," Eva said as she turned and headed down the stairs.

"Bye."

Hanne climbed the stairs, her legs trembling. She turned off the vacuum cleaner and listened in case Frau Kramer returned again for some reason. A car pulled away from the front of the house and she could hear Heidi chatting with her nanny below. She hurried to the open window, pulling a long wire from her pocket. She leaned out the window and attached the wire by winding it several times around the drain pipe and then suspending it down to the garden using the weights. She picked up the cloth bag and used a clasp to hook it to the wire. She dropped the bag out the window and it slipped gently down the wire to the garden below. She listened to the sounds coming from the kitchen before returning to work.

Eleven

Bernie rode his bike down the lane toward the back of the Kramer residence. It was the kind of neighbourhood where tradesmen and domestic servants were a common sight and his straw hat and dungarees allowed him to pass himself off as just another working man. He got off the bike and leaned it against the fence before stepping through the gate to the garden itself. He quickly crossed the grass to the side of the Kramer house.

Moments later he returned to his bicycle and put the cloth bag in the wicker basket before he cycled away. Sticking to the back lanes, Bernie soon pulled up at a wooden shed behind a large house where Peter and Bernie's assistant Allan were waiting for him. The house and shed belonged to a Legation employee who was away on sick leave for several months.

The men entered the shed and pulled the door closed. Allan turned on the light of the Minox copy stand as Bernie started to lay the documents out carefully on the table in the order they were received. Allan picked up two passports and put the glass platen over them. He started to click away, turning the pages as he went.

Peter flipped through the documents and noticed an original memorandum from the PM's office.

"Christ almighty, we've hit the bloody mother load!"

"Everything all right, sir?" Bernie asked with concern.

"Yes, fine, Bernie. Keep going."

Peter put the memorandum back on the table and sat down on a chair in stunned amazement. Bernie hurriedly fed the documents to Allan and then returned them in the right order to the table.

Shortly before one o'clock, Bernie returned to the lane behind the Kramer house with the cloth bag. He left his bicycle leaning against the fence and stepped into the garden, quickly crossing to the side of the house. Moments later, he returned and cycled away.

Hanne was finishing up on the second floor when she heard a sound in the garden coming from the open window. It was time for Heidi's nap in the room off from the kitchen and lunch for Wilhelma. She could hear Wilhelma listening to a German radio program while she had lunch.

Hanne went to the window and looked down at the cloth bag attached to the wire. She pulled on the wire which started to come up followed by the cloth bag. Half way up, the cloth bag hung in empty space and wouldn't come any further. It looked like the wire might have gotten caught on the drain pipe. She tried to move the wire sideways to get around the pipe but nothing seemed to work. She was afraid to use too much force - if the wire became too entangled with the pipe, the bag might get stuck where it was, hanging in plain view. She couldn't take the chance, so she said a silent prayer and let go of the wire. The bag dropped back down to the garden and Hanne breathed a sigh of relief. She shut the window and hurried downstairs to the kitchen.

Wilhelma was eating her lunch and didn't look like she had

heard anything with the German radio program going full blast.

"Everything good, Wilhelma?" Hanne asked.

"*Ja, ja.*"

Hanne collected the bucket from the back door and stepped outside briefly. She went into the garden to fetch the cloth bag. She unhooked it from the wire and put it into the bucket throwing a damp cloth over it. She gave a tug to the wire which was caught on the drain pipe before she returned to the kitchen. She smiled at Wilhelma who had served herself a generous portion of chocolate cake.

She crossed the kitchen and headed for the stairs with the bucket. She entered the study, opened the drawer with her key and slid the documents out of the cloth bag into the drawer. She checked the order of the documents and locked the drawer tucking the empty bag into her pocket. Then she left the room as fast as she could and got on with her cleaning.

Twelve

Peter and Bridget looked up in surprise as Bernie barged into the Consular Services office.

"London has gone mad, sir," Bernie announced, "here are three more messages that came in the last hour."

He said nothing else, just gave Peter the decoded radio messages and left in a hurry. Bridget watched impatiently as Peter read through them.

"Well?" she said finally.

"I told you it was a treasure trove!" he said jubilantly, "the Josefine dispatches are creating quite a stir in London."

"Congratulations, Peter. We did it or H did it."

"Yes, she did."

Peter reread the dispatches and reflected on Kramer's sources. Josefine was the code-name Kramer gave to several sources inside the Swedish Defence ministry. His sources included a Swedish military attaché who made frequent trips to Britain and various young women from the ministry who had access to top secret military reports. He was known to wine and dine the women at his favourite restaurants. Other intelligence he appeared to have simply purchased on the black market and fed to his *Abwehr* colleagues in Berlin. The rumour among his colleagues was that he was faking much of this intelligence in order to collect large payments for his carousing.

Peter had heard through his sources at MI6 in London that the Gestapo suspected Kramer of double-dealing and had a large file on him. They suspected him of providing the Russians with secret information about *Luftwaffe* operations in exchange for Russian intelligence about the Allies.

Peter returned to his dispatches and smiled at Bridget who was busy typing a report.

"Can I invite you to dinner, Bridget, to celebrate our success?" Peter said. "It was you who convinced me to recruit H in the first place. I might not have done it without your forceful presentation."

"Forceful?" Bridget replied with a laugh. "You haven't seen forceful yet, Peter. When you do, you might live to regret it."

"Well, perhaps I should say your highly persuasive presentation of the facts. I am thankful and so is London."

"Then it is a yes for the dinner but we must keep it quiet. I wouldn't want the old busybodies on the first floor chatting about me behind my back."

"7 p.m. then. I will pick you up at your flat?"

"That's fine, Peter."

"You better give me your address."

Bridget nodded and returned to her report.

London

A London taxi pulled up in front of the gatehouse for the Holloway Sanatorium, a mental hospital near Virginia Water in Surrey. The taxi's passenger, Dorothy Furse, wore a WAAC uniform and was Head of Personnel for the SOE. Dorothy got out of the taxi barely glancing at the Victorian facade of the huge mental hospital as she made a beeline for a little man with thick round glasses standing in front of the gate and looking lost. A battered valise sat on the ground beside him. His rumpled clothes looked like he had slept in them.

"How are you, Ewan?" Dorothy asked.

Ewan Butler stared at her but remained silent. He had an absent look on his face. He stepped forward, struggling with his bag. The driver took it from him and put it in the baggage rack as Dorothy opened the door for him.

"Come, Ewan, we need to get you home."

Dorothy and Ewan climbed into the taxi and it pulled away from the curb.

"How long have you been away, Ewan?" Dorothy asked.

"A month, I think."

"How did it go?"

"I slept a lot."

Dorothy looked at the hopeless little intellectual who had been locked up in the sanatorium for drinking problems and was now being let go halfway through his treatment. Poor Ewan, she thought, poor SOE. The little sod would soon be working for them on the front lines.

"Do you feel better?" she asked.

"Better? I don't know."

"Harold Nicolson. You know Harold?" Dorothy asked.

"Harold?"

"Yes, the Member of Parliament. You remember him?"

Ewan ignored the question and watched the traffic.

"He called me and told me to collect you. He's a friend of your family. I am to take you home right away so you can pack your things. You're leaving tonight."

"Leaving tonight?" Ewan repeated, showing little interest.

"Your wife is busy packing for your mission."

"My mission?" Ewan laughed.

"Yes, Ewan," Dorothy said, "you're going to do your bit for King and country. They are sending you on a very important mission overseas."

Dorothy helped Ewan up the steps through the front gate to a redbrick house in an upscale London neighbourhood. The taxi driver has already deposited Ewan's valise at the front door. Dorothy paid him and the driver left. When she turned to ring the bell, the door was already open.

"Welcome home, darling!" Mary Butler said as she reached out to kiss her husband. Ewan stumbled into her arms as Dorothy noticed the hallway littered with suitcases.

"We don't have much time, Mrs Butler," Dorothy said. "You both might want to have a bite to eat before we drive you to the airfield."

Ewan negotiated the baggage in the hall and headed aimlessly for the kitchen.

"Are you sure he is all right?" Mary asked. "He doesn't look himself."

"After a month in a sanatorium, Mrs Butler," Dorothy said, "no one looks themself. I think it's only normal with all the medication."

Stockholm

"So why did you leave your job as a schoolmaster at Rugby?" Bridget asked.

Peter and Bridget were having a drink in a cosy restaurant with a view of the waterfront and the sun setting in the west.

"I was about to get called up when I got a letter from a

Cambridge don," Peter said. "He was on a visit to the college and invited me to tea. It all started there. A few casual questions about my background, my German and French language skills, my desire to serve. I was bored with teaching. I thought I could do something for the country."

"Where did you learn to speak German and French?"

"I ran away from home when I was 15. My dad had a pub in Dartmouth, *The Dauphin,* until he lost it in a wager when I was a kid. Things went downhill from there. He was drunk by 3 o'clock every day so my mum up and left us. She went home to look after my grandma. I had to get away so I took a job on a German channel vessel as a seaman, doing deck and loading duties. The job took me from Dartmouth to Calais, to Bremerhaven and as far as Danzig. It was fun sailing the channel ports and the Baltic coast. I met a lot of very interesting people who spoke a lot of different languages."

It occurred to Bridget that it was the most Peter had ever spoken about himself. Even now it was just the bare essentials, enough to answer her question. Unlike most men in her presence he had made no attempt to embellish or boast about his achievements. She looked down at his hands, his long fingers and nicely maintained nails. In a way they summed him up. They were the hands of a confident man - a man of value - who didn't sweat the fine details and knew where he was going.

"What about you?" Peter asked.

"Oh, me," Bridget flushed with embarrassment, realizing that she'd been staring. "I'm a child of the diplomatic service, Peter. My dad worked in Cairo, Berlin, Rome, and Stockholm. That's why I came back here. I speak German, Italian and some Swedish so it was very easy for me to move here. I feel almost at home in the city."

The waiter brought their plates just as a large group of German Legation officers noisily broke up a meeting in a back room. As they filed out, Bridget noticed with a start that Dr Kramer was among them. Elegantly dressed and supremely confident, Karl-Heinz glanced in their direction.

"Guten Appetit, Herr Faye," Karl-Heinz smiled as he passed their table.

Bridget froze, but Peter managed a nod and a word.

"Guten Tag, Herr Kramer."

Karl-Heinz smiled as he followed his colleagues out the door.

Thirteen

There was the clickety-clack sound of fingers on keys as the secretarial staff toiled over letters and documents for the Enskilda Bank. Britta was one of ten women working in the typing pool and noticed one of the bank's senior accountants walking past her desk. She took a deep breath, got up and followed the man into his office. He was just sitting down at his desk when Britta appeared in the doorway.

"Mr Ahlman, can I have a word?"

"Hello, Mrs Berger. How are you?"

"I am fine, Mr Ahlman."

"Come in, please."

Britta sat down on a wooden chair opposite Ahlman's desk.

"Mr Ahlman, I have been trying to locate my brother Rolf Lagerman. He's in Germany."

"Is he now?"

"My brother disappeared from a concentration camp earlier this year. Now they say he may be in a *Nacht und Nebel* work camp. We have lost any trace of him. My family is very worried."

"I'm so sorry."

"As you know, sir, Enskilda has close relations with the Robert Bosch group," Britta said. "The bank owns shares in several Bosch companies including the American Bosch Corporation."

"I see where you're going with this, Mrs Berger, but I don't..."

Britta interrupted: "My husband and I were thinking that perhaps the bank could inquire at the Robert Bosch company in Stuttgart about the whereabouts of my brother, very discreetly, of course."

"Mrs Berger. You are a valuable employee, but I am not sure whether our management would want to get involved."

"Please, Mr Ahlman, we're only looking for information about my brother. It's a simple request and Mr Wallenberg has always shown an interest in the well-being of the bank's employees."

Ahlman looked lost at sea. He opened his mouth to say something, and then decided to remain silent.

Britta produced a letter from her handbag.

"I have written a short letter," she said, "requesting information about my brother which the bank could simply forward to the Bosch company."

The accountant looked at her, weighing the risk to his position and then came to a decision.

"I will give your letter to Mr Wallenberg. I will tell him you are an employee who is worried about her brother. That is the best I can do. It will be up to Mr Wallenberg."

Britta smiled gratefully and handed him the letter.

"Thank you, sir."

She hurried out of his office before he could change his mind.

Ewan Butler stood in the middle of the Consular Services office in a rumpled suit, holding his hat and looking down at his feet, as Victor Mallet, in a pinstripe suit with a red rose in his lapel, made the presentations.

"Hello, Bridget, Peter. I want you to meet our new employee, Ewan Butler. He's just arrived in Stockholm."

"Hello," Bridget and Peter replied.

In the background Sigge, the desk officer, was busy stamping a document for a Swedish gentleman.

"We are happy to have him," Mallet said. "Butler was a journalist before the war. He speaks fluent German and is a bit of a celebrity, you know, although he will deny it."

"A celebrity?" Ewan asked.

"Yes, he's being very modest but his reputation precedes him. He knew Reinhard Heydrich, the SS butcher, the 'Hangman of Prague'. Didn't you, my boy?"

"That was years ago, sir," Ewan said mildly, "I knew him before the war."

He attempted a smile in Bridget and Peter's direction which quickly became a frown. He removed his spectacles and started to wipe them down with a handkerchief.

"Butler has been working in our office in Cairo," Mallet continued, proud of his new recruit. "He has contacts within the Swedish royal family. You know Princess Sibylla, don't you Butler?"

Ewan looked embarrassed as he put on his spectacles.

"Butler will be working with Joanna in the press office," Mallet added.

"You are both welcome to come down and have a drink with me," Ewan offered in a hesitant voice.

"Thank you, Mr Butler," Bridget said smiling.

Mallet quickly swung around and headed for the door, dragging Butler along with him.

"Ta-ta, Peter, Bridget," Mallet said in the doorway waving goodbye.

Peter and Bridget returned to their desks.

"Butler is SOE," Bridget said. "He's supposed to give Joanna a hand with black propaganda."

"Nice chap but why is Mallet treating him like royalty?" Peter asked.

"The gossips around here are saying that he got the job through the MP, Harold Nicolson. Mallet likes him because of his connection to the Swedish royal family."

"You're amazing, Bridget."

"It's Joanna who hears these things. Everyone is talking about Butler's arrival."

It was ten o'clock when Peter and Bernie arrived at the Grand Hotel waterfront. They checked their watches and looked around. A man appeared out of nowhere and knocked on the window.

"Hello, Mr Faye," Anders said as Bernie slid down the window.

Peter opened the door for Anders who climbed into the back seat.

"We're on time," Anders said. "Our man should be here any moment."

"Who exactly are we meeting, Mr Berger?"

"His name is Saarson. That's all I know."

"So what is he selling?" Peter asked impatiently.

"I think he has something important to tell you, some top secret information."

The lights from a motorcar blinked at the far end of the pier.

"That must be the bloke," Bernie said.

The car approached slowly and then turned away, crossing into the old quarter. Bernie followed it at a distance through the narrow streets of Gamla Stan. After making several turns the car stopped at a Turkish restaurant. Bernie parked the car nearby and they watched as a man left the car and went inside. Peter and Anders exchanged a look, then got out of the car and followed the man.

The restaurant was empty except for a man sitting at a table in the back. He looked up as they came in.

"Are you Colonel Saarson?" Anders asked.

"Yes. You must be Mr Berger."

"Yes and this is Mr Faye of the British Legation."

"Ah, Mr Faye," Saarson said. "A pleasure to meet you, sir. Please sit down."

Peter and Anders sat down opposite Saarson as the waiter approached from the kitchen.

"What can I do for you?" Peter asked.

"I believe the question is what I can do for you, Mr Faye."

Anders stood up as the waiter arrived.

"I think I will let you two talk alone," Anders said. "I will be outside."

"Good idea," Peter replied. "I'm sure we won't be long."

Anders left, returning to the car.

"Coffee, aquavit, Mr Faye?" Saarson offered.

"Aquavit, please."

The waiter left to get their drinks.

"I am from Tallinn, Mr Faye. I work for the Estonian government in exile."

"Would you mind if I checked your credentials with my people in London?" Peter asked.

"Best not to, sir. I could lose my job. This is highly confidential. I'm sure you understand."

"What do you have, Colonel Saarson?"

"Soviet material, sir. Top secret."

Fourteen

In the kitchen of his flat, Anders sipped his morning coffee, being careful not to spill any on his grey suit. Britta looked up from spoon-feeding little Nils in his high chair.

"I will call Ahlman at the bank today," she said, "and follow up on my letter to Bosch company. He's had time to give it to Wallenberg."

"Keep on him, Britta. You are not asking for much. All he has to do is give it to his boss."

"He's my brother. I won't give up on him, Anders."

Anders finished his coffee and grabbed his hat.

"So what did Lundquist say?" Britta asked.

"Lundquist wants a tourism piece. I'm giving him tourism with a twist if you like."

"Lundquist likes you, Anders. He's a nice man ."

"Yes, he's a good man but he may be a bit upset by my new piece."

"Don't be so dramatic, Anders. If he doesn't like it, he'll have you change it or simply suppress the publication."

"But I want him to publish it. It will be a hit with readers."

"Well, best of luck," Britta said. "You better be going."

Anders grabbed his briefcase and kissed Britta and Nils before leaving.

In the basement document room, Michael and Peter were looking at some photographs taken by Bernie.

"I took these at Henry Denham's party a couple of weeks back," Bernie said.

"You haven't met Henry yet. He's our naval attaché, Peter," Michael said, "and very well connected."

"Yes, I've heard about Denham when I was in London."

"The Swedes have tried several times to have him declared persona non grata and sent home, but he is still here."

Bernie sifted through the B&W prints. One of them showed a man on the roof of Henry Denham's house with headphones listening to the conversations of the guests visible in a large glass enclosed hall below.

"Bloody hell, that's a nice shot, Bernie," Michael said. "I believe I have seen that chap before. He's 'Svestapo'."

" 'Svestapo' meaning 'Swedish Gestapo' I presume?" Peter asked.

"That's right," Bernie confirmed, "the tossers are keeping a close eye on us for their Nazi mates."

"We've complained in the past," Michael said, "but they're still doing it."

"I've a contact that might be able to use this picture," Peter said. "Can I keep the print?"

"Sure, Peter. It's yours, no problem," Bernie said.

Bernie put the print in an envelope and Michael and Peter headed back upstairs.

"Did you meet Butler?" Michael asked.

"Yes, he seems to be a nice chap."

"He's nice enough, but he's also a hopeless drunk. He has quite a file. I would steer clear of him if I were you. He can only get you in trouble. I don't know why they sent him here."

Ewan Butler was reading a German magazine, *Der Deutchen in Schweden*. He took off his spectacles and rubbed his eyes. He turned to Joanna who was working at her desk behind a huge pile of newspapers.

"The German Legation is putting on quite a show for their people at the Borgarskolan auditorium," Ewan said. "The actor Georg Alexander from Berlin is coming here to play in a comedy."

"Yes, I saw that," Joanna replied.

"Georg Alexander is good, you know. I saw him in Berlin before the war. Attendance is by invitation only. I would expect their legation to invite a number of Swedish Nazis. What do you think?"

"They do like to do things in style, sir."

Ewan looked at Joanna with a boyish grin.

"We could have some fun with this."

"What do you mean?"

"You know it could get to be quite chaotic if we were to invite a large crowd of Swedes with fake tickets."

"Fake tickets?"

"That auditorium must hold at least 500 people," Ewan said. "Suppose we print 1000 fake tickets and offer them to well-to-do Swedes. They'd be happy to put on their best clothes to get a look at Berlin's finest."

"Oh, no," Joanna laughed, "the poor dears won't be able to get in."

"Exactly," Ewan beamed, "it'll be absolute chaos at the door."

"That is a devilish plot, sir. Rather a step up from our humdrum itching powder and stink bombs."

"Don't minimize the havoc caused by itching powder and stink bombs, Joanna. Itching powder can drive a man mad but this kind of thing can drive a wedge between influential Swedes and their German friends."

"I like it," Joanna said. "When do we start?"

It was a rainy day as Bernie cycled along the lane behind the Kramer residence. He laid his bike against the fence and stepped through the gate quickly, crossing the grass to the side of the house. A moment later, he returned to his bicycle and cycled away down the lane with the cloth bag secured in a plastic wrap in the basket.

Bernie arrived at the shed and stepped inside where Peter was waiting for him. Allan turned on the lights of the copy stand as Bernie laid the documents on the table one at a time. Peter started to rifle through the documents with great interest.

Gustav Lundquist stopped by Anders' desk at the newspaper .

"I like the article, Berger. I like the tone. German tourists having the time of their lives in neutral Stockholm while their cities are bombed by the Allies and their soldiers are fighting on the Russian front."

"Yes, sir."

"I like the matter-of-fact tourism approach. There is nothing here to warrant any serious criticism."

"It's quite harmless, sir."

"Yes, it is."

"It's not anti-German, sir, it should go on the front page."

"Of course, it must go on the front page if we want make a splash with it," Lundquist said. "Let me run it by the owner but I think it's just what we need."

As Lundquist left, Anders beamed with delight at the good news. As a young journalist he struggled to make a name for himself among the established names on the roster. He was still treated as a freelance hack and his income depended on getting his work published.

Fifteen

Dr Kramer pulled up at a hangar at the Bromma airfield near Stockholm in an unremarkable Opel sedan. There were a few Ju52s, DC3s, and Lockheed 14s scattered about the airfield. He got out of his car and went inside, passing a mechanic working on a small plane. Kramer paid no attention to him and went directly to the freight manager's office. Sven Ekstrom in shirtsleeves looked up as Kramer appeared in the doorway.

"Hello, Dr Kramer."

"Morning, Herr Ekstrom. I need your shipping invoices."

"What's the hurry? You get them every Friday."

"A bit of a crisis. What have you shipped this week to Scotland?"

Ekstrom searched his shipping invoices.

"The usual loads of SKF bearings, sir," Ekstrom said, "ABA and BOAC flights to Aberdeen. As you know the British have orders with Svenska Kullagerfabriken AB in Gothenburg."

Ekstrom showed Kramer the invoices and he quickly jotted down the total load for the week in a small notebook.

"Thanks, Herr Ekstrom. I will be on my way. Good day."

Kramer left the office, leaving Ekstrom frowning. He was already breaking every company rule in providing the Germans with sensitive information about shipments of SKF bearings, and now the man was coming around mid-week hungry for the latest. If this continued, Ekstrom could lose his job.

A secretary stopped by Anders' desk on the press floor.

"A letter for you, sir."

Anders ripped open the oversized envelope and took out a large black and white photograph and letter. The photograph showed a man on a rooftop wearing headphones. From the figures in the lighted windows on the floor below it looked as if some kind of party was going on and the man with the headphones was listening in to conversations. Anders picked up the letter which bore the letterhead of the British press office. It read simply: 'Gestapo spies working in Sweden.'

Anders dialled a telephone number and then lit a cigarette. The phone rang several times until it was picked up.

"Press Office," Tennant speaking.

"Hello, I am Anders Berger at the Stockholms-Tidningen newspaper."

"Yes, Mr Berger. What can I do for you?"

"I just got the photograph, sir."

"Sorry, I don't know anything about a photograph," the man replied, sounding confused.

"The Gestapo man with headphones on the roof."

"Oh, that one. The Gestapo man, yes I remember it now."

In the Legation Press office Michael Tennant suppressed a laugh. Nearby Joanna pricked up her ears listening to Michael's side of the conversation.

"Oh, yes, very troubling that photograph, sir," Michael said, playing it for all it was worth.

"Can you tell me when it was taken?" Anders asked.

"In July, I believe during a Legation reception."

"Has Gestapo surveillance been a problem for you at the Legation?"

"It's been absolutely terrible!" Michael complained, suddenly irate. "We can't turn around here without running into some kind of surveillance. It's been going on for several years."

"I'm sorry to hear that, sir," Anders replied.

"We are having a terrible time trying to keep a low profile in this country and getting no help from the authorities."

"I will take this to my boss. You won't mind if we publish the picture?"

"Of course not, Mr Berger. Good-bye."

Michael hung up and then turned to Joanna.

"You remember Bernie's photograph of that man on the roof from Swedish Intelligence services."

"Of course."

"Peter must have sent it to Anders Berger at the Stockholms-Tidningen newspaper," Michael said. "He thinks the man works for the Gestapo. He's going to publish it."

"But the man is a Swede, he's easily identifiable."

"I know, but wouldn't it be wonderful if they make that mistake? We embarrass both the Gestapo and the Swedish government at the same time."

"What will the 'angry rabbit' say about that?"

"The angry rabbit can shit a brick. I don't care what Mallet thinks. Let's see how it unfolds first."

Michael laughed, thinking about the implications.

"It will be very embarrassing for the Swedes," Joanna said.

"They've earned it," Michael said. "The people working for the 'Svestapo' are complete idiots. Don't they know that the Germans are losing the war?"

"My boss is very happy with your work," Bridget said.

"Wonderful, Bridget. I had no idea whether it was working for you or not," Hanne replied.

At the Ansell house Hanne and Bridget were sitting comfortably in the living room as Elsa served them tea. The gramophone played Mozart in the background.

"I have brought you some money, Hanne, for your services," Bridget said, putting an envelope with Swedish krona on the table. Hanne looked annoyed.

"I am not doing it for money, Bridget, please."

She pushed the envelope back towards Bridget.

"Take the money, Hanne," Elsa said. "Bridget knows that you do not do it for money."

"Hanne, please take it, we pay our people," Bridget replied. "This is hard work and dangerous. You need the money."

Hanne looked at Elsa and then at the envelope.

"You're too damn proud, Hanne," Elsa said. "You take the money now, please!"

Hanne looked undecided.

"You take it or I take it and hold it for you."

Hanne nodded her acceptance reluctantly.

"Thank you, Bridget," Hanne said in a whisper. "Dr Kramer is off to Berlin next week. He has meetings with Schellenberg and Schmidt."

"How do you know this, Hanne?" Bridget asked.

"I saw it in his agenda and Frau Kramer mentioned his travel plans. He leaves on the Wednesday."

"So we must do a pickup on the Tuesday," Bridget said, "just before his departure. Then we await his return."

Sixteen

Peter pushed through the barrier at the Consular Services office with several decoded messages. He sat down at his desk and looked up at Bridget who had just put down the phone.

"Kramer's dispatches are providing Berlin with the loads on those SKF shipments to Britain. I think they've spotted our supply weakness in ball bearings and may target BOAC flights."

"I thought London had solved the problem," Bridget said.

"They have a fast blockade-runner, the Gay Viking, on route for Lysekil on the west coast."

"The Gay Viking?" Bridget laughed. "What a funny name!"

"Yes, it is. They sailed last night into the Skagerrak (the strait between Norway and Denmark) and are scheduled to return to the Humber in two days with a full load. Let's just hope they succeed."

Bridget thought about Peter's other life in the merchant marine and realized that he would know about ships and their speeds on the water. He would be at home on a ship like the Gay Viking. He wasn't the typical English diplomat with a superior air who couldn't hold a screwdriver.

"It's a converted gunboat with a speed of 28 knots," Peter noted, "so it should bring home a substantial load of ball bearings for the war effort."

"But don't the Germans have faster S-boats in the Skagerrak?"

"Yes, they do. The *Schnellboots* go up to 43 knots, ergo the night mission. How did it go with H?"

"At first she didn't want to take the money," Bridget said, "but Elsa convinced her."

"Good."

"She says Kramer is off to Berlin next week and guess who he's meeting in Berlin? Schellenberg and Schmidt."

Peter raised an eyebrow at this revelation.

"How does she know this?" Peter asked.

"The names are in Kramer's agenda."

"Well, isn't that something. H is becoming an incredible asset, Bridget."

"She's very courageous. I don't know how she gets up the courage to snoop in that drawer."

"London thinks that the *Abwehr* is on its last legs. The Gestapo has it in for Canaris. Schellenberg may be trying to recruit Kramer for his *SD Ausland* service."

Suddenly the door to the outer office swung open and Michael Tennant barged in with a copy of the Stockholms-Tidningen paper.

"Have you seen this?" Tennant said grinning.

He showed Bridget and Peter the front page. It was dominated by Bernie's photograph of the man on the roof and the headline: 'Gestapo Spies in Stockholm!'

"A marvellous prank," Michael said.

"I never would have thought," Peter laughed."I sent it to Anders to see what he might do with it and he goes and puts it on the front page."

"You sent it, Peter?" Bridget asked.

"Well, it wasn't doing us any good sitting in a file in the basement, so I thought we might have a bit of fun with the Swedish authorities."

"Well, we have that," Michael said gleefully, "the director of the Säpo called the angry rabbit this morning. I hear they practically begged for Mallet's forgiveness."

"You're pulling my leg?"

"No, it's true. It looks like Berlin was outraged by the photograph and the Swedish authorities are getting an earful."

"That's wonderful news," Bridget added.

"The Säpo has promised to stop their surveillance of British Legation activities," Michael said. "Mallet is overjoyed and I am hearing good things from London. Bye now."

Michael waltzed out of the office with the newspaper.

"It's quite astonishing. I don't think Anders is the kind of chap to make a mistake like that," Peter said.

"You think that he knew the identity of the man in the picture?"

"Of course, he must have. He thought he could get more traction from the picture by allowing the mistaken identity and he was right."

"He doesn't look that devious," Bridget said.

"Oh, but he is. Anders is a very clever chap."

Bernie and Peter were on their way to a second nightly meeting with the mysterious Colonel Saarson. They drove through the narrow streets of Gamla Stan, doubling back occasionally to check for tails. They arrived at the Turkish restaurant and Peter crossed the road to the restaurant while Bernie remained in the car.

Bernie was parked under a street lamp, but it was dark in the street. He pulled out his Webley MkIV revolver and laid it on the seat beside him.

Peter sat down opposite the colonel who was sitting in a dark corner of the restaurant drinking aquavit. Peter dropped an envelope on the table and watched Saarson count the money.

"Mr Faye, this is not enough," Saarson complained. "I gave you some very sensitive material. There are risks involved, lives at stake, as you say in English."

"Look, Colonel, I sent the document to London, but they are not offering more money. My superiors are highly sceptical of black market information. Give me better material and perhaps we can come up with more money in the future."

"I can get you anything you want, sir. Top secret material, anything you like, but I need to pay my sources."

"I understand," Peter replied.

"Do you?" Saarson asked.

"Of course I do." Peter said. "The best way to proceed with London is to keep improving on the quality and they will pay handsomely. That's all I can say. I am simply the messenger, but I am sure you know how it works."

Saarson was hoping for a big score, but was clearly disappointed by the result. He stood up quickly, dropping coins on the table.

"OK, Mr Faye. We'll do it your way. I'll bring you better material but I've got to go now."

Saarson and Peter left the restaurant, but Saarson quickly pulled Peter back inside. A car had just pulled up in the street. Two rough-looking men got out and headed towards the café. From across the street Bernie noticed the two men and started his car, slowly driving away.

Peter and Saarson left the restaurant through the back door which opened onto an alley. They ran down it to a side street just as Bernie caught up with them with the car. They jumped into the back of the Legation car and Bernie whisked them away.

"Crikey, that was a close call," Bernie said. "Those two bully-boys are Russian."

"How can you tell, Bernie?" Peter asked.

"Their faces and clothes, sir. They look like Ivans."

"They're NKVD," Saarson said dolefully. "We must be very careful."

Saarson said nothing else until they dropped him off at a street corner near the city centre.

"Good night, Mr Faye. Thanks for the ride. I will contact you again through the journalist in a week or two."

"Good night, sir."

Bernie drove away heading towards the British Legation.

"Why is the NKVD after Saarson, do you think, Bernie?"

"They like to beat up Baltic tossers, sir. Finns, Estonians and their like. Throw them in the canals as sport."

Seventeen

The theatre manager's satisfaction with the glittering crowd had quickly changed to alarm as he realized the number of people swelling the lobby threatened to exceed the number of seats in the Borgarskolan theatre. Something was wrong and he was already on his way to the front of house when he heard the first angry voices.

"You're telling me we can't go in," a big Swede in evening dress yelled at the hapless theatre employee. "We are patrons of this theatre and we have tickets to this event."

"Sir, you see this ticket," said the young man holding it up to the light, "it is not a good ticket. It is white. Our tickets are light blue."

That only served to make the man and his elegant wife even angrier. The confrontation had attracted the attention of others in the crowd and some were checking their own tickets. The manager used the distraction to pull his employee aside.

"Let me see that," he said.

The employee handed the ticket over. The manager only had to glance at it to know his employee was right. It was obviously a counterfeit.

"When did you notice?" the manager asked.

"Just now," the man said sheepishly.

The manager blanched. He could only guess how many people holding these tickets had already gotten in. He hurried inside to take a look.

The theatre was in complete pandemonium. German VIPs arrived at their seats to find them already occupied by wealthy Swedes or Swedes found their seats taken by Germans. Neither party was accustomed to giving way and loud, heated arguments were breaking out everywhere in the theatre. Some had already escalated into shoving matches.

"*Was ist los?*" an angry voice demanded.

The manager turned to find a red-faced and angry German minister at his elbow asking what was wrong.

"A mix-up over tickets, sir," the manager said with a confidence he did not feel. "I am sure everything will be sorted out soon enough."

"This is appalling, sir. Who's responsible?" asked the minister.

The manager had no idea. He was saved from replying by a commotion only a few feet away. Someone had thrown the first punch and the victim was struggling to his feet, blood streaming from his nose.

Wealth implies entitlement and couples in evening dress with counterfeit tickets were now streaming into the hall having knocked down the barrier and were picking fights with German Legation employees and people with valid tickets. Fistfights were breaking out across the hall.

The manager and minister were temporarily blinded by the bright flash of a camera. When his vision returned, the manager recognized Anders Berger standing beside one of the newspaper photographers. He could have sworn that Berger was smiling.

Peter was reading a decrypted message from London in the document room when Bernie came out of the darkroom and laid out several wet prints to dry on a table.

"We must be doing something right, sir," Bernie said, "the messages from London just keep coming."

"Yeah, the Stora Essingen operation is a huge success. We have another pickup on Tuesday."

"I'm ready, sir."

"Good. Bernie, you wouldn't happen to know anyone in cargo operations at the Bromma airfield? Somebody is leaking our SKF shipment loads to the Germans."

"No, but I can ask around."

"I am off to London for a few days. Keep in touch through Bridget, will you Bernie? Thanks."

Peter got up and left the room.

It was late as Peter returned to his flat. As he started up the stairs in the darkened lobby, he noticed a man in the shadows smoking a cigarette. The man lifted his head to look at Peter.

"You played me with that photograph, Mr Faye."

"It worked out very nicely, didn't it Anders? Please call me Peter. Now don't be a spoilsport, I'm sure your newspaper sold a load of copies."

"The man was a Swede from the Säpo."

"Yes, he was."

"Tell me about Kramer, Peter."

"Kramer?"

"Yes, Dr Karl-Heinz Kramer. You seem to have an unusual interest in the man."

"Why don't you come up and have a drink, Anders?"

Peter led Anders up the stairs to his flat. He opened the door and they entered the living room. Peter went to the

81

portable gramophone in the corner and put on a 78 rpm record of a Chopin concerto turning up the volume. As the music filled the room, Peter invited Anders to sit down.

"Please sit down, Anders. The office sweeps the flat for microphones from time to time but you can never be too careful."

"This is a nice flat, it must cost a pretty penny," Anders said with an attempt at cynicism. "Nothing is too good for members of the diplomatic service."

"Aquavit, Anders?"

"Yes. So how do you like Stockholm, Peter?"

"I love it, you live in a wonderful city."

Peter poured two glasses of aquavit.

"No hard feelings about the photograph, Peter."

"I reckoned you knew the chap on the roof and would know it was a mistake."

"This is our patch, Peter," Anders said with a grin. "We know everyone, but sometimes we too make mistakes. We sold the entire print run. It was amazing."

"Cheers, Anders."

Peter and Anders clinked their glasses and drank their aquavit.

"I have some information for you, but I also need to ask you a favour."

"Of course, Anders."

"That Saarson chap has not been back?"

"I can't discuss it. I think you understand."

"Of course, you secret-service types can't have a chit-chat with the ordinary citizen," Anders said with a smile, "it wouldn't do."

Peter shrugged.

"I have heard that Dr Kramer is often seen at General Onodera's house. They are allies, you know, the Japanese and the Germans. I have heard that the General has some Soviet material for sale."

"Makato Onodera, the Japanese military attaché?" Peter asked.

"Yes. Onodera is an interesting man. He speaks Russian and worked in Latvia before the war so he has lots of contacts in Russian and Baltic circles."

Peter stood up suddenly and walked around the room.

"Who put you up to this, Anders?" Peter asked with a suspicious air. "Who are you working for?"

"No one, I'm a journalist," Anders replied casually.

"Someone wants you to shop this information to me? How much are they paying you?"

"No one is paying me, Peter. I won't lie to you. I have a close friend working with Saarson, Reinhard Massing."

"You are very well connected for a journalist."

"Yes, I have to be. As you know, I am also a sympathizer for the Allied cause. I am tired of the German presence in Sweden. Two years ago no one talked about it, but now everyone is talking about the downfall of Germany. It is time for Sweden to show its colours and stand up to Germany."

"I would ask you to be very careful with the information you have. Lives depend on it."

At the Berger flat Britta was asleep when her husband entered the bedroom. Anders started to undress as Britta awakened with a start.

"So how did it go, Anders?"

"He can't promise anything. He's going to check with his people in London."

"Well, that's good, isn't it?"

"We'll see. I don't know whether the British can find Rolf.

The official channels haven't found him yet and your Bosch people were no help."

"No one wants to touch it in Stuttgart and Enskilda won't push them."

"There is some hope, Britta. Count Folke Bernadotte and the Swedish Red Cross are trying to organize prisoner releases in Germany so they should have access to the lists soon enough."

"We'll talk in the morning. It's late. Good night."

"Good night, darling."

Eighteen

On a snowy night at the Bromma airfield, Peter stepped out of the British Legation car and walked through the gates to the tarmac where a BOAC de Havilland Mosquito, a converted bomber, was loading passengers for the night flight to RAF Leuchars in Scotland. Peter put his bag on a rack on the tarmac and started to climb.

At the top of the ramp he looked around at the airfield with its Deutsche Luft Hansa Ju52s, ABA DC3s, BOAC Lockheed 14s and a Curtis CW-20 parked on the tarmac with snow accumulating on their fuselages. Peter was taking what was commonly known as the 'ball-bearing run' from Sweden to Scotland. The Mosquito was a fast, civilian-registered aircraft with all its armaments and guns removed - a legal requirement to fly to neutral countries. The Swedish ABA airline had already lost two DC-3s on flights going to Britain, shot down over the North Sea. From Leuchars, Peter would fly south in a military plane to RAF Northolt near London.

London

There was an odour of dust and decay in the air as Peter

descended from a taxi at MI6 Headquarters at 54 Broadway, near the St. James's Park underground station. London stood in stark contrast to immaculate Stockholm. Many of the buildings on Broadway off Victoria Street were bombed out shells.

Peter met with his old friend, Major Keith Linwood, in a small anonymous office on the third floor.

"I'm sorry it has taken so long to have this meeting, Peter."

"That's all right, Keith. Who's coming?"

"Hollis and Liddell aren't available I'm afraid," Linwood said. "You'll be meeting with Anthony Blunt, the senior MI5 liaison officer, who is in charge of the file."

"Blunt? Is he meeting me here?"

"No. He's waiting for you at his club, the Reform Club on Pall Mall. I know it is a bit unusual, but with all the renovations going on in the building, I think you will better off over there."

Peter raised an eyebrow.

"Isn't this a bit unusual, Keith? MI5 conducting business from a private club."

"Well, Blunt does have quite the pedigree. Takes his tea with the Queen Mother in Mayfair. So be careful with the man."

"Well, I'd better get over there. Pleasure seeing you again."

Major Linwood stood up and gave Peter a parting hug.

"Say hello to Ethel and that lovely daughter of yours," Peter said in the doorway.

"I will. Good luck with Blunt. Nice to see you again, Peter."

The Reform Club on Pall Mall had somehow escaped the ravages of the bombing and the silence within was a welcome refuge from the din of nonstop repair work going on outside.

Peter admired the club's vast atrium with its marble columns and portraits of political leaders as he was led down a hall to a quiet club room for his meeting. Major Anthony Blunt stood up as Peter arrived. He was a tall, aristocratic man with an upper class accent. Peter had been initially prepared to dislike him but Blunt was both charming and obviously intelligent with deep laugh lines and a boyish shock of blond hair going to grey.

"Sorry to run you around town, Peter," Blunt said apologetically, "but since Liddell and Hollis were not available, I thought we might be more comfortable talking here."

Peter was about to reply when a door opened and a man came in bearing a coffee tray. Blunt saw Peter's hesitation.

"It's all right, Peter," he said with a wry smile, "he's one of ours."

The man placed the coffee tray on the table beside a stack of files and withdrew. Peter glanced at the files on the table and wondered just how senior Blunt was. Very few people had the authority to remove files from headquarters.

"We have been over the secret memorandum that you obtained from Dr Kramer's home," Blunt said, "and while you believe it is an original document about the Quebec conference, we think it may be a German forgery."

"With all due respect, sir. It looked very authentic to me."

"You said so in your dispatches that it was an original document and you held it in your hands. Well, our people found some of Roosevelt's comments rather Germanic in their formulation. As you know, that's sometimes indicative of forgeries."

Peter could barely believe his ears and struggled to keep his tone civil. He stared at Blunt silently for a moment.

"Did you notice Roosevelt's obscene remarks about the

letters from Stalin?"

"Yes, of course," Blunt said.

"American presidents are like that, sir. They use profanity constantly to make a point. Roosevelt talks like that."

Blunt looked sceptical.

"In my previous posting I saw parts of the original minutes of the 1941 Newfoundland conference in Placentia Bay, sir," Peter said. "We were shocked by Roosevelt's language. I don't see how this could be a forgery. This is the way American presidents carry on."

"Well, he seems to have a shocking lack of respect for the Soviet leader," Blunt said.

"Yes, he does," Peter replied, "but from what I've heard Churchill finds him amusing."

"Churchill would, of course. His mother Lady Randolph was American."

Peter was surprised by Blunt's anti-American feeling and reminded himself to watch his tone. He stood up for a moment while Blunt busied himself pouring the coffee. Peter looked out the window onto Pall Mall. He could see the ruins of several bombed-out buildings opposite St. James Square. When he turned back, he saw that Blunt was watching him.

"Do you want something stronger, perhaps a sherry or a whisky?" Blunt asked. "You must be quite tired from your flight."

"I'm fine, thank you, sir," Peter said stiffly.

He was indeed exhausted but he was angry with himself for letting Blunt see it. He'd arrived in the early morning and would have to fly back to Stockholm that night.

"I don't want you to misunderstand me, Peter," Blunt said, "we're very happy with your work and the intelligence you've gathered. I will be passing on your comments to my colleagues and we will take them into consideration."

Peter sat down again and looked at Blunt.

"Sir, clearly someone with access to the original drafts is passing them along to the Germans, obviously an agent working at the highest possible level with access to Cabinet documents and War office minutes."

"We're working on it. We'll have results eventually," said Blunt with assurance.

"What's your take on the cabinet document I bought from the Estonian? The one regarding American proposals for the post-war trusteeship of 'dependent peoples'."

"Yes, we think it is credible," Blunt said.

"It has the American State department stamp on it and I'm sure you noticed the snide comment in the margin from the Foreign Office about the American Secretary of State being a 'vindictive old woman'. No foreign intelligence officer can fake that kind of personal touch."

"Yes, I agree."

"One comes from a German source and the other from a Soviet source. Doesn't that worry you a little bit?"

"We're looking into it, but it takes time."

"As you know, there is an absolute glut of secret intelligence in Stockholm and I think most of it is coming from Moscow. The source of the Quebec memorandum may actually be Soviet, purchased by the Germans in Stockholm."

"Yes, you may be right."

"And what about the Josefine dispatches, Kramer's source?"

"We've stopped the Josefine leak. The man was a Swedish air attaché who was reporting back to his masters in Stockholm. We've sent him home."

"Very good, sir," Peter said. "You know that the Swedes are worried about a Soviet invasion, now that the Germans are starting to retreat on all fronts. There is a feeling at the

Legation that the Soviets will soon be a serious threat."

"I doubt that the Soviets would ever attack Sweden. They have enough on their hands," Blunt said dismissively as he stood up and went to the bar in the corner. He poured himself a whisky and returned, looking unhappily at Peter.

"If the memorandum is coming from a Soviet source," Peter pursued, "then Stalin is already reading the minutes of the Roosevelt/Churchill talks. This could compromise future talks with the man."

"About the Quebec conference I can categorically assure you there is no cross knowledge. The Soviets know nothing about this, they are only interested in the timing of the second front."

Peter thought about Blunt's assertion. Since the disaster at Dieppe, the Soviets had been pushing the Western Allies to launch an attack on mainland Europe to open a second front.

"So if it is not a Soviet source, then we have a German agent working at the highest level of the British government who in short order can get his hands on just about any original document. Our chaps must be shitting bricks over this."

There was a long silence in the room before Blunt spoke again.

"Of course we're worried, Peter, but we're not purposely leaking documents to the Germans. So if something is happening here, we'll get to the bottom of it. I promise you."

Nineteen

Stockholm

It was after midnight by the time Peter arrived home from London. It had been all he could do to stay awake during the taxi ride from the Bromma airfield, but when he mounted the stairs in his building he became instantly alert. The door to his flat was ajar and he could see a sliver of light coming from the kitchen. He stepped warily through the open door with his briefcase. He could hear someone moving around in the kitchen.

Peter took a deep breath to steady his nerves and slid along the wall picking up an old cricket bat that he kept near the door. He held up the bat ready to strike as he stepped into the kitchen. He wasn't prepared for what he saw.

Bridget in a dark blue dress and an apron was pulling a casserole out of the oven. She turned and saw him as he hid the bat behind his back.

"Peter, how was your flight?"

It took him a moment to reply. His heart was still pounding in his ears and her expression turned to concern.

"Are you all right?"

"Fine, I'm fine," he managed.

She came up to him and gave him a peck on the cheek.

"You must be exhausted," she said, "I hope you weren't too surprised to find the door unlocked. I did tell you I would cook you a meal on your return."

"How did you get in?" Peter asked as Bridget returned to the stove. He stepped quickly back into the living room and got rid of the bat which he leaned against the wall.

"Oh, the concierge took pity on me and opened the door. What a lovely flat you have? I envy you field agents, you get the best accommodation."

"I suppose we do. London Central wants the best for its agents."

"I could never afford a furnished flat like this on my diplomatic staff salary. How did it go in London?"

Peter found his mind wandering. Bridget looked very fetching in her dress and red lipstick.

"It didn't go very well I'm afraid. I met that tosser from MI5, Anthony Blunt. I don't know how they put up with the man."

"Take off your coat. Have a drink."

"I expected a proper meeting at headquarters with Hollis, Liddell, and Keith Linwood, but instead I wound up with the MI5 liaison officer at the Reform Club on Pall Mall."

"Very posh I've heard."

"It's almost as if Blunt were trying to diminish the importance of our work. He even suggested that Kramer's documents were forgeries."

"No!" Bridget exclaimed, looking stunned.

"It's absurd. I did my best to argue otherwise but all I got was the usual blather about taking my comments into consideration."

"Well, I'm sorry to hear that," Bridget brightened, making an obvious effort to cheer him up. "I've made us a wonderful dinner and I even found a bottle of that German Mosel wine you like."

"Thank you, Bridget. That's very sweet of you."

Peter removed his hat and coat and went to close the door. He returned to the kitchen as Bridget put two steaming plates of English beef stew on the table.

"I hope you're hungry, it's very late," Bridget said.

"Famished, thank you."

Peter opened the bottle of wine and poured them both a glass. Bridget picked up her glass.

"Here we are enjoying a glass of excellent German wine," Peter said, "which would be quite impossible to get anywhere in England."

"Most of the wine here is Spanish or Portuguese."

"Yes, and very good it is, but a Mosel white is very special."

"Cheers, Peter."

"Cheers, Bridget. Thank you for this. It's a wonderful surprise."

It was very late when Peter drove Bridget back to her rooming house. He stopped the car opposite the block of flats and went around to open her door.

"Here you go, Bridget. Thank you so much for the meal and the conversation."

"It was fun, wasn't it?"

Peter took Bridget's hand and drew her nearer. He planted a kiss on her lips before she pulled away.

"Good night, Peter."

Bridget crossed the road as it started to rain and entered her building. She climbed the stairs quietly and opened the door to find three British women in pyjamas playing a game of gin rummy at the kitchen table.

"Bridget, did you have a nice evening?" asked Wendy from the typing pool.

"She's seeing that new chap in Consular Services I bet," said Betty, a rather plain blond woman with her hair wrapped in a towel.

"I met him at the party. His name is Peter Faye. He's a nice catch, quite handsome, Bridget dear," Wendy said.

The third woman Carly laid her cards on the table and turned to look at Bridget.

"There's a message for you, Bridget, from a woman named Elsa. I put it on your bed."

"Thanks. Are you winning again, Wendy?"

"No, Betty's ahead."

Bridget went to her room and collected the message. She went to the hall phone and was going to dial Elsa's number when she looked at her watch. She put the receiver back on its support and returned to her room.

It was a cold and windy day as Bernie on his bike approached the back garden of the Kramer residence. He noticed the Gestapo car backed into the end of the lane so he continued on the road and pulled over under a tree a hundred yards away. He hid behind a shed with a view of the Gestapo officers. One was asleep in the back seat of the car while the other was watching the road in front of the Kramer house.

Bernie had to sneak around a house behind the Kramer's to get into the lane. Then it was just a matter of crossing into the Kramer back garden and collecting the bag. A short time later, he retraced his steps to the bicycle and casually cycled away out from under the nose of the Gestapo.

Bernie arrived at the shed where Peter and Allan were

waiting. The assistant adjusted the Minox camera as Bernie put the first documents on the table.

"The Gestapo car was backed into the lane just as you said it would be," Bernie said nonchalantly.

"We got the message this morning from our contact," Peter said. "Are they still watching the house?"

"If they are," Bernie snorted, "they're not very good at it."

Peter hid a smile as he leaned over to peruse the documents on the table.

The British Legation Christmas party was going full swing as Ewan Butler arrived at the door with his wife Mary. A bar was set up along one wall and a crowd had gathered around including numerous Swedish and American VIPs.

Butler was drunk and nearly stumbled into a Swedish couple standing near the door. Mary pulled him away at the last moment but in the process they ran into Michael.

"Ewan, Mary. How did it go?"

"It was marvellous, wasn't it Mary?" Ewan asked, looking at his wife for corroboration.

"Yes, it was. Princess Sibi was absolutely wonderful," Mary said.

"The Swedes are profiting from the war and it shows them in a very bad light," Ewan said, slurring his words. "They are living in another world."

"But they are a neutral country, Ewan," Michael protested quietly. "They are at peace."

"No, they're not. Europe is in flames and the bloody Swedes are profiting, selling to both sides. It's scandalous!"

The chief of the British Legation Victor Mallet heard Ewan's drunken ranting and approached.

"Cool it, Ewan. Mallet's coming this way," Michael

warned.

"Butler, what are you doing here?" Mallet demanded.

"Having the time of my life! We just arrived from Princess Sibi's reception. The royal family has the very best food and drink, you know. Don't they, darling?" Ewan asked his wife who nodded her assent.

Mallet turned to Michael who was standing nearby.

"Tennant. Can you look after Butler? I think he's had a bit too much to drink."

"I'm fine, sir," Ewan protested.

"Not if you keep carrying on like that. Please go along with Michael."

Michael and Mary took Ewan's arm and led him away towards Peter and Bridget.

"Hello, Peter, Bridget. Have you seen Joanna?" Ewan asked.

"She left early, Ewan," Bridget said.

"I believe the angry rabbit is vexed that he wasn't invited to Sibi's Christmas party," Ewan said.

"Better put a lid on it, Ewan," Michael said as he moved in closer.

"How was it over there?" Peter asked.

"In a word: extravagant, bloody rich, with a lot of sodding aristocrats playing for favours," Ewan declared.

"It was lovely," Mary said. "Princess Sibi is such a sweet person."

"Mary, get me a drink please. A Scotch will do."

"I think you have had enough, dear."

"But I have only just started," Ewan protested. "I am quite sober, you know. After my run-in with the angry rabbit, I need something to fortify myself."

"I will get it, Mary," Bridget offered as she put down her plate on a nearby table. "Why don't you two have a bit of food?"

"Thanks, Bridget."

"No, no. I'm not hungry," Ewan told her. "I want to talk to Peter. I haven't seen him in a while."

Bridget left as Ewan approached.

"Did you see him stamp his feet?" Ewan asked Peter.

"No, I wasn't looking."

"Well, I saw it. No wonder they call him the angry rabbit!"

Twenty

"Hot off the press, Anders. Take a look!"

Stefan looked very pleased with himself as he handed Anders the morning edition of the Stockholms-Tidningen paper. The headline seemed innocent enough: GERMAN TOURISM ON THE RISE.

Under the headline there was the photograph of Dr Kramer and his colleagues carousing on the pier.

"Wonderful!" Anders laughed. "There's Kramer, plain as day. Swedish nationalists will be furious as will most of the German Legation. Great picture, Stefan."

"And to think we pulled that picture from a camera which fell into the canal," Stefan said in amazement.

"Imagine the number of copies the paper will sell with your photograph, Stefan," Anders said with a grin, "you should be asking for a raise."

"She's looking for her husband," Bridget said. "He went missing when his plane was shot down. They were on a bombing raid on Kiel when they were hit. She says that they tried to make it to the Swedish coast."

"It's not that far, you know," Peter said, "I've been to Kiel, it's only about 100 miles from the south coast of Sweden."

Bridget and Peter were finishing a late evening meal in the Grand Hotel restaurant with its traditional bone china dinnerware, its white tablecloths and crystal glassware. The place was almost empty on a weeknight.

"Betty is going to take the woman around to talk to the Swedish authorities."

"If they made it to the coast, there should be a report of some kind."

"Not necessarily," Bridget said. "I told her that her man could already be in a camp. British and American airmen are usually sent to the Falun area. They often don't even bother to contact us."

"So the crew wouldn't be in a police station in Malmo?"

"I doubt it. The Swedes operate under the principle that anyone, friend or foe, flying illegally into Sweden is guilty. Things have improved over the last year or so since the country became less pro-German."

"Tell me about your time in Berlin?" Peter asked.

"Berlin. I loved Berlin," Bridget said. "We were there for five years. We lived in Charlottenburg. Do you know the city?"

"Yes, a bit. I went there for a long drunken weekend with a bunch of German sailors."

"Charlottenburg is a beautiful part of the city west of the *Großer Tiergarten* park with the palace and the *Bahnhof Zoo*. My father had a senior position at the British Legation. I went to a *hochschule* with my brother until 1936 when we returned to England with my mother. She couldn't stomach the Nazis."

"Where's your brother now?"

"He's with the Eighth Army in Italy, Peter. We worry about him."

"I'm sure you do."

Peter was silent for a moment.

"What?" Bridget asked.

"I heard you were married for a time?"

"Peter!" Bridget exclaimed. "You must have seen my file or Keith told you?"

"Keith showed me your file," Peter said, "he thinks the world of you."

"Flattery won't get you anywhere," Bridget laughed. "You know I've never met Major Linwood."

"Well, he's not the only one to have fallen under your spell," Peter said with a grin.

Bridget smiled and picked up her glass.

"I met Allan in 1937 where he clerked for an insurance company in London. We were married a year later. We lived in a flat in Guilford. That summer Allan signed up for military training with the Coldstream Guards and I was hired for a job as a typist in the Foreign Office through my dad's contacts. Allan enjoyed the Guards. It was a way of escaping his marriage and a conventional life."

"What happened to Allan?"

"He was killed in Norway in April 1940."

"I'm sorry to hear that," Peter said.

"All water under the bridge. Our marriage was over by the time he left for Norway. Allan was not good marriage material I'm afraid. He was constantly out drinking with his chums and when he did come home, we would fight. I was happy when he went away. So what about you, Peter? Didn't you ever want to get married?"

"No woman in her right mind wants to marry a seaman off on frequent voyages, Bridget. I had one chance at it, but I blew it. I was a schoolmaster at Rugby at the time. My fiancée wanted me to move with her to a new school in Norfolk where she had obtained a teaching post. I liked Rugby and didn't want to make the move. After a term of separation we just seemed to lose interest in one another. So how did you get to Stockholm?"

"My dad left Berlin for Stockholm shortly after we had returned home. My mother and I joined him in 1940. It was wonderful being abroad again. It was an adventure being in not so neutral Sweden. We had our friends but a lot of the Swedes we met were pro-Nazi. There were several Swedish National Socialist parties vying for power at the time."

"So you have been with the Legation for three years?"

"Yes, my dad retired in 1941 and my family returned home. I stayed on."

Peter called for the bill, leaving a generous tip for the waiter, and they went to retrieve their coats. They were just outside the cloakroom when Bridget waved at someone.

"Is that Joanna?"

Peter looked up just in time to see a woman cross the lobby and disappear behind a marble column.

"It looks like Joanna," he said.

"I waved but she didn't see me," Bridget shrugged.

"Perhaps she's meeting somebody," Peter smiled. "We don't want to embarrass her."

Peter and Bridget left the restaurant.

Inside the hotel lavatory Joanna was applying rouge to her cheeks in front of the mirror as a dark-haired woman wearing a blue scarf and coat came in.

"*Hallå.*"

The woman ignored Joanna's greeting and went into a cubicle. Joanna finished her makeup and hurried out, leaving an envelope between the washbasins. The woman quickly left the cubicle and picked up the envelope, slipping it into her handbag before leaving.

Bridget pressed a sheet against her bare breast and picked up her martini glass as she noticed snowflakes falling on the darkened city through the bedroom window.

"Isn't the snow lovely!"

"I think there is something else quite lovely around here," Peter laughed, embracing Bridget under the sheets.

"Peter, stop. I'm very ticklish."

"Yes, you are."

They were silent as they watched the snow falling. Bridget played with the olive in her martini glass.

"You've known Keith Linwood for some time?" she asked.

"Keith and I went to school together. I've known him forever."

"How did you come to work for Keith?"

"A complete coincidence, my dear," Peter said. "I had no idea he worked for MI6. I thought he had a humdrum desk job in the army and then he pops up on my first day at work."

"It must have been a big surprise?"

Peter looked at Bridget and laughed.

"It was. Keith seemed to think that I had made a wrong turn and mistakenly turned up in his office. 'Faye', he says, 'what the hell are you doing in military intelligence?'"

"I wanted to tell him that I had received all the necessary training to be a spook. I was ready and willing to serve."

"'Go back down those stairs', he says, deadly serious, 'and tell the man at the desk that you're looking for the navy recruiting office. Run along now.'"

"'But I've been recruited, Keith, I say.'"

"'You a spook?' he says. 'You've got to be joking.'"

"I said, 'Keith, I'm serious. I'm going to be a spook.'"

"'Well, you must be right' he says, ''cause I've got your name on the list right here. Welcome to the company, Peter.'"

"He was pulling your leg," Bridget said.

"Yeah, Keith is like that. Always the funny one."

It was snowing heavily as Peter drove Bridget back to her lodgings. They parked nearby and chatted in the car for a long time before Bridget kissed Peter and got out.

"Good night, Peter. I had a lovely time."

"Me too. See you tomorrow."

Bridget crossed the road to her rooming house. She turned to wave at him as she entered the building. Peter drove away into the snowy night.

Twenty-one

Bernie was taking a picture of an employee for an identity card in the basement document room. The young Swedish woman stepped away from the white wall.

"I will send it up to you later, miss."

"Thanks, Mr Dixon."

The employee left the room, almost running into Peter on her way out. Bernie looked up from his camera.

"Thanks for coming down Peter. I have some information for you. The freight manager at ABA is Sven Ekstrom. I heard from a contact that he knows Kramer."

"So you think Ekstrom reports to Kramer?" Peter asked.

"It looks like it. Kramer has been seen out there several times."

"So Ekstrom must be their source of information."

"Ekstrom is the freight manager so he knows all about those SKF shipments."

Peter thought about Kramer using Ekstrom as a source and what to tell London.

"I hope you don't mind, Peter, but I need to talk to you about a personal affair."

Peter nodded and sat down.

"You met Sabrina at the Christmas party. She's worried

about her dad. He's locked up in the Florsberg camp."

"The Florsberg camp. Isn't that one of those Swedish internment camps? I have seen the name somewhere."

"Yeah, that's it."

"Isn't it for Swedish communists?"

"Yeah, Reds, anti-Nazis, German refugees, anybody the government doesn't like. They chuck them in a camp and throw away the key. Aksell is an artist and anti-Nazi, but he's not political."

"What do you think I can do?"

"Well, Aksell was a music composer before the war. He wrote music. I don't know whether he was any good, but he did play in a symphony orchestra years ago. He's a fuckin' musician, gormless and about as useful as tits on a door."

"I don't know, Bernie. This sounds like a matter for Swedish internal affairs."

"The minister is all piss and wind. Sabrina has written several letters to him complaining about her dad's treatment, but nothing ever happens. The Legation has had some success releasing Allied airmen, Peter."

"Look, Bernie, this is way outside my remit."

"Sabrina is worried. Aksell's committed no crime. She thinks the Legation could put in a special request to release him on humanitarian grounds."

"I'll talk to Tennant. That's all I can promise."

"That's fine, old chap. Any help from the Legation would be a leg up for Sabrina and Aksell."

The normally calm atmosphere of the *Abwehr* station was suddenly shattered by heavy footsteps and the bark of shouted orders.

"*Achtung! Achtung!* We're taking control of the office," yelled a loud male voice from the entrance.

Kriminaldirektor Golcher was getting up from his desk to investigate when a tough looking man in a fedora and dark coat barged into his private office.

"Herr Golcher, we have orders to take over this station," the man announced. There was a scar on his face and he had a nervous tic as his left eye blinked incessantly.

"This is outrageous!" Golcher snarled. "I will call Canaris and have you sacked."

"Admiral Canaris has been arrested, Herr Golcher."

"That's not possible."

"It's not only possible," the man smirked with his blinking eye, "but it has already been done. We have orders to secure this station. You are being taken over by the SD (the *Sicherheitsdienst* or security services). We are sending your people home."

Golcher looked flabbergasted. He glanced over the man's shoulder to see four Gestapo agents in fedoras and dark coats herding his staff out of the main office. Among them were Kemper and his secretary.

"Tomorrow, sir, we will start to reorganize the office," the Gestapo man said. "Do not look so unhappy, Herr Golcher. If you cooperate with us, you might still have a job."

Golcher looked at the man's self-satisfied grin and sat down defeated.

Twenty-two

Anders Berger entered the office of the Swedish Red Cross office and met with a receptionist.

"Can I help you?"

"I need to talk to Count Folke Bernadotte."

"Do you have an appointment, sir?"

"No, I am a journalist with the Stockholms-Tidningen newspaper."

"Just a moment. I will check with him."

The receptionist left the room and Anders looked at the photographs of Red Cross events on the walls.

Moments later, Anders was ushered into the office of Folke Bernadotte, Count of Wisborg and vice chairman of the Red Cross. He was a small man in his late forties with a penetrating gaze.

"It's a pleasure to meet you, Mr Berger," Bernadotte said, "but I think you are too early. There's no story to tell. I have only just received the mandate from the minister to negotiate the repatriation of Swedish prisoners from camps in Germany. There is absolutely nothing to report at this time."

"I am not here as a journalist, sir. I am here for a personal matter."

Count Bernadotte frowned.

"You know that the minister has recently imposed a blackout on any information concerning our discussions with the Germans. We want to keep this very low key."

"I am here on behalf of my wife, sir," Anders said. "She is looking for her brother, Rolf Lagerman. He disappeared from the Neuengamme camp several months ago. My wife fears he may be in a *Nacht und Nebel* camp."

"Mr Berger, we have people coming here every day looking for family members who have disappeared in Germany. We cannot help them because we don't have any information yet."

"I'm sorry, sir."

"Don't be," Bernadotte sighed, "I sympathize with your wife. She's living a nightmare. These are Swedish people, innocent people who have done nothing wrong. And now with the war coming to an end, we must repatriate them before it is too late. We must bring them home."

In the press office Ewan Butler furtively pulled out a flask of whisky and had a quick drink before slipping it back in his desk drawer. He had a vicious hangover and nothing seemed to help. He looked up to see Joanna coming toward him.

"How are you this morning, Ewan?" Joanna boomed, looking concerned.

"Keep your voice down," Ewan told her, "I'm extremely sensitive to loud noises."

She took pity on him and lowered her voice.

"I have an idea for another project," she ventured.

"Our last escapade was a huge success, wasn't it?" Ewan managed a weak smile and put down his copy of *Der Deutschen in Schweden* magazine.

"Yes, it was. The papers were full of it."

"So what do you have in mind?"

"I was reading about the *Waffen-SS*. They are losing a lot of men on the Russian front now that the war is going badly for them. I was thinking that the German fund for the wives and fatherless families of the *Waffen SS* could mistakenly put out a missive to various Swedish Nazis requesting money."

"Damn, that's wonderfully insensitive of you, my dear."

"I thought you would like it."

"We could put out a forged circular in the name of the National Socialist *Auslands* organisation," Ewan said, holding his hand to his forehead and trying to will his headache away.

"It could be in a letter from the big boss himself - *Reichsführer-SS* Himmler," Joanna said, "calling upon those loyal to the National Socialists to make a donation to a pension fund to support SS widows and children."

"It would need to tell its readers about the magnificent contribution of the *Waffen-SS* to the Fatherland," Ewan said, "with so many heroes dying in battle for the Nordic ideal."

"We could send it to known Swedish anti-Nazis too. It would inflame the population."

"It's a brilliant plan, Joanna. I never would have thought you had so many devilish ideas hidden behind that angelic face of yours."

Joanna broke into a laugh.

"Devilish ideas are my trademark, Ewan dear," Joanna smiled. "I live to confound the Nazis."

"There are a lot of people locked up in Swedish prisons, so I wouldn't get my hopes up," Michael said. "We'll do what we can, but London will have to make the final decision."

Sigge was closing up shop for the day as Michael and Peter

discussed the Aksell case with Bridget in the office.

"I understand the difficulty," Peter said, "but Bernie is a valuable employee. I think we owe it to him to try."

"Couldn't we simply bestow some kind of award on Aksell?" Bridget said. "After all he is a music composer, an artist. Perhaps a bogus music award in recognition for his extraordinary contribution to the arts."

"That's bloody brilliant," Peter said. "We can't award the prize if the man remains in prison."

"We could get an arts group to invite him to go to Britain to collect the award," Bridget said. "Then they would have to release him."

"You know your idea of an award sounds better than anything we can do through our services," Michael said, "but I will put in a request to London."

"Thanks, Michael," Peter replied.

"London isn't going to help us," Bridget said crossing her arms. "I wouldn't hold out any hope from that quarter."

"You may be right, Bridget," Peter said. "I'm going out for a bit with Michael."

He collected his coat and hat and followed Michael to the door. It was snowing as Peter and Michael emerged from the British Legation building and walked along the nearby canal.

"Mallet's done it," Michael said, enjoying a moment of schadenfreude at his superior's misfortune. "His meetings with *SD Ausland* Chief Schellenberg and Himmler's man, Dr Schmidt, have attracted attention in London. I heard it from a friend."

"Good God!" exclaimed Peter.

"The Soviet government has asked London to recall Mallet on the grounds that he has been providing the German High Command with details of Soviet army operations."

"I doubt Mallet knows anything about Soviet army operations," Peter said, "unless you know something I don't. I thought he was representing banking interests and working with Marcus Wallenberg."

"He is," Michael confirmed. "Our bankers are looking for German assets on the cheap. The question is what are we offering in exchange. Immunity from prosecution for the German leadership at the end of the war or what?"

"So you think Mallet will be recalled?" Peter asked.

"Absolutely and soon. Anyone in that job would be better than the angry rabbit."

"So what will happen to us?"

"Nothing, I suppose. We'll just soldier on."

Outside on the main boulevard it was snowing as Peter and Bridget with their Legation friends embarked on an evening cruise on an old river boat, the M/S Gustafsberg VII. Peter and Bridget remained on deck to watch as the ship passed the old town with its Christmas lights, and then Södermalm before entering the lock into Lake Mälaren. The wind was cold on the lake so they went below to the bar and restaurant where a party was in full swing.

A crowd of lively young Swedes was celebrating the Christmas season and dancing to Tommy Dorsey's *Boogie Woogie*. Peter and Bridget joined Betty, Wendy and Carly from the rooming house and their Swedish boyfriends, near a window table overlooking the water.

"Peter, this is Samantha whom I told you about," Bridget said. "Her husband was the flight engineer on the Lancaster bomber that was shot down."

"Hello, Samantha," Peter said, shaking hands with a thin

dark-haired woman drinking a martini cocktail.

"Hello, Peter," she replied with a doleful expression.

She was poorly-dressed and sat next to Betty and the girls who were all smartly turned out. The women were drinking martinis and were all in various stages of drunkenness while the men stuck to beer and argued in loud Swedish voices about the war.

"I hope Bridget is treating you all right, Peter," Wendy laughed as she flirted openly with him, "she tends to be rather bossy with her employees."

"I do not," Bridget replied sharply.

"Well, the last one took fright," Wendy smirked, "and left his post in a hurry, didn't he?"

"He did not," Bridget laughed. "He was transferred to New York, the lucky devil."

"Bollocks," Wendy said, grinning at her friends.

"Wendy, stop it. Stop slagging Bridget," Betty smiled at Peter. "Don't be an old harpy. I'm sure Peter has nothing to complain about. Right Bridget?"

"You bloody well better believe it," Bridget said, glancing at Peter who remained quietly amused.

"How did it go with your search for your husband ?" Peter asked, turning to Samantha.

"The crew were picked up by the Swedish coast guard," Samantha said. "I'm just so happy Harry is alive and well."

"Were any of the men injured when they crashed their plane?" Bridget asked.

"One of the gunners was in bad shape and needed medical attention," Samantha said. "They took him to a hospital in Malmö. He will be joining the others later."

"They were sent to the internment camp in Falun, according to the man at the minister's office," Betty added. "I must say that the Swedish authorities are being much more helpful. Quite a change over a year ago."

"How long will they be interned?" Peter asked.

"We don't know," Betty said. "That's up to the minister. Allied airmen are put up in hotels and rooming houses in the Falun area and have relative freedom compared to the other prisoners."

"It's a bloody disgrace, if you don't mind me saying so," Wendy exclaimed, "they get full pay sitting on their arses and drinking good Swedish aquavit."

"I'll drink to that," said Betty's boyfriend.

"Cheers, Wendy, cheers Betty, cheers, everyone."

Twenty-three

It was very late as Peter returned to his flat and climbed the stairs. He stopped near his door when he saw a very drunk Ewan Butler sitting on the floor drinking Black & White whisky from the bottle.

"Ewan, what are you doing here?"

"*Guten Abend, Herr Faye*. How was your evening?"

"It was fine, Ewan."

"You know Sir Richard Boord of the SOE in London?" Ewan asked.

"No, Ewan."

"Joanna tried to reach him for me. He's my boss. He's a nice chap but he's out of commission. He can't be reached."

"I'm rather tired, Ewan."

"Look old chap, I need your help," Ewan said in a pleading tone. "I need you put in a word for me with the angry rabbit. I need time off, I can't do this damn job anymore. Mallet's got me working evenings and weekends."

"I don't understand, you're SOE. Why are you working for Mallet?" Peter asked.

Ewan took a swig from the whisky bottle.

"Want some whisky, Peter?"

"It's late, Ewan."

"The angry rabbit won't take no for an answer. I saw your background report on Dr Kramer, Peter. Good work, solid intelligence."

"Tennant requested it some time ago."

"You know Kramer's got a deposit box at the Enskilda Bank for those Bosch shares of his."

"Bosch shares?"

"Yeah, the bastard is holding them for his boss Schellenberg until the deal is done."

"What's the deal, Ewan?"

"Don't play dumb with me, Peter. The royals have been buying up German assets since before the war."

"Swedish royals?"

"Not just the Swedes, Peter, our own British royal family. Everyone is buying up German assets. Marcus Wallenberg thinks we can get a better deal on Nazi assets if we delay. Time is in our favour."

Ewan drank some whisky from the bottle.

"*Festina lente*," he said grinning at Peter, "make haste slowly."

"What are we giving them?" Peter asked.

Ewan looked surprised by this innocent question.

"We can't give the losers in this war the crown jewels, now can we? We are giving them table scraps, that's all Peter."

"What do you mean?"

"Free passage to Sweden and immunity from prosecution. That's it."

"What do we get in exchange?"

"Schelli's secret SD files and a load of German overseas assets, shares in Bosch, I.G. Farben, Kruppe, Rheinmetall, AEG, Siemens-Shuckert and others."

"This is insane, Ewan. Schellenberg and Himmler are

bloody war criminals. They need to be tried in a court of justice."

"Don't I know it."

"Have you requested leave, Ewan?"

"Course, I have."

"Well, what does Mallet say?" Peter asked.

"He won't hear of it. He says that he needs me. I'm his joker, his pitiful buffoon to laugh at and my German is better than his."

"What can I do for you, Ewan?"

"You are SIS. Tell your boss you want to get your old friend Ewan out of Stockholm on the next flight. Say anything you like. Tell him I'm a security risk. I don't care. I have told the angry rabbit that I don't like meeting with Nazi swine but he won't let me go."

"Come in, Ewan. You can sleep it off on my couch."

Peter helped Ewan to his feet and they staggered into the flat.

It was early as Karl-Heinz arrived at the German Press office. He expected to see his colleagues hard at work, but the office was almost empty except for his secretary Nadja.

"*Guten morgen, Nadja.* Where is everyone?"

Heinrich, Fritz and Helmut were missing from their desks. Nadja sniffed and wiped a tear away.

"What happened, Nadja?"

"The Gestapo came for them yesterday, sir."

"The Gestapo?"

"They're going to make an example of them, maybe send them to the Russian front."

"I'm so sorry, my dear, all because of that damn

photograph. What did that husband of yours have to say?"

"He's leaving me," Nadja said, "he says I'm destroying his career. He says that I'm lucky not to have been arrested."

"He may be right, Nadja. We must be very careful."

"There's a man in your office, sir."

Karl-Heinz frowned and walked through the empty room to his office to find Herr Golcher slumped in a chair opposite his desk.

"Hello, sir, I heard you lost your position."

"It's terrible, *Herr Doktor*. The Gestapo has taken over my office. We have no idea when we'll return to work."

"Don't worry, your staff will soon be reinstated. I just came back from Berlin. I've been officially transferred to *SD Ausland* under *Brigadeführer* Schellenberg."

"That's very good news," Golcher exclaimed.

"As you can see, we've been visited by the Gestapo too. My colleagues Heinrich, Fritz and Helmut were arrested."

"I saw the picture in the paper. You're lucky not to have been arrested yourself."

"Not lucky, Herr Golcher," Karl-Heinz said with a confident smile. "I think a better word would be 'untouchable'. No one is going to arrest me. I'm Himmler's special representative in Sweden."

Nadja arrived with the coffee tray. She poured coffee for the two men and left.

"Take heart, Herr Golcher, everything will return to normal shortly."

"Thank you, Dr Kramer."

"You remember that you asked me what the term 'Egmont' meant the other day."

"*Ja*, I remember the term."

"In Berlin I learned that Egmont refers to top secret SD

reports that are compiled from SS battle assessments coming from the front. With the war going so badly," Karl-Heinz searched for the right words, "these reports can at times be a bit depressing."

"So why is the Gestapo so interested in these reports?"

"The Gestapo thinks the Egmont documents are defeatist propaganda," Karl-Heinz said, "and my boss Schellenberg is responsible for circulating them. So they want to use them to bring him down."

Golcher nodded uncertainly.

"By the way I have requested," Karl-Heinz said, "that you be put in charge of the *SD Ausland* station here in Stockholm."

"Thank you, Dr Kramer, thank you. You are very kind," Golcher said gratefully.

"Now, I hope you will excuse me, but I have other things that require my attention."

Twenty-four

Bridget knocked lightly on the door to Peter's flat and slipped inside to find Ewan Butler fast asleep on the couch and Peter in the kitchen drinking coffee.

"Thanks for coming, Bridget," Peter said, embracing Bridget. "How are you darling?"

"I'm fine. What's Ewan doing here?"

"Sleeping it off."

"I can see that, but why is he here?"

"A long story. I am seeing Michael Tennant in an hour and I don't think we should leave Ewan alone for an instant."

"Why? What happened?"

"He was sitting by my door drinking whisky when I came home last night, completely sloshed. He's very anxious and unstable. He wants to return to London, but Mallet won't allow it. Can you look after him for an hour or two?"

"Of course, I love to babysit drunks," Bridget said with a laugh, "it's just my idea of having a good time."

Peter grinned at Bridget as she pulled out a hankie and wiped the lipstick off his face.

"Are you sure?"

"Go along, Peter, I will be fine but I would like a cup of coffee before you go."

Peter nodded and poured her a cup before he went to fetch his coat.

Kramer had been as good as his word. Golcher was already installed in the new *SD Ausland* station on Nybrogatan street and his entire staff had been reinstated. He looked up as his assistant Kemper appeared in the doorway.

"*Brigadeführer* Schellenberg is in Stockholm!" Kemper said excitedly. "He flew in an hour ago."

Golcher was horrified. He feared that things could easily change for the worse as quickly as they had changed for the better.

"*Mein Gott!* Is he coming here?"

"I have no idea, sir," Kemper shrugged.

In his haste Kemper had left the front door to the SD office open and Golcher turned in time to see Dr Kramer shaking the snow off his boots. There was no sign of an impromptu visit from Schellenberg, at least for the moment.

"Later, Kemper," Golcher said, dismissing his assistant.

Kemper left the office and gave a salute to Dr Kramer on his way out.

"*Guten Tag,* Dr Kramer. What can I do for you?"

"Have you heard the news," Karl-Heinz asked, "perhaps you know already."

Golcher got up and closed the door behind his visitor.

"Yes," he said as he returned to his desk. "I just heard that the *Brigadeführer* has arrived."

"Well, at least your sources are good."

Golcher inclined his head at the compliment.

"Is he coming here?" Golcher asked.

"No, Herr Golcher. We need to keep quiet about his arrival.

We don't want the press to know, so you need to keep a lid on rumours. Can you do that?"

"Of course, sir."

"He's having several top secret meetings, I can't tell you anything more."

"Kramer's got a deposit box at the Enskilda Bank filled with Bosch shares," Peter said.

"Butler said that?" Michael asked.

"Yes, I think he thought I was party to Mallet's secret negotiations."

"Who are the shares for?" Michael asked.

"I don't know, but Schellenberg is holding on to them until some kind of immunity arrangement can be worked out with the British and Swedish authorities."

"Bloody hell, talk about dealing with the devil."

Michael and Peter were sitting in a very ordinary Legation car in front of the Grand Hotel when a luxurious Duesenberg Model J sedan pulled over. Marcus Wallenberg stepped out, followed by Victor Mallet carrying a briefcase.

"There's the angry rabbit," Michael said.

"What do we do about Ewan?" Peter asked.

"Nothing. Mallet is looking for an excuse to get rid of me after I leaked that anonymous report to London. I have to keep out of it."

"Ewan's a security risk."

"I don't know how Mallet puts up with him," Michael said. "Stay here, I am going to have a look."

He stepped out of the car and headed towards the hotel.

At the Bellmansro restaurant a waiter entered the back

room with steaming plates of food. *Brigadeführer* Walter Schellenberg, Dr Schmidt, Marcus Wallenberg and Victor Mallet sat at a large table with a white table cloth. Mosel wine and hors d'oeuvres were served. The men stopped talking as the food was served.

"*Guten Appetit, meine Herren*," proposed Schellenberg.

"I love your city, Herr Wallenberg," Dr Schmidt said. "It's wonderful even in the winter. Berlin is so dreary."

"I think it is the peace, the tranquillity," Schellenberg said. "You can feel it in the air."

"I agree, Herr Schellenberg, but I think the canals are the secret," Mallet said. "The city is surrounded by water."

"Let's drink to the coming peace, to health and prosperity. Skål," Wallenberg said with a jovial air.

The men echoed his toast and raised their glasses.

Michael Tennant ran back to the car and climbed into the driver's seat. Peter was busy working on *The Daily Telegraph* crossword puzzle.

"They're not there, I checked Mallet's suite."

"They must have moved the meeting."

"I think Mallet reserved the suite as a diversion."

Michael and Peter drove off.

"Ewan might know where they are meeting," Peter said.

"Good idea," Michael said. "Let's go have a chat with him."

They drove to Peter's flat and climbed the stairs. They found Ewan Butler wide awake on the sofa. He was in a nasty mood, evidently hung over and suffering from a severe headache. His hair was sticking out at all angles and he reeked of alcohol.

Bridget came in with a tray of coffee and biscuits.

"Thank you, Bridget," Peter said.

She rolled her eyes and gave Peter a disapproving look before returning to the kitchen.

"So Butler, we hear Mallet is having a meeting with Wallenberg and some top German brass," Michael said. "Do you know where they are having the meeting?"

"Bugger off, Tennant. Even if I knew, I wouldn't tell you," Ewan said sharply. "It's way above your pay grade."

"We know about Mallet's secret financial negotiations."

"It's none of your business. Mallet has the confidence of our top people in intelligence."

"I don't believe a word of it," Michael said angrily. "He must be doing it for personal gain."

"Bloody hell, Tennant. Are you daft? I report to Blunt, it's all top secret stuff. I can't tell you the half of it."

Peter looked shocked.

"Anthony Blunt?" Peter asked. "That tosser from MI5. That can't be right."

"I said the top people, that's all I can say," Ewan warned, with a frown that quickly turned into a self-satisfied smirk. "Stay out of it, Tennant. If Mallet hears about this, you're gone."

"You silly bugger," Michael said, exasperated, "you don't have any intelligence connections, you old boozehound."

"You haven't seen the reports that I send to London."

"You're talking bollocks, because there haven't been any."

"My material goes out via the Swedes, that's why. This stuff is way too sensitive for the diplomatic bag. They set it up just for me," Ewan retorted with pride.

"You mean the royal courier, the Swedish crown?" Peter asked.

"Of course, old chap."

Michael suddenly looked cowed. If Ewan was using the

Swedes to courier Mallet's reports to London, then this was a secret negotiation at the very highest level of power, approved by London and the Swedish authorities.

"We better get you back to the office," Michael said in a friendly tone, "before the angry rabbit comes looking for you."

Michael's dark mood was gone. He just wanted to be rid of Butler. Peter picked up on this and called to Bridget.

"Bridget, are you ready to move?"

"Yes, Peter," Bridget said, coming in from the kitchen.

"I need a drink please," Ewan begged Peter as Michael left to get the car.

Peter nodded to Bridget who went to the drinks table to fetch the whisky. She poured Ewan a glass and then went to get the coats.

"Are you OK, Ewan? We need to go," Peter said.

Ewan savoured his whisky as Bridget and Peter put on their coats.

"Yes, I feel better already. Thank you, Peter."

Twenty-five

Brigadeführer Schellenberg and Dr Kramer were drinking tea with General Makoto Onodera in his western style office at the Japanese Legation residence in Stockholm. An assistant walked in and bowed respectfully near a wall of bonsai and bamboo before handing Onodera a large envelope. He dismissed the man who disappeared behind the painted screen.

"I have the information you requested, Herr Schellenberg."

"Soviet?" Schellenberg asked.

"Yes, GRU," Onodera said, pushing the envelope across the table. "It comes from a source at the highest level of military intelligence in Moscow."

The GRU was the main military foreign-intelligence service of the Soviet Union, a rival of the NKVD which also collected foreign intelligence.

"You should come to Berlin, Herr General," Schellenberg said, "we would show you a good time."

"I would love to, Herr Schellenberg, but my government will not allow me to leave the country. We are fighting a war with the Americans and I have to keep my ear to the ground here in Sweden."

Schellenberg nodded his understanding as Karl-Heinz reached for his briefcase.

"Dr Kramer has your payment, sir," Schellenberg said.

Karl-Heinz took out a small box and placed it on the table. Onodera raised the lid only enough to see a one kilogram bar of illicit gold, worth approximately $36 per troy ounce. He lowered the lid and looked up as Karl-Heinz put three more boxes on the table. A total value of over five thousand US dollars.

"Thank you, gentlemen," Onodera said, "these are difficult times for Germany and for Japan."

"Yes, they are," Schellenberg agreed solemnly. "When do you expect to have the other documents, Herr General?"

"Give me a few weeks to assemble them."

"Good. Dr Kramer will collect them when you are ready," Schellenberg said. "You can reach him at the Press Office."

Onodera nodded as Schellenberg stood up.

"I'm sorry I can't stay any longer," he said. "My plane departs for Berlin in one hour. Thank you again for your help."

General Onodera smiled at the *Brigadeführer* as they shook hands and nodded at Karl-Heinz.

It was a very cold night and even with the car heater going full blast both Anders and Stefan were uncomfortable. They had been waiting outside the Japanese Legation in the dark for over two hours, hoping to get a photograph of the German VIP that their contact at the airfield had tipped them about.

A door opened at the side of the building.

"Over there," Stefan called to Anders.

Two men walked briskly toward a dark unmarked sedan waiting at the curb. A chauffeur hurried around the vehicle and opened the rear door for his guests, then got in behind the wheel.

Stefan ran toward the car with his camera. He took a picture, his flash illuminating the car just as the chauffeur saw him and accelerated away.

"Did you get it?" asked Anders as Stefan returned to the car.

"I don't think so," Stefan said. "I could only see Kramer. He had his arm up hiding the other man's face. Do you want to try the airfield?"

"We would only be wasting our time. They won't let us in."

Anders turned the car around and they headed back to the city.

Victor Mallet was working late at the Legation as Ewan stumbled into his office.

"Bloody hell, Butler. Where have you been?"

Ewan looked decidedly drunk and ignored the question as he leaned over Mallet's large desk pulling a sheaf of quarto-size SD reports with purple stamps from his briefcase and slinging them onto the table.

"I studied the documents you requested, sir," he said.

"Bloody hell, you're plastered again," Mallet said, standing up angrily. "I can't have a drunk working in this office. Don't you have any shame, man?"

"Send me back to London, sir, that's all I ask," Ewan pleaded.

"I need you here in Stockholm, Butler. We're in the process of negotiating a very important step towards the peace. I'll have Bernie drive you home. Tell your wife to hide the drink or I will have you locked up in your office here at the Legation. Is that clear?"

Ewan stumbled out of Mallet's office, shedding secret reports. Mallet shook his head in disgust and turned to sort out the mess on his desk. He could hear Ewan mumbling to himself as he retreated down the hall.

"I drove Ewan home," Bernie said. "He's a bloody alky. Mary refused to let him in, told me to put him up in a hotel until he stopped drinking."

"He's a hopeless case I'm afraid," Peter said. "I don't know what Mallet is going to do with him."

They were having a drink in Peter's living room listening to Verdi on the gramophone. Bernie had just finished his aquavit and was getting up to leave when there was a knock at the door. With a brief look of concern because of the late hour, Peter got up to open it. Anders Berger stepped inside.

"Sorry, Peter. I didn't know you had a visitor," Anders said.

"It's all right," Bernie said, putting on his coat, "I'm on my way out. See you tomorrow, Peter."

"Good night, Bernie."

Bernie left and Peter could hear the sound of his footsteps on the stairs.

"Sorry for the late hour, Peter, but I had to see you."

"Aquavit, Anders?" Peter asked.

"Please."

Peter poured the aquavit into shot glasses.

"What can I do for you? I still have had no news about Rolf Lagerman."

"I am off to Germany with Count Bernadotte and the Swedish Red Cross next week. Bernadotte is taking me with him as his assistant. It is all on the QT. We fly to Berlin."

"This is not for the newspaper, I presume?" Peter asked.

"No, no. Bernadotte is going there to try to negotiate the release of the Scandinavian prisoners in the camps. I am taking a week off. It should be easier to find my brother-in-law Rolf in Germany than working from here."

"Who are you meeting there?"

"Bernadotte has organized it through Himmler's personal masseur, Felix Kersten. We go first to the Neuengamme Camp."

"Excellent, Anders. Excellent."

"If you hear anything from London, I am leaving on the Monday."

"Of course."

Twenty-six

It was snowing heavily as Bernie approached the back garden of the Kramer residence pushing his bike through the snow. The Gestapo had disappeared with the cold weather. Bernie climbed up on a snowbank to step over the gate into the Kramer's back garden. He walked through deep snow to the house keeping his head down.

He collected the cloth bag with the documents and slid it under his coat as he made his way back to the lane. Half way across the yard, he heard a voice from the house. He turned to see Wilhelma standing at the back door looking at him.

Bernie stopped dead in his tracks.

"What are you doing?" Wilhelma asked.

Bernie looked at the nanny and smiled.

"*Elektricitet, kraftledning,*" he said in Swedish pointing to the power line.

Wilhelma said nothing and quickly shook out the bread crumbs on her table cloth before going back inside.

Bernie hurried away.

"We're snookered," Bernie said, dumping the cloth bag on the table in the shed. "The Kramer nanny saw me."

"When?" Peter asked with concern as he watched Allan setting up ready for work.

"Just now as I was leaving the house. I hear this voice coming from behind me. So I turn around and there's the nanny standing at the back door. I tell her I work for the electricity company."

"What did she say?"

"Nothing. She went back inside."

Peter tried to make sense of this encounter.

"I'm not sure she noticed anything out of the ordinary," Bernie said, "but I can't be sure."

"Did she see you collect the shoe bag?"

"I doubt it. I was half the way across the lawn when I heard her voice."

"I see," Peter said. "You better be very careful when you return the documents. I don't want you walking into a trap."

"Don't worry, I'll keep my eyes open."

"We may have to wait to see whether your presence there has set off an alarm."

"Yeah, I reckon we will. It was bloody stupid of me to be caught crossing the back yard."

"It could happen at any time, Bernie."

Bernie removed the first document from the bag and handed it to Allan.

"Let's get to work," Peter said as Allan laid the first document on the copy stand.

"H is still at it, Bridget. Amazing stuff!" Peter said as he entered the office. "Kramer has access to British cabinet papers at the highest level. The source is Soviet, GRU."

"GRU?" Bridget asked. "How on earth could they get their hands on that kind of intelligence?"

131

"It's extremely sensitive material. There must be a mole in our security services. This should light a fire under that arrogant prick Anthony Blunt, but we've got a problem."

"A problem?"

"The nanny saw Bernie crossing the back garden."

"Oh, God, that's Wilhelma," Bridget said.

"I'm not sure the game is up ,"Peter said. "Bernie told her he worked for the electricity company and was out there checking on the line."

"He's quick-witted, Bernie is."

"Yes, he is."

"Well, I'll call Elsa and tell her," Bridget said. "You have mail, Peter."

Peter picked up the decoded message on his desk. He read the message and frowned.

"What is it?"

"It's Keith Linwood. He's telling me in no uncertain terms to keep my distance from Ewan Butler. He threatens to have me recalled. This is my old friend Keith talking."

"But why, Peter?" Bridget asked in disbelief.

"He seems to think that Michael and I have been bullying Ewan and are responsible for his nervous breakdown."

"Keith obviously doesn't want you poking your nose into this business with Mallet."

Peter nodded.

"I better contact Michael and tell him."

"Good idea."

"I'm being forced out, Peter," Michael said. "I'm being transferred to the Paris office. Mallet can't wait to see the back of me."

"Paris?" Peter asked.

"Yeah, it does sound good, doesn't it?"

Michael and Peter were walking along a snowy path next to the canal where several river boats were tied up.

"With the liberation of France and the war now on Germany's doorstep," Michael said, "they need help reorganizing SOE personnel at the embassy. My new title will be 'information counsellor'. It's got a nice ring to it."

"How's your wife taking it?"

"She's fine with it, she's never been to Paris. I'm happy that I won't have to put up with Mallet any longer."

"That's wonderful, Michael, but I still don't understand what Anthony Blunt has to do with these negotiations. What's his role?"

"Security, Peter. From what Ewan told you, I would think he's working for the royals trying to keep a lid on any rumours about Mallet and the bankers pursuing Nazi assets."

"You think so?"

"What else can it be?" Michael asked. "You need to keep your nose out of it and be very careful."

An old Ford drove into the camp car park. Florsberg, a Swedish concentration camp near Söderhamn, was on the north coast several hours drive from Stockholm.

Bernie and his wife Sabrina stepped out of the car and headed towards the entrance of the old sanatorium. There were no observation towers, but an armed guard at the gate controlled visitors. The man waved them through and they checked in at the front desk. Minutes later, a guard arrived to take them back to a meeting room where prisoners were permitted to talk with their families.

Saturday was visiting day and there were numerous people gathered in the room waiting to see loved ones. There were left-wing activists and communists from the labour movements, German refugees, anti-Nazis, and common criminals. They were all imprisoned without trial, nor with any idea of the accusations made against them. Most were foreigners.

A tall, very thin man in his sixties dressed in prison garb was brought in. Aksell looked like an intellectual with his round glasses and short beard.

Sabrina jumped up from her seat and ran forward.

"Pappa."

Sabrina kissed her father while Bernie stood up and came over to shake hands.

"Good to see you, sir," Bernie said.

"You too, Bernie," Aksell replied.

Sabrina and her dad sat together chatting in Swedish while Bernie listened.

Twenty-seven

"Have you heard any recent gossip from Wilhelma?" Elsa asked as she met Hanne in the city centre. She had just disembarked from a bus and Elsa was waiting for her at the bus stop.

Together they walked along the snowy waterfront opposite the buildings of Gamla Stan on Stadsholmen island.

"She doesn't say much and certainly not to me," Hanne said. "I'm a Jew so good Nazis like Wilhelma don't talk to us."

"She saw our courier leaving the house the other day, Hanne?"

"Oh, no. What happened?" Hanne asked.

"Our man told her in Swedish that he worked for the electricity company and was inspecting the power line. We think that he may have convinced her."

"Her Swedish is not very good, Elsa, so I doubt she would recognize a foreign accent. She certainly hasn't mentioned anything to me."

"Bridget wants you to keep an eye on her. Maybe she'll tell Eva about the man, maybe not."

"She's not too bright," Hanne added, "so I wouldn't worry too much about her letting the cat out of the bag."

"I had our people run the name," Peter said. "There is no Lagerman at Neuengamme, Bergen-Belsen or Ravensbrück, but you know this already. So he could be somewhere else in one of the work camps."

Peter and Anders were leaning against the British Legation car near the Bromma airfield fence watching a plane coming in to land on the snowy runway.

"Why would they move Rolf to a work camp?" Anders asked.

"Perhaps they think he has a special skill."

"~~A music composer~~?" A Construction worker?

"My contact says he could be in one of the Gross-Rosen camps or, worse, in Dora-Mittlebau."

"A *Nacht und Nebel* camp?"

"It's possible, Anders. The whole point of the *Nacht und Nebel* camps is to have the prisoner disappear without a trace and to keep all information from the next of kin. The families are to know nothing."

Peter took out a cigarette, offered one to Anders and lit up. He remembered his instructor telling him about the NN camps. *Nacht und Nebel* meant "night and fog". Himmler himself had issued the directive back in 1941. The aim was to intimidate people into submission by denying them any knowledge of their loved ones. Even the SD ignored where these people were. Their names appeared in files with the letters NN after them. The conditions in these camps were reported to be abominable.

"You must find Rolf quickly and try to have him moved back to Neuengamme or Ravensbrück," Peter said. "If Bernadotte is talking to the *Reichssicherheitshauptamt* (RSHA), then they should be able to locate Rolf if he's not in an NN camp."

"I hope so for Britta's sake."

Peter realized just how impossible the task of finding Rolf in Germany must appear to his friend.

"You know Sweden is the best friend Germany ever had in this war. Germany owes the Swedish people, Anders. It is a huge debt paid in iron ore transiting across the country. Bernadotte just needs to push the right buttons to find Rolf."

"I hope you're right, Peter."

Anders glanced at the Luft Hansa Ju52 that would take him to Berlin. The ground crew had finished their work and the first passengers were already walking out to the plane. He picked up his valise.

"Tell those German bastards that they have a huge debt toward Sweden," Peter said, "don't let them forget it."

Anders nodded and they shook hands.

"Thank you, Peter."

"Good luck."

Peter was at his desk in the office going through a bunch of visa application files with Sigge. Peter pulled a file noting the comments of a visa applicant.

"What do you think?" Peter asked Sigge.

"I think this fellow is hiding something, sir," Sigge replied.

"So we reject the request for a visa or we ask him to come back and provide additional information?"

"We reject it, he can always come back and reapply."

"Alright."

Peter ticked the rejection box and signed the form. Sigge collected the files and returned to the front desk.

Bridget came over and sat on the edge of Peter's desk.

"Wendy's gone."

"Gone?"

"Don't look so unhappy," Bridget said, teasing Peter. "I know she liked you."

"What happened?"

"She left last night after she was caught stealing some money from Betty in the typing pool."

"She really went after you at the party, Bridget."

"Yes, she did. Betty had a slugging match with her in the office yesterday. She punched her out and then slammed a wastepaper basket on her head. All the girls on the floor were laughing at her."

"Bloody hell, what will the diplomatic service think of such high jinks in its offices? Did Mallet hear about it?"

"Nobody said a word. The girls said it happened very fast. And then Wendy took off. Just up and left town."

"Well, good riddance is what I say."

"Me too."

Bridget showed a list of names to Peter.

"Here's a list of music groups who might be interested in celebrating our Swedish music composer, Peter. I have circled several of them."

Peter looked at the list.

"You circled the Rugby Music Society in Warwickshire. Very good," Peter said with satisfaction.

"What about the others?"

"They're all fine. Let's try several and see what they say."

"I will send out the request. Perhaps a personal note from you would be helpful."

"Of course, Bridget. I may even know some of these people. I was a schoolmaster at Rugby after all."

"It has to be an official looking letter awarding Aksell an important prize and an invitation to go to Britain to receive it."

"Absolutely. Let's do it."

Saarson appeared at the canal only moments before the ferry's departure. Peter had arrived early and was watching from the ship's railing. Saarson quickly crossed the road and paid for a ticket, descending to the deck.

"Good morning, Mr Faye," Saarson said.

"Thanks for coming. How about a cup of coffee, aquavit or perhaps a sherry?" Peter asked.

"Good idea, let's go to the bar."

Peter and Saarson went into the bar with its 180-degree view of the canal just as the ferry slipped its moorings. They sat near a window in the corner and ordered their drinks.

"I don't have anything new for you," Saarson said.

"I realise that. I am interested in your GRU material."

"GRU material?"

"London wants to know where it's coming from. Who is giving it to General Onodera?"

"I wouldn't know. He has his sources."

"This is a rogue agent working for the GRU. He's selling to the highest bidder. Who is his control here in Sweden? I want to talk to the man, Saarson. I will pay a very generous bonus if you can get me a meeting with him."

Saarson finished his coffee and drank his aquavit in silence. The ferry turned towards the open sea and the wind picked up.

"My country fought the Soviets in 1940 and now we're fighting them again with German help. With the war winding down, the Germans will be pulling out and we will be back to fighting the Soviets alone."

"Those were NKVD thugs the other day, weren't they?" Peter asked, "What do they want with you?"

"They want to beat me up, put me in the hospital for a few months, make me disappear. They don't care. You are worried about this intelligence?"

"Yes."

"You know you British have too many communist sympathizers, I think. They are helping their friends in the Soviet Union."

"I agree, Saarson, but can you help me?"

Saarson smiled at Peter.

"I am a friend, Mr Faye. Britain and Estonia have always been friends and never enemies. Of course, I will help you."

"Thank you."

"You know the old lady of the October revolution, Alexandra Kollontai. She's now the Soviet Ambassador in Stockholm and she's trying to negotiate an armistice between the Finns and the Soviets. The NKVD are very active here. You must be careful."

In the SD boardroom in Berlin a team of German officers sat across the table from Count Folke Bernadotte of the Swedish Red Cross and Anders Berger. Coffee was served and the conversation was conducted in German.

"So Herr Bernadotte, what brings you to Berlin?" asked the *Oberführer*, a man with a pencil moustache and a dark complexion. He was surrounded by a group of young, blond German officers.

"It is the wish of Christian Günther, our Swedish Foreign Minister, that we enter into talks about the repatriation of all your Scandinavian prisoners."

There was a rude remark from one of the German officers and the *Oberführer* looked sternly at the man to shut him up.

"Herr Bernadotte, we have no knowledge of this project."

Bernadotte hardly seemed put off by the German reaction to his request.

"Herr Oberführer, we estimate there are around 13,000 Scandinavian prisoners in your camps and about half of them are Swedish. We are here to visit the camps. We want to determine the numbers of prisoners who can be repatriated and also to determine their state of health."

"I see, Herr Bernadotte. This is a very big responsibility, I am not sure..."

"Of course, the RSHA will save a vast amount of money if you no longer need to accommodate these prisoners in your camps."

"Yes, I can see that."

"So where are you keeping *Brigadeführer* Schellenberg?" Bernadotte asked, "I am here to meet him."

The *Oberführer* smiled dismissively.

"The *Brigadeführer* is a very busy man, I don't think..."

The door suddenly opened and the *Oberführer's* eyes widened in surprise. *Brigadeführer* Schellenberg himself in his military uniform walked in, trailed by an assistant. There was a cacophony of chairs scraping the floor as the *Oberführer* and his men scrambled to attention. Schellenberg ignored them and went directly to the Count.

"Count Bernadotte! I'm so sorry to be late. I am Walter Schellenberg."

The other men stood rigidly to attention as Schellenberg glanced at their stricken commander.

"I think we can handle this business without your help, *Herr Oberführer.*"

There was a flurry of salutes and the men left the room nodding politely to Bernadotte on their way out.

"I am so happy to see you in Berlin, Count."

"The pleasure is mine. This is my assistant Anders Berger. I was elaborating on our plan to repatriate the Scandinavian prisoners in your camps. We think the best plan is to collect them at one camp so they can travel to Copenhagen in buses."

Schellenberg smiled. He knew the Swedish plan would prove difficult to execute, but he had nothing to lose by indulging them. A *quid pro quo* might be advantageous for the Nazi leadership now facing attack on German soil from both East and West.

"This is quite a plan you have. It sounds very practical and I certainly see a lot of advantages for our government, but we still need the permission of various people including Herr Himmler, Kaltenbrunner and others. You will be meeting them tonight."

"Thank you, Herr Schellenberg."

"Now, you must be hungry so let's dine together and then later we will have our meetings."

Twenty-eight

Peter and Bridget followed Ewan Butler and Victor Mallet into the salon of the Grand Hotel for a formal luncheon hosted by the Russian ambassador to Sweden. In spite of her seventy years and a handicap that confined her to a wheelchair, Alexandra Kollontai had insisted on greeting her guests at the door. The ambassador was a remarkable woman who had lived through the Russian Revolution, survived the purges under Stalin, and continued to work after suffering a stroke in 1942. The stroke had not only claimed the use of her legs but left her with paralysis on one side of her face. She had fought through these adversities the same way she had with everything else in her life, and was treated with great respect by the diplomatic community.

"Hello, Sir Victor. Good of you to come."

"The pleasure is mine, Madam Kollontai. I heard you were ill."

"I am back now and feeling much better. And you are?" Kollontai turned toward Ewan Butler.

"I am Ewan Butler, an assistant to the chief. A pleasure to meet you, madam," Ewan said with a cheerful air.

"Please meet my colleagues," Kollantai said, "Major Vladimir Petrov and his wife Evdokia."

The Petrovs stepped forward to shake hands with the British Legation staff. Vladimir was a squat bespectacled Russian with a round face while his wife was an attractive younger woman with blond hair. The Petrovs had worked as cipher clerks for over a decade in the Special Cipher Section of the OGPU, which later became part of the NKVD.

"So you both work in Consular Services?" Evdokia asked Bridget and Peter as the ambassador turned her attention to the arrival of a Swedish minister.

"Yes, it is a bit slow at the moment, not such a good time to visit Britain," Bridget said.

"It's the same for us, you know," Evdokia said as a waiter arrived with a dozen glasses of champagne on a tray while another man carried a tray of salmon blinis.

"You and your husband are from Moscow?" Peter asked.

"No, I'm from Kiev and my husband from Siberia, Mr Faye."

"How do you find Stockholm?" Bridget asked.

"A wonderful city. We love it here," Evdokia said. "You are a new arrival, aren't you Mr Faye? I haven't seen you before."

"Yes, just a few weeks, Mrs Petrov."

Peter and Bernie took the Legation car northeast towards the coast. The road, a narrow two-lane blacktop, had been recently cleared of snow but was still treacherous in some places.

"I know Kapellskar, Peter. I come out this way with Sabrina a lot in the summer," Bernie said.

"Good, I am meeting Saarson there."

They made good time as they drove past dark pine forests and numerous bays and inlets. After a while Bernie pulled over near a 'falu red' cottage near the water. Bernie took out his Webley revolver and handed it to Peter.

"You better have this."

"I don't think I need to be armed, Bernie. Do I?"

Bernie turned to look at Peter.

"I won't leave you here unless you take the damn gun, Peter," Bernie insisted as Saarson left the cottage and started to cross the road.

"Are you trying to put the frighteners on me, Bernie?"

"No sir, no need to, these Estonian blighters already have me worried sick."

Peter pocketed the revolver just as Saarson arrived at the car and got in.

"You haven't been followed?" Saarson asked.

"I don't think so," Bernie replied.

"Okay, let's drive back the way you came."

"Why?" Peter asked.

"Those are my instructions, Mr Faye. They want to be sure we don't have a tail."

Bernie turned the car around and they headed west.

Kapellskar, Sweden

On the forest road Bernie drove slowly looking for a sign. The snow banks were thick right up to the pine trees bordering the road. There was no traffic on the road. Saarson peered intently out the window looking for a break in the trees.

"Stop here," he said.

Bernie braked to a halt beside a snowy path that led into the woods. Saarson tapped Peter on the shoulder.

"Mr Faye, my instructions are for you to walk along the track to a lake which will appear on your left. It is there that they will collect you. Maybe a five or ten minute walk. It is not far."

"Good," Peter replied.

"My advice, sir," Bernie said, "shoot first and ask any bloody daft question you like later."

"I'm sure that every diplomat in our service knows that, Bernie," Peter said, winking at him.

Peter and Saarson got out of the car.

"Good luck, Mr Faye," Saarson said, shaking hands.

Saarson got into the front seat as Peter set off down the forest track. A moment later he had been swallowed up by the woods. Bernie and Saarson drove off.

Twenty-nine

Peter followed the snowy track and soon arrived at a lake. He walked around the perimeter under the snow covered trees. In the quiet of the winter morning Peter soon relaxed and lost himself in speculation about the Soviet source of intelligence. The GRU agent must be selling the documents through a Swedish source and, if Peter could get exclusive access to this material, MI5 might be able to hunt down the Soviet moles in their services.

Peter followed the track around the frozen lake near several summer cottages locked up for the season. Suddenly, out of the woods two men in trench coats and trilby hats appeared. One of the men was armed with a Suomi submachine gun.

"Mr Faye, this way please," the man said.

"Hello," Peter managed.

"Good day to you, sir," the second man said, "we're going north, our car is parked nearby."

Peter nodded and followed the two men through the woods to their car. They got in and drove away. The driver turned to address Peter in the back seat.

"Mr Faye, I'm Mads, this is Hendrik."

"You are Finns, right?" Peter asked.

"Yes, sir. We're from Helsinki. We should arrive in about ten minutes."

The British Legation car returned to Stockholm with Bernie and Saarson sitting in front. Off the road two cars hidden in a copse of trees observed them drive by. A moment later the first car driven by Evdokia Petrov drove back onto the highway going towards Kapellskar followed by a second car with three NKVD men on board.

Evdokia drove slowly looking for a turnoff or track into the woods. She stopped several times to look for traces in the snow left by the British Legation car. After a while she pulled over near a snowy forest track and got out. She examined some fresh footprints in the snow heading off into the woods and went to talk to the agents in the second car.

Mads and Hendrik headed north and brought Peter to a rambling old cottage with a red tile roof overlooking the Baltic sea. They climbed out of the car and followed Peter up the steps to the house.

An older and strikingly handsome man stepped out of the cottage. He wore the uniform of a senior officer in the Finnish army. He fixed Peter with a penetrating gaze.

"You must be Mr Faye from the British Legation. It's a pleasure to meet you, sir."

"The pleasure is mine."

"I am Colonel Reino Hallamaa, Mr Faye. I'm in charge of the Finnish radio intelligence in my country. RTK, Radio interception and cryptanalysis. You've met my adjutants, Mads and Hendrik."

"Why the subterfuge, Colonel?" Peter asked.

"We are Finns and friends of Sweden but we have many enemies here. I believe your Estonian friend had a run-in with the NKVD recently. We are at war with the Soviets."

"And the British, I might add."

"Yes, but we never wanted war with Britain. It was only because you were allied to the Soviets that you had to declare war on Finland."

"We tried to help you during the Winter War in '39 with our French allies but if I remember correctly, Norway and Sweden wouldn't allow our troops to cross their territory."

"A very sad story. Let us go for a walk. Then we will have a nice meal here before my men take you back to Stockholm."

Peter waited a moment as the colonel entered the rustic cottage to fetch his coat. There was a log burning in the fireplace and the room had an excellent view of the sea and a dock, jutting out into the water.

Peter remembered the Winter War which began on November 30, 1939 when the Soviets invaded Finland. On December 14, the League of Nations deemed the attack illegal and expelled the Soviet Union from the organisation.

The Finns put up a vigorous defence of their country against impossible odds. The Soviet Union had three times as many soldiers, thirty times as many aircraft and a hundred times as many tanks. The Red Army, however, was ill-equipped for a winter war both in regard to clothing and vehicles which couldn't cope with the cold. Soviet troops were obliged to fight on a small front since large parts of the border were impassable. The Finns attacked the Soviet convoys on the roads by using their knowledge of the terrain to get behind them, blocking their retreat. So the Soviets had to dig in and were soon surrounded.

There was an outpouring of support for Finland across Europe. A Franco-British expeditionary force was organized with a plan to disembark at the Norwegian port of Narvik and proceed by rail toward Finland, passing through the Swedish iron ore fields on the way. The request to travel across Norway and Sweden was sent to the government authorities on January 6, 1940, but was rejected six days later when Germany threatened to invade Sweden to protect its access to Swedish iron ore.

After several months of desperate battles, Finnish resistance collapsed and a peace treaty was signed with Moscow in March 1940. The Finns were forced to give up a large swath of land in the Karelian Isthmus, including Finland's second largest city Viipuri: approximately 11% of their territory.

Colonel Hallamaa and Peter walked along the snow-covered beach near the grey and forbidding Baltic sea. Breaking waves crashed among the ice floes creating a thunderous noise.

"We have made our peace with the United States and we will soon do the same with Britain. Germany has been helping us with our war against the Soviets, but that is coming to an end."

"Aren't you negotiating a peace treaty with the Soviets?" Peter asked.

"There have been some discussions but there can never be peace with Stalin. We will need your help to stand up to Stalin."

"I am not sure what help we can give you. The war has been a disaster for everyone."

Colonel Hallamaa pointed towards the horizon.

"You can just see Finland from here. See those clouds over there? Those are the Aland Islands, a distance of about sixty kilometres. They're an autonomous state under Finnish control."

Peter could just barely see the islands shrouded in mist.

"Mr Faye, I believe you are looking for moles in your intelligence services?" Hallamaa asked.

"Yes, we are. London was impressed with your Soviet sourced material."

"Of course they are. Your intelligence service is riddled with Soviet spies. The GRU collects intelligence on a daily basis from numerous sources in Britain."

"The GRU has sources at the very highest levels of the British government, Mr Hallamaa," Peter said. "This is causing great concern within our intelligence services."

"You British have a saying when things are going terribly wrong. You say let's close it down and start from scratch," Hallamaa grinned at Peter. "That would be my advice to you, sir, start from scratch. Your secret services are hopelessly compromised."

"I'm not sure our government would agree with that."

"Your plans for an atomic bomb are now well known so you can be sure that the GRU will redouble its efforts for nuclear intelligence both in England and in America."

Peter was astonished by the depth of the colonel's knowledge.

"Finnish codebreakers have broken Soviet military and NKVD cipher codes. We can read almost all of their communications. We are also reading American, British, and German codes. It's not a problem for us, Mr Faye."

They walked around a large chunk of ice brought in by the tide.

"We can help you identify the spies by their code-names but we want a commitment from your PM to stand up for Finland when peace with Germany comes."

Peter looked at Hallamaa in disbelief.

"Let's go back now and have some food. You must be hungry and this wind is picking up," Hallamaa said, turning his back to the wind.

Colonel Hallamaa, Mads and Peter were served a meal of codfish and pickled herring by an elderly Swedish cook. Mads poured copious amounts of aquavit for the colonel and his guest.

"We started in 1927 with radio interception and cryptanalysis of Soviet material, Mr Faye. So we have always had an advantage over you British. We started earlier. Before the Winter War, we had some 75 employees and now we are close to 1,000 people working on codes. Your people at Bletchley Park have done very well in a short time but RTK is in a class of its own. We read everyone's code without exception and we can provide fast decryption services for our friends."

"You have contacts at Bletchley?" Peter asked.

"Of course, we exchange information whenever we receive a request. We are also helping your American colleagues who are only just getting started in codebreaking."

Mads got up and went outside to check on his colleague. Suddenly shots were heard from the front of the cottage as Hendrik and Mads rushed back inside. The colonel and Peter hit the floor as a volley of bullets slammed through the bay window at the back of the house.

Thirty

Neuengamme, Germany

Count Bernadotte and Anders Berger walked through the Neuengamme concentration camp under the machine gun towers accompanied by the SS camp commander *Obersturmbannführer* Max Pauly and his assistant. They entered the administration building and were invited to sit down in a conference room with the unsmiling portrait of Adolf Hitler on the wall. An adjutant brought in a tea service and placed it in front of the visitors.

"What exactly are you interested in seeing, Herr Bernadotte?" Pauly asked as the adjutant left the room.

"We're interested in your Scandinavian prisoners. Do you have the prisoner lists so we can go over them?" Bernadotte asked.

"Of course, Herr Bernadotte," Pauly said, gesturing for his assistant to fetch them. "We can show you the lists, but I don't think there are many Scandinavian prisoners here."

"What about the work camps, *Obersturmbannführer*?"

"I really wouldn't know," Pauly replied.

"How many work camps are we talking about?" Anders asked.

"We have around one hundred *Baubrigade* (construction labour brigades) in different locations."

"One hundred!" Anders exclaimed.

"They are all over Northern Germany, sir."

Pauly's assistant returned with a large record book and opened it on the table.

"Here you go," Pauly said, "these are the lists for Neuengamme. See for yourselves."

Bernadotte turned the pages of the record book as Anders looked on. There were literally thousands of names.

"This is volume 25," Anders said, "how many volumes do you have?"

"There are some thirty volumes, sir," replied the assistant.

"How many prisoners?" Anders asked.

"The record books contain over 100,000 names, sir."

Anders was clearly impressed by the huge number of prisoners and the camp organisation.

"The names here are for 1943," Bernadotte noted. "They are not in alphabetical order nor by citizenship or origin."

"We put a name in the book each time a new prisoner arrives, sir," remarked the assistant.

"What is this column with the 't'?" Bernadotte asked.

"*Sie sind tot*, Herr Bernadotte," the assistant replied. "These are prisoners who died in the camp."

"We've lost many prisoners to sickness," Pauly said.

Bernadotte and Anders were shocked by the large number of names with 't's next to them.

"A large number of prisoners have died here," Anders said.

"Yes, it is very unfortunate," Pauly replied.

"How many prisoners are present in the camp now?" Anders asked.

"We have around 12,000 prisoners at the moment," Pauly said. "We can help you identify your people but as I say, you will not find too many."

"How many prisoners are in the *Baubrigade*?" Anders asked.

"We have around 37,000 prisoners in the work camps," the assistant said.

"They are processed here at Neuengamme before being sent out to the work camps," Pauly said. "A doctor sees them so we know they are healthy. Would you like to see our medical ward, Herr Bernadotte?"

"Of course, Herr Pauly."

Pauly and his assistant led Bernadotte and Anders out of the administration offices and across the way to the medical ward. The place was spotless and clearly a mise-en-scène had been put on for the Swedes' benefit. Several doctors and nurses were waiting to show them around.

Bernadotte and Anders shook hands with the senior doctor and they started the visit. The doctor described the medical problems of each patient as they went from bed to bed.

Kapellskar, Sweden

At the cottage bullets slammed into the walls, smashing picture frames and windows. Mads grabbed a Suomi submachine gun from a gun rack and handed another to the colonel who pushed Peter towards a trap door in the floor. Hallamaa lifted the door and slid down the steps followed by Peter, the distraught Swedish cook, and Mads. In the darkness of the basement the colonel lit the wick of an oil lamp and they headed into a tunnel leading to the shoreline. The cottage had once belonged to Swedish smugglers who used the house to hide illicit goods brought in by fishing boats from Finland and Estonia.

On the main floor Hendrik went from one window to the next firing wildly. He then followed the others into the tunnel, slamming the trap door shut behind him. Mads led the way down the tunnel which opened into a boathouse some fifty yards from the cottage. One at a time they climbed a ladder into the boathouse. Once inside Mads and Hendrik left to engage the attackers while the colonel, the cook and Peter slipped out a side door and made a run for the dock. Mads and Hendrik worked their way around the cottage to attack the NKVD agents from behind.

At the dock the colonel jumped into a wooden motorboat and started the engine while Peter helped the cook climb in and threw aside the lines. The motor turned over almost instantly with a gurgling sound and they quickly headed out to sea. The colonel skilfully steered the craft through a cluster of ice floes before turning south towards Kapellskar. On the shore the exchange of gunfire around the cottage was intense.

"I'm sorry about that, Klara," the colonel said. "They must have followed Mr Faye somehow. We'll get you to safety shortly."

Peter looked at the cook and felt a wave of guilt. She was an old woman, a civilian, and he had put her in harm's way. He touched her shoulder as she cried silently still in shock from the ordeal.

The exchange of gunfire at the cottage finally slackened when the NKVD team heard the motorboat heading out to sea. They realized the game was up and raced back towards their car. The Finns continued to blast away at them and one of the

NKVD men slumped forward with a bullet to the back of the head. The men quickly hauled their dead colleague to the car and drove away at high speed. The Finns tried to follow the Russians but they had taken the precaution of shooting out their tyres.

A mile away the NKVD car pulled over to allow Evdokia to pull up alongside in her own car. She exchanged a few words through the window with the senior agent and ordered them to hide the body of their colleague in the boot.

Evdokia finished giving instructions and then left for Stockholm in her car followed by the second vehicle.

Thirty-one

Hamburg, Germany

Obersturmbannführer Pauly and his assistant drove to a remote railway work site with Bernadotte and Anders in the back of a German military staff car. At the *SS-Eisenbahn Baubrigade* camp, there were some fifty prisoners in rags hauling iron rails from a truck parked near the tracks. With the frequent Allied bombing of German railways, the SS had organized special work teams to repair bombed-out sections of track.

The staff car pulled over so Bernadotte and Anders could get a look at the prisoners. They got out of the car and approached the work crew.

"They are Russian prisoners who work for the *Reichsbahn* repairing bomb damage," Pauly said. "It's good work, you know, and not too dangerous."

Pauly waved to a guard carrying a Schmeisser machine gun who saluted him. Bernadotte and Anders approached the prisoners who sneaked looks at them. They were rough-looking men with scowling faces but they looked relatively well fed to do the hard work of laying track.

There was a *Deutsche Reichsbahn* rail repair vehicle and a rail carriage on the tracks for transporting and feeding the prisoners. Anders peeked inside the carriage where there was a man cooking food for the prisoners on a gas stove. He waved at Anders who looked at the wooden benches and tables where the prisoners ate.

Pauly and Bernadotte joined Anders at the carriage door and looked in.

"These men are well cared for, Herr Berger," Pauly said. "They have to work fast and move quickly to new sections of track. Allied bombing is destroying our rail links and yards. It's terrible."

"What do your other *Baubrigaden* do?" Bernadotte asked.

"All kinds of jobs. We have them clearing buildings after air raids, removing bombs and recovering bodies, repairing fortifications, it is often very hard work."

Stockholm

Peter was in the office early typing up a report to Keith Linwood as Bridget came in.

"Peter, how did it go yesterday?"

"Very well. Saarson's contact was Colonel Hallamaa of the RTK. I had lunch with him. He's a very knowledgeable man."

"Good, but aren't the Finns officially off limits?"

"They are and they aren't, their intelligence is just too good to ignore."

"I'm happy it went well, Bernie was worried about you."

"No need to worry, Bridget. The Finns can provide us with top secret intelligence, but in exchange they want help from the British government in their war with the Soviets."

"The Soviet Union is our ally in the war, Peter. That won't go over well with the government."

"I agree. I am putting it all in my report to Keith. London can deal with it."

"Got a minute, Bernie?" Peter asked, entering the document room as Bernie looked up. He was hunched over a table under a very bright light examining something with a jeweller's loupe. Several tiny objects glittered on a lint-free cloth near Bernie's lunch box.

"Bernie, are those diamonds?" Peter asked.

"Yes, they are, sir," he said proudly, "I've got me a new hobby. See these stones, I bought them from Sabrina's brother Magnus. He's a jeweller in town. Diamond traders are selling them at bargain prices, a lot of them are war booty."

"I heard most of the dealing was in gold."

"Gold, diamonds, silver, art works. You name it, there is someone out there selling it. Diamonds are going at half price but you've got to know what you're buying with a diamond, right? Cut, colour and clarity."

"I suppose so, Bernie."

"You want diamonds. I can fix you up, old chap, even have them assessed for you. When you return to Britain, you sell 'em for a profit and Bob's your uncle."

"I think I will stick with sterling, Bernie."

"What about an original work of art? Something you can put on your wall or maybe gold that you can hide in an old shoe?"

"No thanks."

Peter removed the Webley service revolver from his pocket and put it on the desk.

"Any news from Stora Essingen?" Peter asked.

"I went out there this morning to take a look but the window was closed, so no documents today."

"We're still waiting for confirmation that everything is okay with the nanny. It may be a while before we resume the operation."

"Peter, I heard from Saarsen about the shooting," Bernie said, picking up a diamond with his forceps. "Did you know that the Finns shot one of their attackers?"

"No, I didn't, but please don't tell Bridget," Peter said. "I haven't mentioned the shooting to her yet."

"My lips are sealed, old chap."

Bernie picked up the revolver and handed it back to Peter.

"You need to keep this," Bernie said. "It could save your life."

"I don't know, Bernie."

"Please, Peter, do it for Bridget. Stockholm can be a dangerous place what with the natives settling grudges and the bad blood between friends and enemies."

"We were having this wonderful meal and suddenly, all hell broke loose," Peter said. "Men were firing into the cottage through the front door and through a window at the back. I was on the floor with the colonel and the cook."

"Peter!"

Bridget and Peter were naked in bed together in the darkened bedroom of his flat.

"We managed to escape through a trap door to a tunnel in the basement."

"You could have been shot," Bridget said.

"We got to the dock and escaped by taking a motorboat back to Kapellskar. We were very lucky. The NKVD has it in for the Finns."

"Who have you told?"

"No one, absolutely no one," Peter said. "Bernie knows, he heard it from Saarson."

"I hope you didn't mention it to Keith, he could have you recalled after an incident like that."

"No, of course not, I didn't mention it."

"That nice lady Evdokia is NKVD," Bridget said. "You think she is involved?"

"Absolutely, she must be. Her husband is Major Petrov who runs the NKVD in Stockholm. He has to know about the attack."

"You better keep it to yourself, Peter, if what you are telling me is true."

"The colonel says that the Soviets have several moles in our intelligence services."

"You don't suspect me, do you?" Bridget asked.

Peter laughed.

"You were my first suspect. I thought I would torture you with kisses to get you to talk."

Bridget pinched Peter.

"Go on then, let's see some more torture."

They kissed briefly and Peter caressed her shoulders.

"Peter, I think you like dishing out torture. Just like any man."

"Is this like any man?"

"No, but keep going, darling, you're getting better at it all the time."

"You know what the colonel said. Our intelligence agencies are so compromised we should get rid of them and start over."

"What are you going to do, Peter?"

"I can't talk to Blunt, I don't trust the bastard." Peter said. "I thought I might be able to talk to Liddell, but he's working with Blunt so that would just alarm them. I was thinking of a plant."

"What do you mean a plant?"

"Just that, slip a planted document into the Kramer file."

"But Peter, that could get you fired?"

"I agree, but anything I do can get me fired!"

Thirty-two

Joanna was reading a German newspaper when Peter entered the press office.

"How are you, Joanna? Where's Ewan?"

"He doesn't come in until after lunch these days, Peter."

"I was hoping to have a chat with you about something. Can you come up later?"

"Of course, Peter. It's gotten to be rather boring around here, with Tennant leaving for his new posting and Ewan not around as much."

"I can imagine."

"This has nothing to do with Ewan's work with Mallet, has it?"

"No, no. I just need your particular skills, Joanna."

"OK, fine then. See you later."

Peter left the office.

"Is there any news from H?" Bridget asked.

"She's out sick this week," Elsa said, "she's got the flu and won't be back at work until next Tuesday. She told me that Wilhelma hasn't said a word about your man in the backyard."

Bridget and Elsa were sitting on a bench in the Berzelius Park in central Stockholm near the statue of the great chemist.

"So she hasn't been to work at all this week?" Bridget asked.

"Frau Kramer doesn't want her cleaning woman sniffling in the house near young Heidi. Shall we walk?"

"Yes, but I can't stay for long."

The two women started walking along the snowy path towards the *Chinateatern*.

Karl-Heinz followed the guard through the basement cell block of Gestapo HQ, then waited as the guard unlocked the cell door. He stepped aside and Karl-Heinz walked in.

Herr Golcher looked up at him from where he sat on a crude bed. He looked miserable.

"Dr Kramer. They came for me this morning at my flat."

"Yes, I received a courtesy call at my office."

"I've done nothing, Dr Kramer."

"I had a talk with the people here. It appears you were arrested for payment irregularities at the *Abwehr* office. They think you absconded with some money, Herr Golcher."

"That's ridiculous. I had a fund for special operations. All intelligence agencies have such funds. I even provided you with some funds, didn't I?"

Karl-Heinz scratched his chin, looking perplexed.

"Of course you did. I understand, but it is going to take some time to sort this out. How long were the Gestapo in your office?"

"They were there for a full week, sir."

"So they had their accountant go through your books. They say you have a Swedish mistress."

"Yes, it's true. My wife returned to Berlin to be with her mother a year ago."

"Good for you. Is she pretty?" Karl-Heinz asked.

"Yes, Dr Kramer. She's a delightful woman."

"Well, I hope she is and the skimming was worth it. You will have a chance to defend yourself when they send you to Berlin."

"Berlin?" Golcher said aghast. "Please, Dr Kramer, I will do anything. Please!"

"I will talk to my people but I cannot promise you anything," Karl-Heinz said knocking on the cell door. A guard appeared and opened the door.

"Good-bye, Herr Golcher."

Peter and Bridget were having a drink in a waterfront restaurant during the lunch hour.

"Don't look now, Peter, but that Russian woman Evkodia just walked by with her husband."

Peter risked a quick glance in their direction, then turned back to Bridget.

"Well, well. This is a small town. You never know who you might run into."

"So what did Joanna say?" Bridget asked. "Will she do it?"

"Yes. She writes *Deutsche Kurrentschrift* better than anyone. I think you should keep out of this, Bridget, for your own good."

"Peter, I don't mind helping," Bridget said.

"It's easier to deny something," Peter said, "when one has no knowledge of it."

Peter took Bridget's hand and kissed it.

"You mentioned Major Linwood?" Bridget asked.

"Keith will listen, Bridget. He has a mind of his own."

"Have you written to him?"

"Yes, I have," he said. "I remember we used a similar ploy to flush out a teacher's snitch back when we were at school. In that case it was a bogus test question. So Keith knows how it works."

Thirty-three

Peter entered the room where Joanna was helping Bernie produce a bogus German *Abwehr* document on Soviet airplane production. She signed the document with a flourish using her Mont Blanc fountain pen and then employed a rocker-style blotter to dry the ink.

"I signed 'Hans Weber' as you suggested," Joanna said.

Peter picked up the document and looked very closely at the signature.

"Very good, Joanna. That certainly looks like a man's signature. We'll need an *Abwehr* stamp."

"Piece of cake," Bernie said, handing Joanna a rubber stamp, "try this one."

Joanna tested the stamp on a piece of paper and examined the result. Peter pulled Bernie aside.

"Are we good tomorrow for a pickup?"

"Of course, Peter."

Joanna applied the stamp to the *Abwehr* report and handed it to Bernie. He positioned it under the lights of the Minox copy stand and took a picture.

The trip had been a total waste of time. After three days of aimlessly touring the Neuengamme subcamps it had become clear that Schellenberg, *Obersturmbannführer* Pauly, and the SD were simply going through the motions. Frustrated and angry, Count Bernadotte and Anders had decided to cut their search short when it became clear that it was not a genuine search at all. They had said as much to Pauly, requesting immediate transfer back to Tempelhof Airfield in Berlin so they could fly home. Pauly had made a clumsy effort to talk them out of it but in the end he had reluctantly complied.

They had booked tickets on the next Luft Hansa flight to Stockholm and were on the way to the aircraft when someone called out to them. They looked back at the air terminal and were astonished to see the *SD Ausland* Chief Schellenberg and his aide get out of a military staff car and walk towards them across the tarmac.

"Can I have a word, Herr Bernadotte?" Schellenberg asked.

"Yes, of course."

"Let's go into the office for a moment."

Anders and Bernadotte exchanged a look.

"Don't worry, gentlemen," Schellenberg assured them. "You won't be late. My men have informed the crew. They will be waiting for you."

They returned to the terminal and a hastily vacated flight office. They sat down while Schellenberg's aide closed the door on them and waited outside.

"There has been an unfortunate misunderstanding," Schellenberg began.

Count Bernadotte was having none of it.

"Herr Schellenberg, we requested the names of the Scandinavian prisoners and their locations, but we have received no names and very little assistance. Sweden is a neutral country and a friend of Germany. When you needed our help, we gave it to you and we were very generous. This kind of treatment is quite unacceptable among friends."

"Herr Bernadotte, I am very sorry for the wasted time but we are making real progress now. Herr Himmler has agreed to your proposition to regroup all the Scandinavian prisoners in the same camp. It must be done very discreetly. Not everyone agrees with this idea so Himmler's approval is important."

"I don't see," Anders said, "how we can regroup prisoners if we don't know where they are, sir. I don't see how this can be accomplished."

Bernadotte shot him a reproving look but Schellenberg acknowledged Anders' question with a nod.

"I will have our people do an exhaustive search, Herr Berger. We have the records. Don't worry, we will find all of your people."

"The Swedish Red Cross has lists of names," Bernadotte said. "Some of these people have already been identified on your prisoner lists, but there are many names that we have lost track of."

"The SD will work very hard to please you," Schellenberg said. "Send me the lists and we'll find them."

They stood up and Schellenberg smiled as he shook their hands.

"Don't worry," Schellenberg said, "we'll find your people. Now you better go to catch your flight. I'll be in touch."

He then summoned his aide to escort them to their plane.

Joanna collected her coat and slid a brown envelope into her handbag before leaving the Legation building. She walked past several old river barges tied up at the waterfront and crossed the street to the main post office. She bought a postcard and took it over to a side table where a dark-haired woman wearing a blue scarf was putting stamps on some letters. Joanna rummaged in her handbag, taking out the brown envelope and placing it on the table. She found a pen and wrote a brief note on the back of the postcard before addressing it to a friend.

Joanna quickly left the post office, dropping the postcard in the mail box on her way out. The other woman remained behind and picked up Joanna's envelope on her way out.

Thirty-four

Peter had just left the Legation offices and was on his way to lunch when a car pulled up beside him. The driver was Mads with Saarson in the passenger seat.

"The colonel wants a meeting, Mr Faye," Saarson said after rolling down the window, "it's urgent."

"Will this take long?"

"No, sir, we'll have you back after lunch."

Peter looked around and then got in the back of the car. Mads took off, doubling back on their route several times to shake off anyone who might try to follow. They drove to the port and stopped beside the gangway to a cargo vessel. Peter got out of the car and looked up to see Hendrik smiling down at him from the main deck. He was armed with a Suomi submachine gun slung from a shoulder. He waited for Peter to come up and then led him to the galley where Colonel Hallamaa was having lunch with some of the ship's officers. He looked up as they arrived, and gestured for them to wait outside. They retreated to the deck and idly watched the cargo loading operations until Hallamaa joined them a few moments later.

"Good day, Mr Faye," Hallamaa said. "I'm sorry for the inconvenience, but I had to see you before I leave."

Hallamaa nodded at Hendrik who moved out of earshot, keeping his eye on movements on the dock.

"I'm sailing tonight for Finland and won't be back for a while."

"What can I do for you, Colonel?" Peter asked.

"There have been some new developments. You know Wilho Tikander over at the US Legation?"

"Not well, I'm afraid. He's OSS."

"The Americans didn't believe we could break their codes so we did it to show them that we could. Now we're providing them with Soviet code material and deciphered messages. We give them everything and they finance our operations."

"Very impressive, Colonel," Peter said.

"I have two names for you: 'Sonia' and 'Elli'. That is S-O-N-I-A and E-L-L-I. These are the GRU code-names for two Soviet agents working in Britain. At least one of them has been providing information about tube alloy research and the British nuclear program to the Soviets."

Peter was gobsmacked. The implications were staggering.

"In return," Hallamaa continued, "I need your help with my request to meet senior representatives of your government."

"Yes, of course," Peter managed.

"Please be careful, Mr Faye," Hallamaa said with grave concern. "You must only communicate these code-names to your most trusted people. By giving you these names, I am putting your life in danger and anyone you contact with this information."

"I understand, sir. I will take precautions. Thank you, Colonel, thank you very much."

"I hope so, Mr Faye. I hope so. You like Stockholm?"

"Yes, sir. I do."

"You will love Helsinki," Hallamaa said. "You must come and visit Finland after the war. So what about my meeting with your government?"

"I can get you a meeting with our Legation chief, Victor Mallet," Peter said, knowing as he said it that it would not be enough.

"No, not Victor Mallet. He's too busy buying up German assets to show any interest in Finland."

"I don't see who else, sir," Peter replied when an idea suddenly dawned on him. "I do know an individual who has close personal contacts with a Member of Parliament, someone who could perhaps get you to Anthony Eden at the Foreign Office or perhaps the PM."

"Mr Faye," Hallamaa smiled, "now you are on the right track. Eden or Churchill, that would be splendid."

Peter smiled back. He could only hope that Ewan Butler's contacts were as good as he said they were.

Evdokia Petrov chain-smoked as she sat at a table in front of a glass of red wine at a waterfront restaurant. It was a stressful job running secret NKVD operations for her husband in Stockholm and she needed the wine to relax. Still, her life in Sweden had many compensations. She and her husband Vladimir much preferred Stockholm to Moscow, not only in material terms but professionally as well. Their job was to keep an eye on the ambassador and to do Moscow's bidding in forcing a peace settlement on Finland.

The door opened and a woman with a blue scarf stepped inside. Evdokia ignored her as she walked towards the back of the restaurant and dropped a brown envelope into Evdokia's lap on her way by. Evdokia slipped the envelope into her handbag and took her time with the wine. After several minutes she stood up, left some krona on the table to pay her bill before collecting her coat and heading for the door.

It was after midnight and Ewan Butler was drinking whisky in his study looking over several reports for Victor Mallet. A knock at the front door was heard. He got up and stumbled into the hallway running into his wife Mary in her night gown.

"Who is it, Ewan?"

"I have no idea," Ewan said as he opened the door.

"Peter!" Ewan exclaimed.

"It's very late, Mr Faye," Mary said. "You better come back tomorrow."

"Peter, what are you doing here?" Ewan asked.

"Where have you been, Ewan?" Peter asked. "I've been trying to reach you all day."

"I just got in an hour ago. I've been busy working with Mallet the whole day."

"Get dressed, Ewan," Peter ordered, "you're coming with me."

"Let's have a drink first, Peter. Come in please."

"I know it's very late, but this is very important. It's Legation business."

Ewan looked at his irate wife and then put on his coat and hat.

"I'll be back soon, Mary. Don't worry, my dear."

Ewan and Peter quickly left the flat and headed down the stairs to the car where Mads and Hendrik were waiting for them. They were bundled into the car and Mads raced away heading toward the old city.

After a few minutes in the car Peter was already fed up with Ewan who was slurring his words and stank of whisky and cigar smoke. He seriously doubted that Hallamaa would be impressed by Ewan, but there was no time to worry about it as they drove up beside the big freighter in the dock area. The four of them got out and climbed the gangway with Hendrik watching the shadows for NKVD surveillance. Peter kept a discreet hand on Ewan's arm as he stumbled up the gangway.

On the deck Mads muttered something to Hendrik in Finnish and Peter thought he could hear Hendrik snicker. Peter felt a flush of embarrassment but kept his expression impassive as they followed Mads into the galley. Hallamaa rose from a chair to greet them.

"Ewan Butler," Peter said. "This is Colonel Hallamaa of the RTK."

If the colonel was alarmed by Ewan's befuddled appearance, he showed no sign of it.

"I apologize for the lateness of the hour, Mr Butler," he said, "I am sailing for Finland at dawn so I wanted to meet you before I left. Have you ever been to Helsinki?"

"Helsinki, no I'm afraid not, sir. I prefer warmer climes for my travels."

"You must have enjoyed your previous posting in Egypt then?"

"Yes, Egypt was very nice and much warmer."

"Mr Faye has kindly brought you here because we need your help."

Peter cringed as Hallamaa gestured for Mads to pour some drinks. Ewan brightened noticeably.

"I'm afraid I don't understand, Colonel," Ewan said. "I work in the press office at the British Legation."

"Yes, you do but you also work for the SOE," Hallamaa smiled. "We need your help in our war against the Soviets."

"My help?" Ewan laughed. "Sir, I'm a civil servant in His Majesty's government. Totally useless, if you ask me. Peter here will tell you."

"No, Mr Butler. You are my knight in shining armour. I believe that is what you British people say. So you are going to save a damsel in distress, our beloved Finland."

The colonel and Peter laughed heartily at this as Ewan looked on in a state of puzzlement. He recovered just enough to accept the glass of aquavit Mads was offering him.

"Me, a knight in shining armour?" Ewan grinned as he lifted his glass. "Well, I suppose that calls for a toast."

Thirty-five

Gustav Lundquist stopped by Ander Berger's desk at the newspaper.

"So how did it go, your trip to Germany, Anders?"

"I am not allowed to talk about it, sir," Anders said, "and we're not allowed to publish anything."

"I know. We received the gag order from the government."

"I can't say it was successful, sir. Bernadotte and I spent three days at the Neuengamme camp getting nowhere."

"How many Swedish prisoners do they have?"

"I really don't know. Bernadotte estimates there are 13,000 Scandinavian prisoners. The Germans estimate the number at around 3,000."

"So what's the plan now?"

"The SD has agreed to regroup the prisoners at Neuengamme to facilitate their removal. I'm to follow up with our own list of people who have disappeared in the camps. The Red Cross is helping me draw up the list."

"Keep me posted on developments. We want to be the first to publish this story when the gag order is lifted, Anders."

"Of course, sir."

Bridget looked up and smiled at Peter as he walked into the office. She held up an official looking letter on thick bond paper. The letterhead looked vaguely familiar. Peter removed his hat and coat and stepped closer.

"The Rugby Music Society," Bridget said.

"Really? They actually replied."

"Yes, Peter. They did more than reply. They're awarding Aksell a prize for his music compositions."

Peter was astonished. He took the letter and quickly read it over once and then read it again.

"Bloody hell, I never would have thought," Peter paused a moment, "I didn't think those old sods would be capable of helping an unknown Swedish composer get out of prison, but clearly they did their part."

"You better take this down to Bernie and see what he thinks," Bridget said.

"Maybe they remembered me at Rugby?"

"Of course, they remembered you, Peter. A handsome, young housemaster, good with languages. A little slow sometimes with staff."

"Slow! No way, Bridget."

"Maybe sometimes," Bridget laughed, "so how did it go with H?"

"She's still producing," Peter said. "The documents keep coming. They went out last night by diplomatic bag with our bogus report."

"When will you know something?"

"Keith has been warned to be on the lookout. The aim is to target Blunt or Hollis."

"I don't get it. So what if Blunt sees the report?"

"You remember the uproar in London concerning H's first delivery. Well, it contained a top secret memorandum with the private discussions of Churchill and Roosevelt at the Quebec

Conference in August 1943. I can tell you about it since apparently it is no longer a secret for anyone."

"Of course. The Quebec conference was discussed in the papers."

"Did I tell you I was posted to the Atlantic conference in Newfoundland back in 1941? Churchill and Roosevelt issued a joint declaration, the Atlantic Charter, at the Naval Station Argentia in Placentia Bay."

"No, Peter, you didn't tell me. You do live an exciting life."

"It was my first posting. We sailed on the HMS Prince of Wales with the PM's people."

Peter sat down near Bridget.

"In retrospect it wasn't really all that exciting, we were sea sick most of the time," Peter said. "Anyway we had access to the minutes of the meetings between the American president and the PM. We were shocked by the obscene language used by Roosevelt in the talks. This is the same man speaking at the Quebec Conference in 1943. The language is so similar that it must be the real thing, not some German fakery as Blunt suggested."

"I don't understand, Peter. It can't just be Roosevelt's vulgar language that created a panic in London."

"No, of course not. The memorandum at the Quebec Conference contained an agreement for a nuclear partnership, a top secret project to build an atomic bomb in collaboration with the Americans. Only the chiefs of staff were allowed to see this part of the document and I estimate it took less than two weeks for a mole in London station to leak it to Moscow."

"So you want to know the time it takes to leak your bogus report to Moscow?" Bridget asked.

"Precisely and who is doing the leaking?"

"That's brilliant, Peter."

"Well, it's a start. It's the least we can do from here and who knows? We might get lucky."

Thirty-six

"Her brother is a scientist in tube alloys at Oxford. He has helped us in the past," Evdokia said.

She looked out the window at the frosty garden of the Soviet Legation.

"She could be a plant," Vladimir Petrov said, sitting at his desk. "It could all be disinformation."

As NKVD chief in Stockholm his job was to look at all the possibilities and to second guess his people. No one had his ear. He was a shrewd operator and a bad decision could instantly ruin his career. On the other hand Evdokia was smart and sometimes saw opportunities when he did not.

"Faye is no fool, Vladimir. I don't understand why they are doing a mock-up *Abwehr* document on Soviet airplane production. They have the resources in London to fake any kind of documentation. This is MI6 in Stockholm winging it. They had to ask a bunch of amateurs at SOE to help them."

"You're right, it does look odd."

"Something is going on with Peter Faye and the Finns are behind it. You need to inform Moscow."

"So what happened last night? Did you find anything in the ambassador's office?" Evdokia asked.

"We went through Kollontai's desk and opened her safe. She has no secrets that I can tell. They won't be happy in Moscow. They've been trying to arrest her for years."

"I like her, Vladimir, and so do you, but this is not good news for us."

"What can we do?" Vladimir asked. "We have nothing."

Evdokia thought about Kollontai's extraordinary career as a colleague of Lenin and one of the few among the old guard Stalin permitted to remain alive. Her husband Dybenko had been shot in 1936 on a charge of being a Trotskyist. Now their job was to find anything of a compromising nature that their NKVD bosses could use against her.

"I don't know," Evdokia said, "but we need to find something fast or they may send us back to Moscow."

Vladimir took a cigarette case from his pocket and stood up. He went to stand near his wife in the window. He gave her a cigarette and they both lit up. They stood there in silence smoking as they looked out at the snow. The Petrovs were a loving couple, inseparable, but they worked for a frightening secret organization involved in kidnappings and assassinations that often ate its own agents.

"I like it here in Stockholm, Vladimir. I don't want to go home," Evdokia said.

"So do I, my dear."

"It would be a disgrace."

"I've got a surprise for you, Bernie," Peter said.

Bernie looked up from the mundane task of pasting Legation staff photo IDs into document holders. Peter put the Rugby Music Society letter on the table next to him. Bernie carefully wiped his hands before picking it up and reading it.

"Crikey!" he exclaimed, getting up from his chair and hugging Peter. "They're givin' him the bleedin' Nobel prize!"

Peter grinned, surprised by Bernie's uncharacteristic display of emotion.

"It was Bridget's idea," Peter said. "It clearly states that Aksell has to go to England to accept it."

"This is incredible, Peter. Thank you and thank Bridget! You must have put on a good show to get them to play along. The minister can't ignore this. They'll have to release him."

"It does look good, doesn't it?"

"I want to give you something in return, Peter."

Peter looked confused.

"I have a diamond, a nice one," Bernie said. "Sabrina's brother can have it mounted for you. You can give it to Bridget when you ask her to marry you."

Peter just gaped at him in surprise.

"Everybody knows, Peter," Bernie grinned. "We see you around town together. Bridget's in love with you, old chap. She looks so happy since you arrived."

"I don't know whether I can accept it."

"Don't be daft, Peter, course you can. It's for Bridget!"

An elderly woman entered the room and put a coffee tray on the desk between Count Bernadotte and Anders Berger. Neither man looked up, engrossed as they were in their lists of missing people. The two men were busy working late in an office at the Swedish Red Cross.

"I'm off, sir," the secretary said, "I want to get home before the storm."

"Thanks, Rose," Bernadotte looked up. "Take care on the roads and lock the door on your way out."

"I have the lists," Anders said, "but there are still around 700 people missing. Some have been located by Arne Berge, the priest at Neuengamme. Others by Conrad Vogt-Svendsen at Gross Kreuz, and Johan Hjort also contributed a few names."

"So we need to put all the names together into one list with their last known location," Bernadotte said.

"Britta and I can do this at home, sir."

"We must hurry, Anders. Word is out that the Russians will be in Berlin in a few weeks and then the conditions in the camps will become disastrous."

"I will have it for you by tomorrow, sir," Anders said. "We will work on it all night. So let's check first for the surnames that appear on more than one list."

"Very good," Bernadotte said. "Thanks, Anders, for your help."

"It's a pleasure, sir."

Peter left the British Legation building after work and crossed the street to catch a tramway as the snow storm struck the city. Wind blasted in off the Baltic and snow swirled around the streets reducing visibility. He caught a tram heading west and didn't notice a car following the tram at a distance through the snowy streets. After a short ride, he got off and walked several blocks to his flat.

Peter reacted far too late. He had just stepped into the entryway of his apartment building when he found himself staring into the muzzle of a Tokarev pistol. The man holding it said nothing, just motioned for Peter to follow his partner to their car. Even without the weapon there would have been little point in resisting. Both men were obviously NKVD thugs and, if they had wanted to kill him, they already would have.

Still, it was embarrassing. Peter had made the classic mistake of falling into a routine, leaving the Legation at the usual time by the same door and then taking the same tram back to his flat. He'd been complacent, unaware of his surroundings and had blundered into an ambush. He was disgusted with himself.

One of the thugs opened the back door of the car and the other one pushed him inside. Peter wasn't terribly surprised to find Evdokia Petrov waiting for him.

"Mr Faye. It's a pleasure to see you again."

"Aren't we being a little bit melodramatic, Mrs Petrov?" Peter said unamused. "You could have just called my office and made an appointment."

Thirty-seven

The NKVD car sped through the snowy streets heading for the waterfront.

"This is really quite outrageous, Mrs Petrov," Peter said. "I'm going to have to protest to your government unless you tell me right away what this is all about."

"Don't worry, Mr Faye," Evdokia said, with a warm smile. "I am not taking you to the Soviet Legation. There are too many people who might observe you entering the premises."

"What is this about?"

"Ambassador Kollontai wants a word. This is an unofficial meeting. We didn't have time to call you."

The car pulled up at the service entrance of the Grand Hotel and the two NKVD agents accompanied Peter into the hotel followed by Evdokia. They entered through the kitchen and soon found themselves in a luxurious drawing room in a large hotel suite.

"Please sit down, Mr Faye. The ambassador will be with us shortly."

Peter sat down and looked around. The agents had left the room, pulling the door closed.

"How about a refreshment?" Evdokia asked. "Perhaps a martini, a whisky, or do you want a cup of tea?"

"No thanks."

"Relax, Mr Faye. We're colleagues simply having a chat. This won't take up much of your time. Are you sure you don't want a whisky?"

"I think I will indulge myself after all. A whisky neat, please."

Evdokia got up to pour the whisky from the bar in the corner.

"I think I will have one too, to keep you company. Is that the right term, Mr Faye?"

"Your English is very good, Mrs Petrov."

The door to the suite opened and one of the NKVD agents pushed the Soviet ambassador's wheelchair into the room.

"It's a pleasure to see you again, Mr Faye."

Peter stood up as the ambassador appeared.

"Hello, Madam Kollontai."

The ambassador was all smiles and appeared in good spirits as Evdokia brought her a cup of tea.

"Please sit down, sir. My people tell me you have been very busy since you arrived in Sweden."

"I work in Consular Services, Madam Kollontai," Peter said. "It's very boring work and there are not many Swedes who want to travel to Britain right now. Perhaps you should be having this conversation with my superior, Victor Mallet."

"Mr Faye, we know who you are," Kollontai said. "You work for British Intelligence - SIS. I thought we might have a talk about a subject of mutual interest: Finland."

"I know nothing about Finland, Madam. It's not my forte."

"You were seen with Colonel Hallamaa of the RTK a few days ago, Mr Faye. You must know that my government is trying to negotiate a peace settlement with Finland through the office of President Ryti."

"I don't know anything about these negotiations, Madam."

"Colonel Hallamaa is against the peace settlement. He's trying to sabotage the months of work we have put into these discussions. He's a very tiresome man."

"I'm sorry but I really cannot help you."

"Mr Faye thinks we are ignorant of his recent discussions with the colonel," Evdokia said. "We know what the colonel wants, Mr Faye. He wants the British to intervene in his fight against the Soviet Union."

"The Finns are our friends, Madam Kollontai, just as the Soviets are our friends. The British government will never abandon Finland."

"We're only asking you to help us find the colonel," Kollontai said, "so we can enter into a negotiation with him. He trusts you enough to meet you in public."

"I'm sorry, Madam Kollontai," Peter said. "I cannot help you. I haven't the slightest idea where to find him."

"If you change your mind and decide to help us, please contact Mrs Petrov at the Legation."

The grand old Bolshevik snapped her fingers and Evdokia instantly came over to take her cup and saucer.

"Good evening, Mr Faye."

Evdokia wheeled the chair towards the door where one of the guards took over. Peter finished his whisky and stood up.

"I did say it wouldn't take long," Evdokia said.

"I cannot condone your methods, Mrs Petrov. We are in neutral Sweden and your people sent armed men to kill Colonel Hallamaa and his bodyguards."

"I think you are exaggerating a bit, Mr Faye," Evdokia said as she sat down, "it was the Finns who opened fire on us and killed one of our men."

Evdokia sipped her whisky.

"Please sit down, Mr Faye. I have an offer to make you."

Peter remained standing.

"We realise that Finnish affairs are of no concern to you," Evdokia said. "Your job at SIS is to track German spies here in Stockholm. This is our job too. We're on the same side so we should help each other. Would you like another whisky?"

"No thank you, I better be going."

"Ambassador Kollontai is a very generous woman. She is willing to pay a substantial sum of money for information about the colonel. What he is thinking, what he is doing."

"It's not my affair, Mrs Petrov."

"The Finns have very little time to make up their minds, Mr Faye. The Soviet army will crush them unless they negotiate a peace settlement."

"Good-bye, Mrs Petrov." Peter said as he started for the door.

"Mr Faye, you are making it your affair whether you like it or not," Evdokia said with a warning look.

Peter did not look back as he left the room.

"Good-bye, Mr Faye. Thank you for your time."

It was dark in the nightclub as the lights came up on the band playing Hollywood swing and cool jazz. Ten scantily dressed chorus girls danced onto the stage in revealing costumes showing off their navels and long legs. The dance number was professionally choreographed and worthy of any Paris cabaret show.

In a booth near the back Peter and Bridget were enjoying martinis in the company of Bernie and Sabrina. It had been Bernie's idea to invite them and a way of showing their gratitude for obtaining the award for Aksell. Sabrina had just received news from the Swedish Interior Minister that Aksell would be released from prison to collect the award.

As the show progressed Peter noticed numerous young men moving about from booth to booth in quiet conversation showing no interest whatsoever in the floorshow. They sat in a booth, conversed for a minute or two and then moved on to other booths. There were very few women in the audience and clearly something other than ogling the chorus girls was going on.

"After ten o'clock buyers and sellers can circulate, Peter," Bernie said, "and the deal-making can begin."

"What are they selling?" Bridget asked.

"Gold, silver, diamonds, war booty, anything you like," Bernie said. "They don't come here for the floorshow."

"Bernie, I'm sure Peter and Bridget aren't interested in the deals that go on here," Sabrina said as Magnus appeared at Bernie's shoulder.

"Peter, Bridget, I'd like you to meet Magnus, Sabrina's brother," Bernie said.

"Hello, Peter. Bridget, Sabrina."

Magnus leaned in to kiss his sister.

"So what's happening, Magnus?" Bernie asked.

"It's going to be a big night, Bernie."

"Got any great deals going down?"

Magnus pointed to a table off to the side where a very large man with a black moustache and a bald skull was smoking a cigar and blowing smoke at Herr Kemper, the new *SD Ausland* officer.

"*Der Grosse* says it's going to be busy tonight."

"Federmann is making a fortune with German war booty," Bernie said. "This is where it all happens."

"Magnus, please sit with us a bit," Sabrina implored her brother.

"No, I can't Sabrina," Magnus replied looking preoccupied, "I have a booth in back with Emil. We're waiting for the Americans to make their offers."

Magnus smiled at Bernie and disappeared as Kemper left Federmann's booth. A group of Americans GIs in cheap suits joined Federmann, bringing their drinks with them. A waiter appeared and brought a glass of cognac for the fat German but left quickly. Federmann puffed away on his cigar as he listened to the American spiel.

Bernie leaned in to speak to Peter and Bridget.

"Federmann came here from Berlin in the 1920s. He owns half the bars in Gamla Stan. He's the SD contact for gold and diamonds."

"How can you buy stolen diamonds, Bernie?" Bridget asked with real concern. "Surely some of them come from Nazi death camps."

"I don't, I buy them from Magnus," Bernie laughed.

"Magnus is a diamond trader, Bridget," Sabrina argued. "It's just a job for him. He doesn't ask where they come from."

"I wouldn't worry, Bridget," Peter said. "Diamonds are in very short supply with the war on. They are used mainly in industrial applications. I doubt Federmann gets any from the SD. The diamonds are coming from private sources."

"Thank you, Peter," Bernie said watching the floor. "The Americans are leaving."

As soon as the American GIs got up to leave, a number of buyers congregated around Federmann's booth looking for deals. Magnus and his associate Emil were already on their feet heading towards Federmann's booth to bid on a few stones, when gunshots were heard and everyone hit the floor. The music stopped playing and the chorus girls ran off the stage. Bernie grabbed Sabrina's arm and pulled her to the floor along with Bridget and Peter.

"Let's get out of here," Bernie yelled as a second volley of shots rang out.

"What about Magnus?" Sabrina replied worried about her brother.

"Okay, I'll get him," Bernie said. "You go with Peter and Bridget."

Peter ran towards the exit pulling Bridget and Sabrina along with him as Bernie struggled through the frightened buyers looking for Magnus. There was a crush of people at the door trying to leave as the staff looked on. Once outside in the alley, the crowd gathered, waiting for news of their friends inside. After several minutes Bernie appeared with Magnus.

"What happened?" Peter asked Bernie as Sabrina ran to embrace her brother.

"Some poor sod tried to stick up *Der Grosse*," Bernie said. "Federman has an armed bodyguard nearby at all times."

"You think the bodyguard shot someone?"

"Yeah, Federmann's man Karl got one in the arm, but he offed the other chap. They are patching Karl up now. It won't be long before the show starts up again. *Der Grosse* has thousands of dollars and krona on him on any one night so there is always someone out there wanting to pinch his loot."

"Doesn't the Swedish police offer to protect him?" Bridget asked.

"Nobody reports the incidents," Bernie said. "No one wants to tell on Federmann who owns the place."

"Let's go somewhere else, Bernie," Sabrina said. "Magnus, are you going back?"

"They're cleaning up now, it won't be long. They'll be offering free drinks on the house in a moment."

"Be careful, Magnus," Sabrina said as Magnus joined his associate Emil and headed for the entrance.

"Okay, ladies, let's go, the night is still young." Bernie said taking Sabrina and Bridget by the arm.

Peter watched Magnus return to the club and then followed Bernie and the women.

Thirty-eight

It was after midnight at the Berger flat as Anders typed a list of names on an old Remington typewriter. Nearby, Britta called out the names of the disappeared.

"Matsen, Gustav; Nygaard, Benedikt; Pihl, Edvard; Risberg, Knut; Steensen, Harald; Thomason, Jacob. Want some more coffee, Anders?"

"Yes, please."

Britta returned with a thermos of coffee and poured a cup.

"We're half way through," Britta said. "It won't be long before we finish."

Anders stood up to stretch briefly, before sitting back down and starting to type again. He stopped a moment to drink his coffee.

"Count Bernadotte has a secret plan to bring back all the Scandinavian prisoners."

"Really, what's this plan?" Britta asked.

"Well, it's still being debated by the authorities, but Bernadotte wants to send some thirty buses to collect our people at Neuengamme. The buses will be painted white with the sign of the Swedish Red Cross to prevent bombing from the Allies. He wants the army to provide twenty doctors and nurses to accompany the volunteers."

"When do you think they will start?"

"I don't know but the minister must first accept the plan," Anders said, "and they need to hurry."

"Will you go with them?"

"I hope so," Anders said, "I am not giving up on Rolf."

Britta approached and kissed her husband.

"The minister has appointed Colonel Gottfrid Björck to look over the plan. He will be in charge of handling the logistics of the repatriation."

Unshaven and drunk, Golcher was asleep on the couch in his small flat when he heard a knocking at the front door. He awakened as the knocking increased in intensity.

"Herr Golcher. Open up."

Still half asleep, Golcher went to the door and opened it. Karl-Heinz walked in without a word and looked around at the mess. There were empty bottles of beer and glasses on the tables and chairs, and a pile of dirty dishes in the kitchen sink. Worse was the stink of unwashed bodies and rotting food.

"Herr Golcher, you need to get cleaned up and come back to work."

"But I have no work. The Gestapo has barred me from returning to work while they decide what to do with me."

"Who do you think got you out of that Gestapo prison?" Karl-Heinz asked.

"I don't know. They didn't say."

"Schellenberg. Who else? He put in a call to the Gestapo head Müller. That's why you were sent home. I said I would help you."

Kramer lit a cigarette and puffed on it as he looked around the flat.

"Where is your Swedish woman? You should get her to come over and clean this place up."

"She left me, Dr Kramer, after this business with the Gestapo."

"I'm sorry, but you need to pick yourself up and come with me. I have some work I want you to do. It's a temporary job but you'll be paid by the *SD Ausland* office."

Golcher's eyes lit up with hope.

"*Vielen Dank, Dr Kramer*! Thank you. Give me ten minutes."

Karl-Heinz opened a window as Golcher started running around the flat picking up clothes and clearing space for his boss to sit down.

In the Florsberg common room Bernie and Sabrina waited as Aksell was brought in.

"Pappa!" Sabrina cried, rushing forward to kiss her dad.

Bernie gave them a moment and then joined them.

"We're taking you home, sir," Bernie said, "you've been released."

Aksell looked confused standing in the middle of the room in an old threadbare suit.

"Home?"

"Yes, you are free to leave, Pappa," Sabrina said. "We're taking you home today."

"I can go home?"

"The minister has released you," Bernie said. "We have the papers here. Show him, Sabrina."

Sabrina thrust the letter from the Swedish Interior Minister into Aksell's hands but he ignored it.

"I must say good-bye to my friends, Sabrina. I must say good-bye."

"Yes, of course, Pappa."

"The British have given you an award for your music compositions," Bernie said.

"My music?" Aksell laughed. "No, it is not possible."

"Bernie is right, Pappa. The British have given you a prize for your music."

"But I have never been to Britain, Sabrina. This is a joke, yes?"

"No, sir," Bernie said, "with the award you will be able to go to Britain."

"It's not a joke, Pappa," Sabrina assured him.

A short time later after numerous handshakes and hugs from his friends, Aksell walked out of the Florsberg camp on the arm of his daughter.

Spring was in the air as Bernie and Sabrina drove south through the Swedish countryside with its pretty falu red cottages and melting snowbanks. Aksell sat in the back admiring the view.

"So who is giving me this prize?" Aksell asked.

"The Rugby Music Society in Warwickshire," Bernie said.

"I've never heard of these people."

"Nor them of you, Pappa," Sabrina said. "The award was the only way to convince the minister to release you."

"Sweden cannot start putting its prize winners in jail," Bernie said. "Imagine what would happen to the Nobel prize."

"Which composition did they hear?" Aksell asked.

Bernie looked at Sabrina and Sabrina at Bernie. There was a moment of silence before Sabrina turned to address her dad.

"You know my favourite, Pappa."

"You mean my 'Daybreak Symphony'."

"Yes, that is the one. They loved it."

Sabrina smiled at Bernie as Aksell looked positively ecstatic to hear this. He felt honoured that the Rugby Music Society loved his precious symphony.

It was the middle of the afternoon and the restaurant in Gamla Stan was almost empty. Bridget was having tea with Hanne and Elsa.

"Frau Kramer is worried about her mother," Hanne said. "She wants to return to Cologne to see her, but her husband is against it. After the bombings in October, her mother fled the city. She's living with an elderly cousin in a nearby village."

"There's real panic at the German Legation," Elsa said. "I heard that a lot of their employees are trying to stay in Sweden, as they fear that Germany will be overrun by the Red Army."

"Yes, I've heard the same," Bridget said.

"No one wants to go back," Hanne said.

"Is the Gestapo still watching the Kramer house?"

"No, I think they're gone. I haven't seen a car in quite a while."

"Are we good for a pickup tomorrow, Hanne?"

"I think so. It may be the last in a while. I will only be working one day a week if Frau Kramer gets her wish to return to Germany."

Thirty-nine

Karl-Heinz stepped into the Bromma Airfield hangar followed by Herr Golcher, clean-shaven in a business suit and fedora. The two men greeted Sven Ekstrom, the freight manager, who arrived from the tarmac in a leather jacket.

"*Guten Tag, Dr Kramer.* The spring has finally arrived."

"Yes, it has been a very long winter, Herr Ekstrom," Karl-Heinz said. "This is Herr Golcher, a colleague of mine. He'll be in charge of all our shipping interests from now on."

"I have received two packages from Germany for you, Dr Kramer," Sven said. "They are in the 'in transit' cargo."

"Very good. I have to return to town. Why don't you show Herr Golcher how it works?"

"Of course, sir."

Kramer turned and headed back to his car.

"Come with me, Herr Golcher," Sven said.

Golcher followed Sven into his office.

"You want a coffee, Herr Golcher?"

"Yes, thank you."

Sven put the kettle on the hotplate and sat at his desk.

"Now I suppose you know what the term 'in transit' means?" Sven asked.

"Of course, I do," Golcher said. "It means travelling between one place and another."

"I'm talking about freight 'in transit', Herr Golcher?"

"Is it a shipping term?"

"You are new to this I think. What was your previous occupation? No, don't tell me."

Sven smiled at Kramer's man.

"The term 'in transit' refers to freight that we hold temporarily until we ship it out to a new destination. It does not go through Swedish customs."

"Okay, I understand."

"Freight 'in transit' is held in a separate locked warehouse. It never enters the country."

"So these packages are in the 'in transit' section, the international zone?"

"Very good, Herr Golcher," Sven said. "Dr Kramer wants to send them on to new destinations, so they will require a new bill of lading."

Golcher suddenly caught on.

"So I bring you a new bill of lading, which you then stick on the package and send on its way."

"Not exactly, Herr Golcher. It is illegal for me or any Swedish employee to tamper with freight 'in transit'. We will lose our jobs and go to prison."

"You will lose your jobs? Is it illegal?"

"Yes, under Swedish law. So I will get you into the 'in transit' section and you will change the bill of lading and destination as you see fit. There is a room in there where you can do your work."

Golcher looked worried by the illegal nature of the work.

"Don't worry, Herr Golcher," Sven said. "No one will ever see you in there. No one goes into the 'in transit' area except to deliver or remove packages and during daytime hours only."

Golcher seemed reassured.

"Dr Kramer has requested that you be allowed to bring a friend with you to identify the contents," Sven said. "So you may need to open the boxes and repackage them before shipping. Can you do that?"

"Of course, nothing could be simpler."

"Wonderful, Herr Golcher."

Shortly before one o'clock, Bernie struggled down the lane in the wet snow behind the Kramer house. He stepped over the fence into the garden, quickly crossing to the side of the house. Moments later, he struggled back across the fence and disappeared down the lane with the cloth bag. He climbed on his bike and took off down the road pedalling fast. Moments later he arrived at the shed and laid the bike against the wall.

"You look wet," Allan said as Bernie entered the shed.

"I'm wet and bloody freezing," Bernie said, closing the door and stamping snow off his boots. He gave Allan a sour look. The photographer had been waiting for him, sitting comfortably on an old couch and drinking hot tea from a thermos. Allan took the bag from him and opened it. There were several documents inside and he laid the first of them on the Minox copy table.

"Hang on a minute," Bernie said, walking over to the table, "that one looks familiar."

He leaned over and squinted at it for a moment, then clapped Allan on the shoulder.

"Don't just stand there, Allan my boy. Take your pictures. We're about to make the boss very happy."

Allan gave him a quizzical look and set to work.

Several hours later Bernie was in the Legation darkroom when he answered a knock on the door.

"I got your message," Peter told him through the door, "Bridget said it was urgent."

"Just a moment, Peter."

Bernie used forceps to pick up an 8 x 10 B&W print in an acid bath and dump it in a stop solution.

"Come in, Peter. You need to take a look at this."

Peter came in and under the red safelight peered at the bogus Soviet airplane production figures in amazement.

"Seen this before?" Bernie asked, grinning. "It was in with the Kramer documents today."

"Bloody hell. Is it the same?"

"Of course it is. It's got Joanna's Hans Weber signature right there."

"That was fast. What are we today?" Peter asked.

"Tuesday."

"It's only been twelve days," Peter replied in amazement.

"I thought you'd want to know."

"Thank you, Bernie."

Peter hurried out of the office.

Forty

At a Swedish trading company near the docks Karl-Heinz led the way through the dark stock room followed by Herr Golcher. They headed towards a wizened old man with a white beard, Herr Akerson, who was packing a new radio in brown paper for shipping. Around them were stacks of oriental rugs and radios.

"Dr Kramer. How are you?" Akerson asked.

"I'm fine. How is business, Herr Akerson?"

"Business is good for radios and carpets, but very slow for art, Herr Kramer," Akerson said. " Sweden is a small country and with the war we have become even smaller."

"Well, I hope we can help you with some new business. Two packages have arrived, a Matisse and a Chagall. Herr Golcher here will handle the viewing."

Kramer handed Akerson a bill of lading with a description of the art works. Akerson looked at the pedigree of the Matisse and laughed out loud.

"The 'Seated Woman'? You must be joking, Dr Kramer. That's not possible."

"Herr Akerson, the information comes to me from Berlin," Karl-Heinz said. "I have not seen the package. Please feel free to examine the work."

"I would love to see it. If it is really the 'Seated Woman', I will have a buyer for you by the end of the week."

Karl-Heinz nodded.

"Golcher here will look after you, Herr Akerson. He will organize the viewing. All you need to do is to ring him up and fix an appointment."

"Very good, Dr Kramer. I look forward to seeing this 'Seated Woman'."

Golcher left a business card on the table and the two Germans left the warehouse. Akerson picked up the card and looked at the address of the German Press Office.

No, thought Akerson, it was not possible. He knew all about the 'Seated Woman' which he had seen hanging in Paul Rosenberg's art gallery in the 8th arrondissement of Paris in 1939. It had been painted by Henri Matisse in 1921 and until 1940 had belonged to Rosenberg. It was looted by the Nazis as Rosenberg fled France for Portugal on his way to New York City.

Hanne entered the Kramer house through the back door. She took off her winter coat and hat, then changed her shoes before entering the kitchen.

"Guten Morgen, Wilhelma, Heidi."

In the kitchen Wilhelma and the child looked at her as Eva stormed in from the living room.

"Hanne, have you seen Heidi's toy house, the one with the green shutters?" Eva asked frantically.

"No, Frau Kramer."

"Wilhelma says she saw you with it."

"No, that's not possible," Hanne said. "I almost never go into Heidi's room."

"Are you telling me that Wilhelma is lying?" Eva asked with a hint of menace in her voice.

"I don't even remember seeing the toy, Frau Kramer."

"That little house was bought in Berlin by my husband at the *Kaufhaus des Westens*. It was a very special gift for my daughter and quite expensive," Eva said with undisguised pride.

"Have you looked under Heidi's bed?" Hanne asked, "or maybe in the closet?"

"Of course we have, Hanne," Eva said. "This is quite serious. Did you borrow it?"

"I don't have any children, Frau Kramer. I have no need for a child's toy."

Hanne started to collect the plates on the kitchen table and to carry them to the sink.

"Wilhelma thinks you stole it," Eva let slip.

Hanne looked at Frau Kramer in shock and then glared at Wilhelma.

"That's crazy, Frau Kramer."

"*Sie schmutzige Jude*," Wilhelma said.

"*Verrücktes Weib*," Hanne screamed.

Frau Kramer grabbed Hanne's wrist and she lost her grip on the plates which crashed to the floor.

"*Lass mich allein*," Hanne said.

Upstairs in his study Karl-Heinz heard the shrieks from the kitchen. He snatched up his briefcase and hurried downstairs to see what the commotion was about. He stepped into the kitchen to see Eva struggling for a knife that Hanne had picked up off the floor with the plates. Eva slammed Hanne's wrist down on the side board. Heidi was crying, while Wilhelma looked on with satisfaction.

"*Nazi Hündin*, get your hands off me," Hanne yelled as she dropped the knife on the floor.

"Karl-Heinz, this woman stole a toy from Heidi and won't give it back."

"Dr Kramer, your crazy Jew wife is blaming me for a lost toy. It is unbelievable."

"I am not Jewish, Hanne," Eva protested.

"Yes, you are," Hanne yelled. "You are a Jew just like me, but you won't admit it."

Wilhelma looked at Eva with real concern, sensitive to racial issues. Eva stood back in silence.

"Ladies!" Karl-Heinz bellowed. "Let's calm down, please."

"I won't calm down with this woman in our house," Eva said. "I told you we couldn't trust a Jew and you hired her anyway."

Karl-Heinz ignored her complaints and turned to Hanne.

"I think you better go home, Hanne. I will drop you off."

Furious, Hanne headed to the door to put on her coat and boots.

"*Die schmutzige Jude*, I saw her steal it," Wilhelma said.

"Wilhelma, that's enough," Karl-Heinz said. "Eva, I will be at the office."

Karl-Heinz and Hanne left the house and walked down to the waiting German Legation car. The driver held the door as Karl-Heinz and Hanne got in the back. Eva stood in the window and watched them drive away.

Karl-Heinz glanced at Hanne as she took a handkerchief from her bag and blew her nose.

"You are from Vienna, aren't you Hanne?"

"Yes, Dr Kramer."

"Why do you think Wilhelma called you a thief?"

"I have no idea, I have no interest in Heidi's toys," Hanne said. "That bitch called me *'eine schmutzige Jude'*, that's the word Germans use to call out a Jew on the street. It's so easy."

"My wife says I should not have hired you but I think you are from a well-to-do family in Vienna. You know things, you have a good deal of culture. That is my impression."

"My family was chased out of Vienna in 1938, Dr Kramer," Hanne said. "We had a large house in Hietzing. We went to concerts at the Vienna Philharmonic. We went to the *Café Dommayer*, and I was to go to the *Medizinische Universität* but I was kicked out. We lost everything."

"I'm sorry, Hanne," Kramer said with genuine concern.

"My family has lived in Vienna forever. I'm Austrian and proud of it."

Karl-Heinz watched as Hanne dabbed delicately at her nose. He thought she had a very unusual background for a cleaning lady. They drove on in silence until the car pulled up in front of the German Legation at number 2, Hovslagargatan.

"Come in with me for a moment, Hanne." Karl-Heinz said. "I have to drop something off, and then we will be on the way to your flat."

Hanne acquiesced and followed Karl-Heinz inside the building.

Forty-one

Peter walked arm in arm with Bridget along a Stockholm canal during a warm spring day.

"Keith put it on Roger Hollis' desk, that's all I know. He thinks Hollis took it home."

"Took it home. Isn't that against the rules at MI5?" Bridget asked.

"Of course it is, but Hollis is the senior man in charge. Keith had someone search Hollis' office but the file was gone."

"So what did Keith think about the turnaround time on that bogus report?"

"He was as astonished as I was. He's very keen to get to the bottom of this. This Soviet mole business saps the energy of the entire organisation."

"So Keith suspects Hollis?" Bridget asked.

"Keith does but Hollis works with Anthony Blunt so the mole could be either or both of them."

They walked on in silence for a bit.

"We need to be careful, Bridget," Peter said. "That bogus document could get us into hot water."

"You think it might come back to bite you, Peter?"

"We are the pipeline for Dr Kramer's secrets. So if they discover that the report is bogus, then it could get back to us."

"You could lose your job, darling."

"I'm sure Blunt doesn't think that we are much of a threat, he's already cut us off. We're out of the loop."

Bridget stopped walking and looked down into the canal.

"I wouldn't worry too much, Bridget," Peter said, putting his arm around her. "He can't get rid of me without justification. Our operation has been too successful."

"And Keith? What is Keith going to do?"

"Keith is going over Hollis' head to Liddell and to Jane Archer. Jane is not having a good time at MI5 at the moment, but she's our best hope. She's Britain's foremost expert on Soviet intelligence gathering after her interrogation of Walter Krivitsky."

Bridget remembered the name. Krivitsky was a Soviet intelligence officer who had defected weeks before the outbreak of war and subsequently revealed the plans for the signing of the Molotov–Ribbentrop pact dividing up Poland between Germany and the Soviet Union.

Bridget turned towards Peter.

"I'm worried about Keith," Bridget said, "he may be in more trouble than we are."

"Keith can take care of himself. He's tough. No one is going to touch him."

At the end of the day Golcher and Akersen entered the 'in transit' section of the Bromma Airfield hangar. No one was around so Golcher used his key to open the door to an office in the rear where he had set up a viewing room for his art works. On the desk there was an ashtray and a bottle of aquavit and glasses. In the corner of the room sat an easel covered in black cloth surrounded by shipping notices in Swedish on the walls. The wooden shipping container lay propped up against the wall. Golcher turned on two very bright lights illuminating the painting and the room.

"Like a drink, Herr Akerson? I think I will have one."

"If it is what I hope it is," Akerson said, "then this calls for a drink."

Golcher pulled the cork on the bottle of aquavit and served two glasses. He handed one of the glasses to Akerson.

"What do you know about the 'Seated Woman', Herr Akerson?"

"The last I heard was that Paul Rosenberg had it in his gallery in Paris in 1940. He left for New York shortly after so I don't know what became of it."

"Paul Rosenberg had a brother Leonce," Golcher said. "They both had art galleries in Paris: one on the rue de la Boétie and the other on rue de la Baume."

"Yes, I visited Paul Rosenberg's gallery in 1939. He had the most amazing collection of modern art. You know the Rosenbergs were the most famous art dealers in the world until the Nazis chased them out of Paris."

"A very unfortunate time, Herr Akerson. The Rosenbergs were Jews so their paintings were confiscated and deposited in the *Galerie nationale du Jeu de Paume*. Some of them made it to Germany, but a lot of them were considered too degenerate or unworthy so they were sold in Switzerland."

"And some were destroyed, weren't they Herr Golcher?"

"Yes, a terrible tragedy. Many of the unsold works of Picasso and Dali were destroyed in a fire on the grounds of the *Jeu de Paume* in 1942. So we are very lucky to have found the Matisse masterpiece."

The men drank their aquavit.

"Time to take a look," Golcher said building the suspense. "Are you ready, sir?"

"Yes, absolutely."

Golcher slid the black cloth away from the painting and revealed a woman with a veil sitting on a chair. Akerson looked silently at the painting transfixed. He stepped up close to get a better look at the paint texture and colour on the canvas. Akerson was obviously a true connoisseur and from the look on his face he had a keen appreciation for art.

"Take your time, Herr Akerson."

Akerson could barely conceal his excitement. He glanced nervously at Golcher, then took a magnifying glass from his pocket and examined the brush strokes on several parts of the canvas. Finally, he stood back to take it all in.

"This is quite amazing," Akerson exclaimed, "a Matisse in Stockholm."

"Indeed."

"I am not an expert," Herr Golcher, "but if it is a fake, it is a very impressive piece of work."

"Berlin doesn't deal in fakes, Herr Akerson."

Peter and Bridget returned to Peter's flat later in the evening when they ran into Vincent Ansell waiting for them in the entrance.

"Hello, Vincent?"

"Peter, Bridget. I thought I would try to catch you here."

"What happened, Vincent?" Peter asked with concern.

Vincent stamped his feet nervously.

"What's wrong?" Bridget asked.

"Hanne's disappeared," Vincent said. "Elsa went to her flat. Everything was normal but where is she?"

"Could she have gone on a trip?" Bridget asked.

"Not without Elsa knowing. I tell you she has disappeared."

"What about her job with the Kramers?" Peter asked.

"Elsa called the house and asked for Hanne, but the nanny said she no longer worked for the Kramers."

"This is very unusual, Peter," Bridget said. "We need to find her. She can't just disappear like this."

"I agree. It's very worrying."

Forty-two

Elsa hung up the phone, looking shocked.

"That Nazi bitch!" she said, shaking with anger.

Bridget put down her coffee, alarmed.

"What did she say?"

Elsa made a visible effort to control herself. They'd been discussing Hanne's disappearance over coffee for over an hour and still couldn't think of any leads when Elsa decided to put in another call to the Kramer household. The pretext was Elsa's search for a cleaning woman and her desire to hire Hanne for the job.

"She called Hanne *'eine schmutzige Jude'*."

"Why?"

"She said Hanne was a thief," Elsa said. "She accused her of stealing a toy belonging to her little girl."

"That's absurd."

"They fired her."

Bridget had never seen Elsa so angry. She reminded herself that it was going to take a clear head to solve the problem of Hanne's whereabouts and expressions of anger against the Kramers wouldn't be of any help.

"When did this happen?" Bridget asked.

"Tuesday. Dr. Kramer drove her home."

"So Dr Kramer left Hanne at her flat, if I understand correctly."

"We don't know that for sure, Bridget," Elsa said. "All we know is that the last person to see Hanne was Dr Kramer."

"Elsa, you need to go to the police and report her missing. I will talk to Peter to see what we can do."

Bernie was parked down the road from the Kramer house in a copse of trees. All was quiet on the street. He pulled a thermos from the front seat and poured himself a cup of tea. He drank the tea and then heard the noise of a door slamming shut coming from the Kramer house. He picked up his binoculars and saw the German Legation car leave the house with Dr Kramer in the back seat. There was no sign of Hanne so he decided to follow Dr Kramer's car to see where it went.

The car drove into town and left Kramer at the German Legation press office. Bernie gave up the surveillance on Kramer and returned to the house in Stora Essingen. He parked near the lane leading to the Kramer backyard and took off on foot. The snow drifts had almost disappeared, but there was still a lot of water on the road. He approached the house in the usual way stepping close to the first floor windows.

He observed Wilhelma with Heidi in the living room downstairs. He walked around the house peeking in through the windows. He caught Eva Kramer putting on lipstick in a downstairs washroom, but could find no evidence to show that Hanne was being held hostage at the Kramer house. He left muddy tracks in the snow as he returned to his car.

"I came yesterday and everything was in its place," Elsa said as she opened the door to Hanne's flat.

She stepped into the front hall with its pegs for coats and umbrellas, followed by two Swedish police detectives.

"Her mail is on the table," Carlstrom said. "Did you bring it in, Mrs Ansell?"

"Yes, when I came by looking for Hanne yesterday."

"Does she have a boyfriend?" Carlstrom asked.

"No, sir. Not that I know of."

Detective Carlstrom went into the bedroom searching for clues while his partner Detective Norden searched the kitchen. Elsa followed Carlstrom into the bedroom.

"She lives very frugally," Elsa said, looking at the single bed and the books in German on the bedside table. "Hanne likes to read, detective."

"Yes, I was about to say the same thing. How long have you known her?"

"Forever, we grew up together in Vienna."

"When did she start working for Dr Kramer?"

"Last year."

Carlstrom threw open the closet doors and looked at Hanne's clothes.

"Have you noticed any of her clothes missing?"

Elsa came over and looked through several skirts, dresses and blouses hanging in the closet before shaking her head.

"If she had gone on a trip, she would have taken her suitcase, detective. Her toiletry bag is in the bathroom."

It was past midnight and far too late to be calling on Anders Berger at home, but Peter felt he had no choice. He knocked softly on the door. Peter heard movement inside and then Anders appeared at the door. He was fully dressed and looked like he had been working.

"Peter? What are you doing here?"

"It's a bit of an emergency, Anders. Can I come in?"

"Of course, please. Let me offer you a drink."

"Who is it, Anders?" Britta called from the bedroom.

Anders turned to look at his wife who appeared in the hall in her night gown. Peter felt badly about waking her.

"It's all right, Britta," Anders assured her, "this is Peter Faye. He's been helping us in our search for Rolf."

Britta's face brightened immediately.

"I can't thank you enough, Mr Faye."

"My pleasure, Mrs Berger, and I do apologize for calling so late," Peter said, accepting a glass of aquavit from Anders.

"How is it going, your search?" Peter asked.

"Anders has just returned from Germany," Britta said, "and we think there's been some progress."

"That's encouraging."

"Well, it certainly wasn't very encouraging at first," Anders said. "Bernadotte and I were there for three days and got nowhere. We were just leaving Germany when Schellenberg himself intervened."

Peter nodded, impressed. He knew all about Walter Schellenberg.

"The SD has agreed to regroup the Scandinavian prisoners at Neuengamme," Anders continued, "they're giving us a hand with the prisoner lists."

"Keep at it, that's my only advice. Time is running out and the Russians will be in Berlin soon. Then there will be complete chaos in all the camps."

"We're doing the best we can, Mr Faye," Britta said, "but it takes so much time."

"It is very kind of you to ask about Rolf, Peter," Anders said quietly, "but I know that is not why you are here. You mentioned an emergency."

"Yes," Peter said, "you know Dr Kramer?"

"Oh, yes. I remember your activities in Stora Essingen."

"His cleaning woman has gone missing. Her name is Hanne Gabor. She's Austrian. She disappeared on Tuesday after Dr Kramer took her home."

Anders raised an eyebrow.

"And you have a special interest in her?"

"I do. She is the close friend of one of our employees. Her friends have tried to find her without any success. The police are involved. No one has seen her since Kramer drove her home. We're afraid Kramer and the Gestapo are holding her and may force her on to a plane to Berlin."

"Why would they do that?" Anders asked.

"Kramer works for German intelligence. Hanne was seen entering the German Legation on Tuesday. We don't know whether Kramer drove her home afterwards but that is what his wife is saying. We think the Gestapo may have nabbed her, that is all I can tell you."

"I understand," Anders said. "Of course, I will help if I can. What do you want me to do?"

Peter produced a small photograph of Hanne that Bridget had gotten from Elsa. Bernie had already made several copies for the police.

"Put her picture in the paper," Peter said, handing the photograph to him, "and ask the public to call the police if they see her."

Anders looked thoughtfully at the picture.

"I will talk to my boss," he said finally. "How about a title like: 'Cleaning woman for High-Ranking German officer Disappears'? Would that work for you?"

"That would be perfect," Peter said.

Peter drank his aquavit and got up to leave.

"Call me if you need anything else. Thank you both. Good night."

"Good night, Peter," Anders said, opening the door.

In a tiny hideaway in the woods Hanne was asleep on a horsehair mattress. She awakened suddenly feeling groggy due to the drugs she has been given. Inside the moss hut her head almost touched the ceiling. A plate of food had been pushed through the pet flap in the locked door along with a handful of snow flakes.

On her hands and knees she moved to look through the flap hoping to see her jailor, but all she could see was a snow bank and a lighted area in the general gloom. She returned to the mattress and pulled the sleeping bag over her head.

Forty-three

"What's the offer, Herr Akerson?" Karl-Heinz asked, exasperated. "Just give me the figure in sterling or dollars."

Karl-Heinz looked up as Nadja brought in the coffee tray and then returned to her desk near the entrance.

"Are you crazy? It's a fucking Matisse, you've seen it with your own eyes."

Karl-Heinz lit a cigarette and blew smoke into the room.

"I know it's a fast sale, but can't this Spaniard do better than that?"

There was a long pause as he listened to Akerson complain about the timing of the sale and how with a few more weeks he could maybe get a better offer.

"So he's offering the same price for both paintings?"

Karl-Heinz took a drag on his cigarette.

"That doesn't make sense, Akerson."

Karl-Heinz wrote the figure on a pad on his desk.

"Okay, we'll accept the offer. Where does he want it sent?"

He wrote down a name and an address.

"The buyer must first send the funds to our bank in Switzerland. I will give you the details this afternoon. Good day, Mr Akerson."

Karl-Heinz put the phone down and stubbed out his cigarette. He was about to light another one when he heard the door to the front office open. Two men came in and stopped in front of Nadja's desk. Even though they were in plainclothes, they had the unmistakable look of policemen.

"Can I help you?" Nadja asked.

"We are here to see Dr Kramer."

"Do you have an appointment?"

"I will see them, Nadja," Karl-Heinz motioned for the two men to come in and returned to his desk.

"How can I help you, gentlemen?"

"I am Detective Carlstrom and this is Detective Norden," the taller one said, "we are with the Stockholm Police Department."

If they were expecting Karl-Heinz to be nervous about their visit, he was determined to disappoint them.

"Yes?" Karl-Heinz asked, a hint of impatience in his voice.

The two policemen glanced at each other.

"This is personal business, sir," Norden said. "Do you want to go somewhere else to discuss it?"

"No, here is fine. Please sit down."

The detectives sat down, looking about warily.

"It concerns your cleaning lady, Hanne Gabor."

"Yes? What has she done?"

The question seemed to catch the detectives off guard. Finally Carlstrom answered.

"She has disappeared."

"Disappeared? That's not possible."

Carlstom looked at Norden.

"I'm afraid so, sir."

In the Consular Services office Bridget hung up the phone and looked over at Peter who was busy with *The Daily Telegraph* crossword.

"That was Anders Berger. They're going to publish the piece about H in tomorrow's paper."

"Very good. Does he mention a high-ranking German officer in his article?" Peter asked.

"Yes, he does."

"I really don't know what else we can do, Bridget. Bernie said there was no evidence Hanne was still at the Kramer's."

"She'll turn up," Bridget said with a confident air. "Someone will spot her in town or at the airfield. There's no way the Gestapo can take her out of the country now."

"I'm afraid they can," Peter said gloomily. "They can put her on a boat and in a few hours she'll be in Germany. If they suspect her of compromising Kramer's traffic in secret documents, they'll try to get her out of country to interrogate her."

"Have you talked to Joanna? She knows everything there is to know about the German Legation here in the city."

"That's a good idea."

It was getting dark as Joanna spread the Stockholm city map out on the Ansell kitchen table. Vincent, Elsa, Peter and Bridget crowded in around her.

"You say that the last place Hanne was seen was at number 2, Hovslagargatan," Joanna said. "Dr Kramer is Luftwaffe, so he could have hidden her away at the German Air Attaché's office at 99 Karlavägen. That's over here."

Joanna ran her finger over the map.

"What about the old *Abwehr* office at 27 Nybrogatan?" Peter asked.

"They don't own the building, it's just an office on one floor. Not an easy place to hide someone," Joanna said.

"If they kidnapped her, then she's going to be drugged. She could be hidden anywhere," Bridget said.

"I doubt you can hide a drugged woman in the tourist bureau or anywhere else where there are Swedish employees coming and going," Elsa said.

"Elsa's right." Vincent said. "It would create a serious diplomatic incident. It's not worth it. They must have moved her somewhere out of town, somewhere remote."

"I believe they have a retreat for their office staff down near Norvik south of here," Joanna said. "I've seen articles in *Der Deutschen in Schweden* magazine. From the photographs, it's a large house, a pretty place on the water. In the summer the Legation puts on parties there."

"It's probably closed up at this time of year," Bridget said.

Peter tapped his hand on the table thinking hard.

"I would think that Norvik or Nynäshamn on the coast would be the perfect place for an illegal operation," Peter said. "A fast boat from Danzig could pick up Hanne in a couple of hours."

"Hanne could already be in Germany," Elsa said as tears ran down her face, "this is terrible."

"I think we need to take a look at the place," Vincent said. "If it's locked up for the winter, then we can eliminate it."

"What do you think, Peter?" Bridget asked.

"Vincent is right. It's only an hour away by car."

Forty-four

"There is a chance they might fire at us," Bernie said to Peter and Vincent in his old Ford driving south on the two-lane blacktop. The weather had grown milder but the rain and fog made driving at any speed hazardous.

"We need to keep the lid on this," Peter said. "We don't want a diplomatic incident."

"Peter's right, we'll lose our jobs," Vincent said. "We need to keep quiet about this."

"Don't be a fucking pansy," Bernie said with sarcasm. "Crikey, Vincent, do you think for one moment that these Nazi bastards are going to let us take her back without a fight?"

"I'm afraid Bernie's right, Vincent. If she's there, then it's the Gestapo we'll be dealing with. They'll be armed and ready for action."

"I brought three Thompson machine guns just in case," Bernie said. "They're in the boot. Peter, your Webley is in the glove compartment."

Peter pulled out the Webley revolver and put it in his pocket.

"There probably won't be anybody around at this time of the year," Vincent said. "They don't usually open up until May for the summer months."

"If this broad is there, we take her," Bernie said. "I don't care what the consequences are."

"We won't have any choice in the matter," Peter said. "We must get her home."

"I brought winter coats and balaclavas," Bernie said. "They'll never recognize us. The way I see it is we go in, grab the woman and shoot any Fritz that stands in our way."

Vincent looked distraught on hearing the plan.

"Look at it this way, Vincent," Bernie said. "Kramer and the Gestapo kidnapped this woman on Swedish territory in broad daylight. That's a crime. They won't be complaining to any local police if we happen to kill a few of them taking her back, now will they?"

Vincent thought about his wife Elsa and her friendship with Hanne. She would never get over the loss of her friend if anything bad were to happen to her.

"Bernie's right, Peter. Elsa will kill me if I don't bring Hanne back alive. We shoot first if anyone goes for a gun."

It was almost midnight as Bernie took a left towards the town of Norvik. The snow was still heavy in drifts on the side of the road, but the rain had finally stopped.

Bernie pulled up at an isolated two-storey villa off the road after cutting his headlights. The air was chilly near the coast and there was a good deal of ground fog. They climbed out of the car and Bernie opened the boot. They put on the black winter coats over their suits and removed their hats. They slipped the balaclavas over their heads and grabbed the Thompsons. Bernie showed Vincent how to remove the safety on his weapon.

"Since you chaps have no military training, just follow me one at a time keeping your distance," Bernie said. "Walk in my footsteps keeping your guns pointed at the ground. And no noise or talking."

Peter and Vincent nodded quietly and followed Bernie towards the house in a long detour. They sneaked around the villa in the deep snow keeping their distance from the windows. They could see a light on inside the silent house.

After completing their surveillance of the house, they congregated at a side door into the kitchen. Through the window they noticed an older man dressed in workman's overalls pouring himself a glass of water.

Bernie kicked the door open and raced into the kitchen yelling at the man in German.

"*Auf den boden!*" Bernie screamed.

"*Nicht schiessen,*" the concierge replied in fear for his life as he dropped to the floor.

"*Auf den boden,*" Peter repeated the order taking over from Bernie who ran up the stairs to the second floor while Vincent checked the adjoining rooms.

"*Haben Sie eine Frau?*" Peter asked after the man's wife.

"*Ja, sie schläft,*" the concierge replied, indicating his wife was sleeping.

"*Gehen sie finden,*" Peter ordered the man to go fetch her.

The concierge stood up stiffly and went to wake his wife. Moments later, he reappeared with a woman in her night gown frozen with fear. On the upper floor Bernie appeared with a German officer and brought him downstairs. The officer emerged from the darkness and Peter immediately recognized the face of *Oberleutnant* Kemper in a black SS uniform.

"He's the only one around," Bernie whispered to Peter in English.

"So Herr Faye. It's Herr Faye, isn't it?" Kemper asked.

"*Oberleutnant* Kemper, I believe. You are with the SD now. What are you doing here?"

"This is a retreat, Mr Faye, for hard-working German officers."

"Yes, I can see that. We're looking for a woman who has disappeared."

"A woman? Well, you have come to the wrong place. It's just me, the concierge and his wife."

Vincent reappeared and shook his head at Peter.

"She's not here," Bernie insisted, "let's go, Peter."

"Sorry for the disturbance, *Oberleutnant*," Peter said, taking the lead from Bernie. "Good night, sir."

"Good night to you, Herr Faye," Kemper replied, "and good luck finding this woman."

Bernie, Peter and Vincent filed out of the room closing the door behind them as Kemper and the concierge looked at each other and broke into a laugh.

"*Verfluchte Engländer*," Kemper said, remarking on the crazy Englishmen.

Forty-five

Peter, Bernie and Vincent left the villa and headed back to their car. They drove off with the lights on high beams, but Bernie suddenly cut the lights as they pulled up around the corner from the villa. Peter and Vincent got out of the car and crouched behind a snow bank as Bernie drove away.

"Why are we waiting here, Peter?" Vincent asked.

"Something is going on. Kemper had on his SS uniform and was wearing boots. I suspect he's leaving on a boat for Germany some time tonight."

"You think he's got Hanne hidden somewhere?"

"I don't know, Vincent, but clearly he has no intention of going to bed tonight."

Bernie drove two hundred yards down the road and pulled the car over, hiding it in a copse of trees. Peter and Vincent watched the villa for several minutes. There was no sign of activity until the concierge stepped out the side door and headed to the nearby shed. He was wearing boots and a winter coat, and carrying a suitcase. He opened the door to the shed to reveal the dim outline of a motorcar inside. They lost sight of the concierge as he went to the back of the car. They heard the boot open and slam shut. The concierge got in behind the wheel and started up the car driving out on to the road.

As the car idled, the concierge disappeared into the woods behind the shed. *Oberleutnant* Kemper appeared at the side door in a leather overcoat and SS visor cap. He walked over to the car smoking a cigarette. A short time later, the burly concierge reappeared dragging someone through the snow to the car. Peter and Vincent were too far away to see who it was but it had to be Hanne. The person was in a blanket and appeared to be sedated. Kemper tossed his cigarette away but made no effort to help as the concierge opened the rear door of the car and roughly shoved the person inside. The concierge got in behind the wheel and they drove off along the coast road.

From Peter and Vincent's vantage point it clearly looked like Kemper was going on a trip with Hanne. Was he returning to Germany by boat or were they driving their hostage to another safe house?

Peter and Vincent called to Bernie to bring up the car.

At a private dock near Nynäshamn , a fishing boat waited for *Oberleutnant* Kemper and his hostage to arrive. Two sailors were loading a cargo of Bofors anti-tank guns on the exterior deck with a crane, as Kemper's car pulled up on the dock. They got out and waved at the captain. The concierge opened the boot and brought over Kemper's suitcase which he put on the boat deck.

Bernie, Vincent and Peter drove along the coast road near the dock with their lights out. They spotted the Kemper's car on the dock near the fishing vessel shrouded in mist. They stopped the car and climbed out to get a better look. Peter turned to Bernie and Vincent.

"We've got to do something," Peter said, "that fishing boat will be in Danzig in two days."

"We have to get to her before they finish loading," Vincent said.

Bernie quickly sized up the situation.

"Here's a plan," Bernie said with a confident air. "I want you, Vincent, to sneak down there and get behind the shed. Peter and I will drive down to the dock in the car. As soon as we stop the car, I want you to open fire on the boat pinning them down. You think you can do that?"

"Of course," Vincent said suddenly eager to be involved in the action.

"We'll give you ten minutes to get into place. Put the safety on before you go. You better hurry, go now."

Vincent clicked the safety on the Thompson machine gun before he took off running along the road.

"Don't shoot anybody, just keep their heads down."

Peter and Bernie watched Vincent disappear in the fog.

"Okay, Peter, you take the back seat with the Thompson at the ready. If anyone fires at us, you fire back," Bernie said.

Peter nodded in agreement.

Down on the dock the loading of the Bofors was complete and the captain had started up the engines getting ready for their departure. After chatting with the captain, Kemper signalled for the concierge to fetch the hostage. The man headed back to the car just as Bernie drove down on to the dock. The concierge stopped in his tracks seeing Bernie pull up in his car.

Suddenly Vincent opened up, firing wildly at the boat. The concierge ran to his car as bullets slammed into the wheelhouse. Most of the shots were over the heads of Kemper and a sailor hiding behind the bulwark.

The concierge reached his car just as Peter fired a first volley of shots at Kemper. Bernie jumped out of the car and ran after the concierge only to see the man pull a Schmeisser machine pistol from the backseat. He turned and sprayed Bernie's car with bullets. Peter slipped down on the floor in the backseat as bullets slammed through windows.

The concierge stood up and started looking for Bernie on the dock, approaching Peter in the car. As Vincent continued to rain bullets down on the fishing vessel, Peter crouched on the floor hoping to get a shot through the window. The concierge stepped close to the side window of the Ford and fired into the front seat. He heard a cry and looked in but saw no one. He moved along to get a look into the back seat. As he peered in, he saw Peter moving about. He shoved his gun through the window just as Bernie fired his Thompson, killing the man instantly.

"Stay down, Peter. Kemper is coming this way."

Peter struggled to sit up, holding his bleeding arm. A bullet from the Schmeisser had clipped his upper arm. He opened the door on the side away from the fishing boat and looked around for Bernie. Vincent had stopped firing after having run out of ammo. As Peter glanced over at the fishing vessel, he saw Kemper cross the dock going to his car, holding a Luger pistol in the ready. A sailor threw the mooring cables off the dock and quickly jumped back on to the deck as the boat started to move away.

"Bernie, where are you?" Peter whispered.

He stepped out of the car and fired twice at Kemper with the Thompson. Kemper fell to the dock and stopped moving.

"Good shot, Peter," Bernie yelled. "Let's get the woman and be on our way."

Bernie ran over to the German car and checked on Hanne in the backseat.

"Is she okay?" Peter called.

"I think so," Bernie said, feeling for a pulse. "They must have drugged her. She won't wake up for a while."

Bernie looked up as Peter approached.

"Bloody hell, you're wounded, Peter!"

"It hurts like hell, but it must be superficial. I can still move my arm."

They were interrupted by the voice of a night watchman, stumbling drunk out the warehouse door and holding a shotgun pointed at them. Bernie levelled the Thompson at the man as Peter ordered the man to lay down his gun.

"*Legt die Waffen nieder.*"

He goggled at Peter and dropped the gun, backing away and then stumbling away into the warehouse. Bernie watched him go as Vincent arrived.

"Let's take a look at that wound, Peter," Bernie said.

"Not now," Peter replied, "we need to get out of here."

"What happened, Peter?" Vincent asked as he arrived on the dock.

"The bastard clipped me with the Schmeisser. I think it's just a flesh wound."

The fishing boat was clearing the dock on its way out to sea, as Bernie went over to examine his car. The windshield and windows were smashed and the body of the vehicle was riddled with bullet holes. Bernie got into the front seat and started the engine. Steam soon started to rise from a perforated radiator. Bernie lifted the hood and took a look at the engine.

"Vincent, are the keys in the ignition of Kemper's car?"

Vincent went around the German car and sat in the driver's seat. He turned the key in the ignition and started up the engine.

"It's running, Bernie," Vincent said.

"Good," Bernie said. "We'll drive mine into Norvik and dump it somewhere. I don't want the Swedish authorities to find it here."

Bernie took the Thompson and went to have a look in the warehouse. He stopped near the door and glanced inside. The night watchman had returned to a couch in the office and seemed to be fast asleep. Bernie looked at the stack of shipping crates with German lettering in long rows.

On the dock Peter grabbed the concierge's feet and started to drag the man to the edge of the dock.

"Give me a hand, Vincent. We can't leave the bodies on the dock."

Peter and Vincent dragged the concierge to the edge of the dock and dumped his body in the sea. Then they went to collect Kemper as Bernie returned.

"What do we do about the old man?" Peter asked.

"He's too drunk to care. I don't think he saw anything."

"Right. Let's get out of here."

Forty-six

It was a slow drive along the coast road. Bernie's Ford had been riddled with bullets during the gunfight, smashing the windshield and holing the radiator, and now it was a matter of finding a place to ditch it.

Peter, Vincent and Hanne rode in Kemper's Opel trailing Bernie in the Ford as he limped along the two-lane blacktop. After a few minutes Bernie pulled over and turned off the engine. He came back to the Opel.

"I'm going to let it cool down a bit," Bernie said. "Let's have a look at that wound."

Peter pulled off his coat and suit jacket. His shirt was drenched in blood. He shivered as he removed his shirt. Bernie switched on the overhead light and examined Peter's wound.

"It's not too bad, Peter. It's a flesh wound, in and out. I have some whisky in my car. We can clean it up and wrap it tight. You should be alright, old chum."

Driving along the coast road Bernie had had to pull over several times to cool off the engine by packing lumps of snow onto the radiator. They were making progress but it was taking way too much time. Bernie finally pulled over near a bridge spanning an estuary. Vincent pulled up behind Bernie and they got out to take a look.

"What do you think?" Bernie asked.

Peter looked up and down the road. The bridge had a fairly high railing but the road had no fence at all and there was a very steep incline to where the water pooled twenty feet below.

"It'll do," Peter said.

There was no time to waste. Bernie got to work switching out the license plates. So far their luck had held and they had not seen any other traffic on the road. Peter heard the rasp of the Ford's engine and looked up as Bernie swung it out into the incoming lane and pointed it down toward the slope. Vincent ran to the back of the Ford ready to push the car as Bernie climbed out of the Ford.

"Let's give it a push," Bernie yelled to Vincent.

Bernie guided the car down the slope with one hand on the steering wheel and the other on the door frame. The car moved slowly at first but quickly gained momentum as Bernie spun away from the door. It picked up speed leaving Vincent sprawling in its wake. Peter watched as the Ford rolled off the bank into the water.

Bernie laughed as his old Ford settled in the water and started to sink.

Ten minutes later they were on their way to Stockholm with Vincent driving.

"I got a look at that warehouse in Nynäshamn, Peter," Bernie said. "The SD are importing antiques into Sweden. The crates had '*Antiquitäten*' written all over them."

"Stolen antiques for resale?" Peter asked.

"It could be, they are flogging gold, silver, and art works. Why not antiques?" Bernie asked.

"No, that doesn't make sense, Bernie. The cost to ship and the resale value. I think they must be the personal effects of well-to-do German Legation staff. By shipping their personal effects to Sweden, they probably want to protect them from Allied bombing and plunder by the Soviets."

"They might belong to German nationals," Bernie said, "who have acquired visas and are moving here."

"Yes, that's possible," Vincent said. "Lots of Germans are applying for visas to stay in Sweden after the war."

Hanne woke up next to Peter on the back seat.

"Hanna's waking up," Peter said. "We need to give her something to drink. I think she's dehydrated."

"Take my thermos," Bernie said. "Give her some tea."

"Peter, is that you?" Hanne asked.

"You're going to be all right, Hanne," Peter said in a soothing voice, "we're taking you home."

The light was coming up in the east as the car stopped in front of the Ansell flat. Peter helped Hanne out of the backseat as Elsa and Bridget emerged from the house. Elsa ran forward to embrace Hanne and Vincent. Together they led Hanne towards the house. Bridget came over and kissed Peter.

"You're bleeding, Peter!" Bridget said, looking at Peter's arm. "What happened?"

"The Gestapo was sending her to Germany on a fishing boat. We got there in the nick of time."

"Are you alright?"

"It's not too bad, a flesh wound."

"Well, let's go inside and take a look."

"I'm going to fetch Sabrina," Bernie said. "You're going to need stitches. Sabrina used to be a nurse."

"What are you going to do with the car, Bernie?" Peter asked.

"Well, you know my old Ford was in need of some major repairs so it is not such a big loss. I think I prefer this German Opel. It's a newer model and runs well."

"Well, you must keep it then."

Bridget and Peter walked towards Vincent's flat as Bernie drove off.

"One more to go," Sabrina said as Peter winced at the pain in his arm. Sabrina put in the final stitch closing the wound. She had given him a local anaesthetic before thoroughly cleaning the wound and stitching it up, but it was not very effective against the pain.

Elsa had put Hanne to sleep in her bed as the others celebrated their success. Bernie and Vincent were drinking aquavit at the kitchen table as Bridget sat near Sabrina watching her work.

"Bridget, I've cleaned it as best I can, but you'll need to keep an eye on it," Sabrina said. "If an infection develops, he's going to need to see a doctor."

Bridget nodded as Sabrina dressed the wound with a roll of white gauze.

Vincent was getting drunk on the aquavit as he unwound from the events on the dock. "What a night! I can't believe we succeeded."

"You did a magnificent job," Elsa said. "You saved my Hanne. That is the important thing."

"And I've got a new car," Bernie said. "The Opel beats my old Ford any day."

As Sabrina joined the others at the kitchen table for a glass of aquavit, Bridget handed Peter a telegram.

"I went back to the Legation earlier to see whether there was any news," Bridget whispered. "There was this message from London, Peter."

Peter opened the envelope and started to read.

"It's Keith. He wants me to come to London for a meeting - off the books, he says. I will need to request a short leave for personal reasons."

"That's very good, Peter. He must be making progress."

"I hope so."

Forty-seven

Berlin

A car drew up to the curb in front of Gestapo headquarters on Prinz-Albrecht Strasse. Two Gestapo agents stepped out and hustled *SD Ausland* Chief Walter Schellenberg in his black SS uniform through the front door. He was taken to an empty interrogation room in the basement and left there.

Schellenberg was furious and paced the room for several minutes before he finally sat down. He was exhausted and had been working overtime for months on end as the war started to wind down. This was the final outrage being arrested by the Gestapo, a sister organization to his own foreign intelligence service.

The Gestapo was a state-run police department and not a Nazi organisation. Its members came from the *Sicherheitsdienst* (*SiPo*) or the *Kriminalpolizei* (*Kripo*) who were responsible for investigating serious crimes. Very few were Nazi Party members. The rank and file officers came from working class or lower middle class backgrounds.

As Schellenberg napped quietly in a straight-backed chair, the door to the interrogation room sprang open and two men entered.

"Hello, Schelli. We don't get you in here very often."

This was Schellenberg's second unpleasant surprise of the night. The man standing in front of him was none other than Heinrich Müller, the second in command of the Gestapo. Müller's rise through SS ranks was amazing for a man who seemed to have had no interest in politics. He only became a member of the Nazi party in 1939 after Himmler insisted that he do so. He was the protégé of Reinhard Heydrich and after Heydrich's death in 1942, Müller became second-in-command to Ernst Kaltenbrunner. It was reported that he once said that all 'intellectuals should be sent down a coal mine and blown up.'

Schellenberg had envisioned himself berating some terrified, nameless functionary, someone who would apologize profusely and then allow him to leave. Müller was something else entirely - the man had once rounded up five thousand people suspected of involvement in the attempt on Adolf Hitler's life and had ordered the execution of two hundred of them. Schellenberg reminded himself to be very careful with Müller, since guilt or innocence was often whatever the Gestapo decided it was.

An assistant had followed Müller into the room. Schellenberg watched incredulously as the man unpacked a wire-recording machine, a German Reichhalter reporter and a microphone.

"What is this?" Schellenberg said.

Müller ignored him as he opened his briefcase and took out some files. His files were legendary. He was known to be a dogged interrogator with his piercing grey-blue eyes, yet he looked for all the world like a punctilious little bank clerk. He was the man who had hunted down Reinhard Heydrich's killers in Prague using bribes and torture.

"Müller, you are going to be in serious trouble if you keep up this charade," Schellenberg said angrily.

Müller glanced at his assistant and the man flipped the switch to turn on the recording machine.

"Let's begin. *Brigadeführer* Schellenberg, you have been arrested on two very serious charges."

"Really, what did I do?" Schellenberg asked.

"Take that smug look off your face, Schellenberg. You are accused of being a British agent. You can be hanged for treason on a charge like that."

Schellenberg laughed at this comment.

"I have some advice for you, Müller," Schellenberg said in a serious tone, "talk to Himmler before you go any further. He will set you right."

The veiled threat was unmistakable but Müller forged ahead looking at his file.

"Secondly, you have been arrested for giving the British copies of SD documents, several Egmont reports have gone missing."

Schellenberg sighed.

"This is a joke, no?"

"We have also arrested your co-conspirator, Dr Karl-Heinz Kramer, in Stockholm on charges of treason."

"He's a spy, Müller. He works for our side," Schellenberg said in a tone one would use to explain something to a small child. "His job is to provide us with intelligence from British and Allied sources."

"We have had you followed for several months now, *Brigadeführer* Schellenberg. We have read your defeatist Egmont reports and your 'Reports from the Reich'. These reports undermine the confidence of our troops."

Schellenberg shrugged his shoulders.

"They are not my reports, Müller. We only collate what we receive from *Wehrmacht* and SS officers at the front. These are their assessments, not mine, and you know it."

"You are responsible for their publication and distribution and therefore you are committing a crime."

"I am proud to do this work!" Schellenberg exploded. "These officers command men who are dying at the front. This is a war we're waging, and we owe it to them to get their reports out."

"The reports are defeatist."

"They are not released to the public, only to our sister organisations. Look, we are colleagues, Müller, and you know that any intelligence organisation like ours must work with the truth. We don't try to rewrite history like Stalin and the Soviets. To be effective we need to know what the situation really is, not to cover up military setbacks and put it all in a favourable light."

"Why don't you simply admit that you are a British spy?"

Schellenberg laughed, exasperated.

"We're losing the war, Müller, and we all know it. Even the Führer knows it. We cannot hide behind a lie - our soldiers cannot hide behind lies when they are under attack!"

Müller looked in his file as Schellenberg continued.

"You know as well as I do that we cannot compete with Allied tank production. It's a fact. Our soldiers need tanks to defend them at the front. The Americans are building more than two thousand Sherman tanks a month and the Russians three thousand T-34s. Our production figures for the Tiger and Panzer tanks are pathetic. This is not defeatist talk, Müller. This is the reality our men face on the battlefield."

"You talk the worst kind of defeatist language," Müller snapped. "Our Tiger tanks are a spectacular achievement and vastly superior to any Sherman or T-34 tank."

"Perhaps," Schellenberg conceded, "but there are not enough of them to win on the battlefield and there never will be."

"These are lies, *Brigadeführer* Schellenberg. Our soldiers know that the Tiger is a far superior tank and because of it, they know we will win the war."

"Talk to Himmler. He'll put you straight," Schellenberg sighed.

Forty-eight

Walton-on-the-Naze, England
March 1945

Peter got off the train at the picturesque seaside town in Essex. He was walking along the platform heading for the exit along with several other passengers when he was waved down by a lively 47-year old woman.

"Hello, I'm Jane Archer and you must be Peter Faye."

"It's a pleasure to meet you, Mrs Archer."

"Call me Jane," she smiled as they shook hands, "and I'll call you Peter."

She turned and led him across the road to an old Wolseley black sedan. She opened the rear door so he could put his bag on the back seat. She got in behind the wheel and Peter climbed into the passenger seat.

Jane drove out of town at high speed racing along a narrow country lane and turning from time to time to examine her guest. Finally she spoke.

"I have some very bad news," Jane said, "Keith Linwood has had an accident in London. He's going to be in the hospital for a while. He was hit by a car."

"When did this happen?" Peter asked, alarmed.

"Yesterday as he was leaving the office."

"That's terrible. How is his family taking it?"

"I really don't know. I only learned about it this morning when I called his office. His legs were smashed. You know him well, I think."

"Old school chums, Keith and I. You think he will walk again?"

"I wouldn't know, Peter, but you might want to look him up when you return to London. It might help to cheer him up."

"Certainly."

"Keith briefed me on your story. We'll talk after we have had a cup of tea at the cottage."

The car pulled up at a lovely old house overlooking the sea. They left the car and walked through a maze of yellow daffodils heading to the front door.

After showing Peter around the house, Jane put the kettle on and they settled into leather club chairs in the living room with a view of the North sea.

"This is a lovely house," Peter said.

"It belonged to my husband's family. I like it as a quiet retreat, you know, away from the bombing in London."

"Do you get in from time to time?"

"Not so much anymore since they let me go. I suppose Keith told you all about that?"

"Yes, he did."

"Why don't you tell me the whole story, Peter? Don't leave anything out."

"Of course. As you know, I arrived in Stockholm in the summer of 1943," Peter said, as the kettle on the stove started to whistle. Jane got up and went to the kitchen to remove it.

"Go on, Peter. I'll just put the tea on."

"It was in August and very hot at the time," Peter said. "The target was Dr Karl-Heinz Kramer. My job was to try to find anything I could to compromise his activities in Stockholm."

Jane brought in the tea and a plate of biscuits. She put them on the table and sat down to listen to Peter.

An hour later Jane and Peter were in the garden walking among snowdrops and pansies in early bloom. They shivered from the cold wind as they approached the east side of the house overlooking the sea. From the garden, they could see the Naze tower near the wildlife reserve on the peninsula of the same name, jutting out into the North Sea.

"You can see the tower from here, Peter. We get a lot of ducks and brent geese overwintering in the area."

They watched the waves striking the beach below.

"The sea erosion is spectacular here in Walton," Jane said. "The old medieval town and its church succumbed to the waves in 1798 and is now at the bottom of the sea somewhere to the east of us."

They walked on admiring the flowers.

"The sea hath no king but God alone," Jane said with a laugh.

"Dante Rossetti?" Peter asked.

"Yes, I believe it is."

They walked back to the house.

"I gather that Keith gave the planted document to Roger Hollis," Jane said, "and this same document was discovered in Dr Kramer's desk drawer some twelve days later."

"Yes, that's exactly what happened."

"You know Dick White and I rejected Hollis for a job at MI5 back in '37. There was something wrong about Hollis at the time, but the director Vernon Kell hired him anyway and he became my assistant. I have had no reason to complain. He did his job very well and seemed quite competent."

"Keith mentioned that you worked briefly with Kim Philby and Section IX."

"Yes, it was not a happy arrangement. I was side-lined, if you like. I spent most of my time analysing radio intercepts from Eastern Europe instead of looking for Soviet spies. Not my cup of tea really. Guy Liddell recently got me a new job in C division at MI5 which handles security clearances. I will be starting in a few weeks."

"So you no longer have any contact with Soviet counter-intelligence at MI6?"

"I am out of it, Peter. I suppose Keith came to me because of my work debriefing Walter Krivitsky back in 1940. You know Krivitsky was at the top of the NKVD hit list after Trotsky was assassinated in Mexico. I had four weeks to work with him. He was a very brave and interesting man. He gave us a lot of very useful information about Soviet espionage."

"I heard he committed suicide in 1941 in a hotel in Washington DC."

"That was the official version. The non-official version is that it was a hit by the NKVD just like when they killed Ignace Reiss in Switzerland in 1937. Walter would never commit suicide. It was a very effective *mise-en-scène* with a suicide note."

Peter remembered that Krivitsky had painted a target on his head by testifying before a Congressional committee in October 1939 and then, only a month later, publishing a book entitled 'In Stalin's Secret Service'. In February 1941, he was found dead in a room at the Hotel Bellevue in Washington DC, a single bullet wound to his right temple. He had warned his wife that if he were to die in such circumstances, she should never believe he had committed suicide. The 'suicide note' found with his body said it all. It advised his wife and children that the Soviet government and people were their very 'best friends'.

Jane and Peter walked to the end of the property, looking down the cliff face to the beach below.

"So what are you going to do?" Peter asked.

"You have brought me some very valuable information, Peter. There are people who will listen. The code-names 'Sonia' and 'Elli' will be helpful. Colonel Hallamaa and the RTK have done some amazing work. Your adventure with the NKVD in Stockholm is interesting. The foreign office needs to be notified, but it is going to take a good deal of time."

"What do you want me to do?"

"Keep your head down."

"If I find anything new, its goes to Keith?"

"No, send it to me. Keith is going to be out of it for some time. Microdot any documentation. Watch out for Anthony Blunt. Your meeting with him at the Reform Club is revealing. You know the Quebec memorandum leak should have set off a firestorm in our intelligence services, all the way to the PM's office."

Friedrichsruh, Germany

The Swedish Red Cross had set up a tent on the grounds of Friedrichsruh Castle near Hamburg. A crowd of Swedish volunteers listened attentively as Count Bernadotte spoke from a makeshift stage. He was flanked by Colonel Gottfrid Björck, Doctor G. A. Rundberg and *SS-Obersturmbannführer* Karl Rennau.

"I hope you are comfortable in your new lodgings. Tomorrow we will visit the Neuengamme camp where the first group of Scandinavian prisoners will be arriving from Sachsenhausen. The plan is to put them in a special compound within the camp. We will be making numerous trips to collect our prisoners from different camps. We will travel mainly at night to avoid the air raids."

Anders Berger stood up to ask a question.

"What about the group going to Southern Germany, sir? When do they leave?"

"They will be leaving soon. The plan is to go to Dachau, Mauthausen and Natzweiler. Dachau is near Munich, a distance of eight hundred kilometres, so we need to secure enough petrol to make the trip."

"When do we move the prisoners to Sweden?" asked another volunteer.

"We're still working on this," Bernadotte said. "We have permission to move old people, mothers with children, and the sick to Copenhagen, but not the other prisoners. We still do not have the authorization to bring them to Sweden."

Forty-nine

London

Peter walked out of Paddington station, glanced down Praed Street and froze. The destruction was overwhelming. During the Blitz a cluster of three bombs had struck just outside the Great Western Hotel and caused massive damage. Two of the bombs had exploded in the street and the third had crashed through the road into the Circle Line tube station below.

Peter stood transfixed for a moment, then walked northwest to St. Mary's Hospital. He entered the building and asked for Keith's room number, then took the lift up to the fourth floor. Coming out of the lift, he ran into the slight figure of Ethel Linwood and her ten-year old daughter on their way down.

"Hello, Mrs Linwood. I'm a friend of Keith's. I'm Peter."

"Oh, yes. Peter. Keith talks about you a lot. You went to the same prep school, didn't you? You were a master at Rugby before the war."

"How is he?"

"He's in great pain, Peter. The driver ran right over the curb and didn't even stop."

"Can I see him?" Peter asked.

"Of course, but you better hurry. The nurse just gave him a sedative."

Peter said goodbye to Ethel and her daughter and hurried down the hall to Keith's room. He hardly recognized Keith with his bruised face and legs in traction in plaster casts.

"Keith, it's Peter."

"Peter?" croaked Keith, struggling to keep his eyes open.

"I met Jane yesterday, Keith. She told me you had been in an accident."

"Isn't she a sweetheart? The best of the best and sharp as a tack."

"What happened?"

"Gawd, if I only knew. Some arsehole ran up over the curb and hit me. I never saw him coming."

"You think someone hit you on purpose?" Peter asked, incredulous.

"I don't believe in coincidences, Peter old boy," Keith said, "and neither should you."

The sedation was taking effect and Keith was slurring his words with his voice getting more and more faint.

"Watch your back in Stockholm, Peter. Somebody knows about us..."

Keith fell asleep in mid-sentence.

Neuengamme, Germany

Norwegian social worker Wanda Hjort looked into the night sky and saw the reflection of headlights on the road approaching. The lights belonged to a column of buses carrying Scandinavian prisoners from the Sachsenhausen concentration camp.

Wanda, Anders and *Obersturmbannführer* Pauly had been waiting at the gate for some time and, even though the buses were expected, it was still a relief to finally see them arrive. They watched as several white buses with '*Schweden*' and the red cross emblazoned on their sides drove into the camp. A ragged cheer went up from the buses as the headlights swept across the waiting group and the Norwegian prisoners spotted Wanda. She smiled and waved back.

"I think you are well-known to them," Anders said.

"I see them every week," Wanda said. "They've had showers and cleaned up. They're happy to be going home."

Anders thought about Wanda's extraordinary efforts to help her Norwegian countrymen. She and her siblings had brought food supplies in backpacks by bus to the Sachsenhausen camp gates, telling the guards they had packages for the Norwegian prisoners. This started a weekly routine that allowed them to carry messages from the Norwegians to their families and led to familiarity with the camp guards. Wanda knew more about the Scandinavian prisoners in Germany than anyone else.

"How many are we expecting?" Anders asked Pauly.

"Several thousand, I would think."

"We have lists for 2,200, Anders," Wanda said. "I have their numbers here. We shouldn't miss anybody."

"So Herr Berger, you are going south tomorrow I hear?" Pauly asked.

"Yes, we head south."

"I hear the conditions are not so good at Mauthausen and Dachau," Pauly said. "They have had a series of typhus epidemics."

"We are taking our doctor and nurses with us, *Herr Obersturmbannführer*," Wanda said. "We should be okay."

"Have you found your Mr Lagerman?" Pauly asked Anders.

"No, nothing," Anders said with frustration. "His name is on none of the lists I am afraid."

Several days later a long convoy of white buses with their red cross markings set off at dawn for the south of Germany from Friedrichsruh Castle. Each bus had a Gestapo agent in plainclothes sitting up front with a Swedish driver and volunteers.

In one bus there was the Norwegian doctor Bjorn Heger and a nursing staff of five along with Anders Berger and Wanda Hjort. The Swedish volunteers remaining at Friedrichsruh waved good-bye as the bus convoy headed for the autobahn going south. It was going to be a very long drive to Dachau.

Fifty

Stockholm

Peter sat at the kitchen table in his flat naked to the waist as Bridget changed the dressing on his arm. Sabrina had removed the stitches and the swelling had gone down, but it was still a very ugly scar.

"So what did Keith have to say?" Bridget asked.

"Not much. He was sedated."

"Someone attacked him, Peter. Someone must know what we've been doing."

"I've had some time to think about it, Bridget. If Keith is right, someone is trying to prevent an internal inquiry at MI5 into Soviet moles in the service. By putting Keith in the hospital, they will have delayed any kind of action on the matter so I doubt they will feel the need to come after me."

"You think so?"

"Furthermore, we've lost our link to Kramer, so we won't be producing much intelligence from now on."

"I hope you're right, Peter."

Dachau, Germany

It was after midnight when the convoy of buses finally pulled into the Dachau concentration camp north of Munich. They drove into the camp perimeter after passing through the famous gate with its *'Arbeit macht frei'* slogan. The Swedish contingent was dead tired after the long and stressful day on the road. Bjorn and Anders stepped off the bus in a light-hearted mood murmuring the old German refrain:

> *"Lieber Herr Gott, mach mich stumm,*
> *Das ich nicht nach Dachau komm..."*
> (Dear God, make me dumb,
> that I may not to Dachau come.)

The camp guards in the towers watched the visitors with interest, machine guns at the ready. A senior camp officer approached Bjorn and Anders.

"Sie sind doch Schwedisch?"

"Guten Abend. I am Dr Bjorn Heger from the Swedish Red Cross."

"I am *Obersturmführer* Ruppert. The camp commander is *Obersturmbannführer* Weiter, but he is away."

"This is Herr Berger from the Swedish Red Cross, Herr Schultz with the Gestapo, and our Norwegian friend Wanda Hjort."

"Guten Abend, Herr Obersturmführer," Schultz said.

Ruppert ignored the Gestapo man, turning his attention to his Swedish visitors.

"Come with me, please."

Ruppert led the small group into the inner perimeter past the guard towers to an ugly squat building housing the prisoners. In the dark barracks murmurs could be heard from sick men lying in their bunks. Many were starved half to death and dressed in rags.

"Here are your Scandinavian men," Ruppert said. "All are in good health I think."

A man appeared in the doorway speaking very softly.

"I am Norwegian. Have you come for us?"

"Yes, we have come for you," Wanda replied.

"Many are sick, some have the typhus," the prisoner whispered to Wanda and Bjorn.

"They are skin and bones, *Herr Obersturmführer*," Bjorn said with mounting anger. "Please do not say they are in good health."

"This is not acceptable," Anders added.

"We had a typhus epidemic back in November," Ruppert said. "It took the lives of thousands. These are the lucky ones, Dr Heger. We did the best we could to save them."

Bjorn was a small, intense young man, known for his kind and friendly demeanour, but now he was livid and his face was transformed into an apoplectic scowl.

"You did not do your best, *Herr Obersturmführer*. These men are chronically undernourished," Bjorn said. "They are starving to death, no wonder so many died from the typhus."

Wanda pulled Bjorn away from Ruppert and they entered the barracks. Inside the ward the stink was unbearable. Anders held a torch as Wanda touched hands with those prisoners who could sit up on their bunks. Many prisoners lay motionless in the dark, barely breathing. Anders started to tick off the names of the survivors from the list he was carrying.

It was early morning. The Swedish volunteers had cooked a nourishing soup for the prisoners and were serving them in the officers' lunch room. The thin, emaciated men had showered with the help of the volunteers and their clothes had been replaced with clean striped concentration camp pyjamas supplied by Ruppert and the guards. Many had red triangles on their chests indicating they were political prisoners and their camp numbers were pinned to their chests to identify them. They sat at long tables and ate hungrily watched by the guards.

Colonel Björck, Wanda, Bjorn, and Anders sat apart from the men and were busy preparing for the long day ahead. Nearby sat three of the Gestapo men looking tired and unkempt, smoking cigarettes. Schultz sat next to a Swedish nurse who was busy changing the bandage on an infected foot.

"We have 313 Danes and 143 Norwegians who can travel," Björck said. "There are at least 50 who are too sick to travel and some of them have the typhus. We will have to leave them here and return for them later."

"We can't leave them here, Colonel," Wanda said. "They are in a terrible state. We need to get them home."

"I agree, Wanda, but many of them cannot travel in their present condition," Björck said. "We have no choice."

"What about Mauthausen, sir?" Bjorn asked.

"The Dachau prisoners should leave this morning," Björck said. "I think we should split up. I will take the Dachau prisoners north while some of you should go on to Mauthausen in Austria and the others to Nachtweiler."

"It's a good plan, but we need to move quickly," Bjorn said.

"The road to Linz is good," Wanda said. "It can't be worse than what we have seen already. I can go to Mauthausen, sir."

"I'll go west to Nachtweiler with the remaining buses and we'll divide up the nursing staff," Bjorn proposed.

"Good, it is decided then," Björck said.

"I hear Allied bombing is worse in the west, be careful Bjorn on those roads," Wanda said. "What about you, Anders?"

"I'll go with you to Mauthausen."

"Wanda, you need to get in and out fast," Björck warned. "I want you on the road back before nightfall. That doesn't leave you very much time."

"Don't worry, sir," Wanda said. "We won't waste any time."

Fifty-one

Stockholm

Karl-Heinz was locked up in a Gestapo interrogation room in the basement at number 2, Hovslagargatan. He was unshaven and dishevelled after a long day and night in detention. A detective with a briefcase arrived and the guard opened the door.

"Hello, Dr Kramer. I am *Kriminalinspektor* Bauer. You have been arrested for treason under instruction from Berlin."

"How long do you intend to keep me here?"

"That all depends on you, Dr Kramer."

"Why have I been arrested?" Karl-Heinz asked. "I'm a busy man, I have important work to do."

"You remember *Oberleutnant* Kemper who was recently found dead in mysterious circumstances at Nynäshamn, it was in all the papers."

"Yes, I remember *Oberleutnant* Kemper very well. He recently joined the *SD Ausland* office here in Stockholm."

"Our information is that his assailants were British. What was your relationship with *Oberleutnant* Kemper?"

"I hardly knew Kemper," Karl-Heinz said. "He was just another *Abwehr* employee who worked for Herr Golcher."

"*Oberleutnant* Kemper was to take the Austrian Jew Hanne Gabor to Danzig on a fishing boat. You remember the woman?"

"Of course, she was my cleaning lady. I left her with your people."

"We had sent her to Berlin for additional interrogation and *Oberleutnant* Kemper was to travel with her. Somebody tipped off the British to our plans."

"Really. That's very interesting but I am not sure what this has to do with me."

"We believe you informed your British friends of their location and they attacked Kemper and his man on the dock."

"That's a lie," Karl-Heinz said. "I have no idea how the British knew about Kemper's operation."

Bauer stood up and walked around the cell.

"Did you know that your boss Walter Schellenberg has been arrested in Berlin for treason?" Bauer asked. "It appears that he too has been working for the British SIS."

"I don't believe a word of this. That's a ridiculous statement, Herr Bauer. Schellenberg doesn't work for the British, he works hand-in-hand with Himmler."

"We know about your dealings with a certain Josefine working in Britain. Can you describe the activities of this source?"

"I cannot discuss it with you, Herr Bauer," Karl-Heinz said angrily. "You are talking about a top secret intelligence operation. You Gestapo people are ordinary policemen. You are not cleared for top secret RSHA intelligence."

"Who is Siegfried, Dr Kramer?"

"Siegfried is another source, you moron," Karl-Heinz snapped. "You have been through the *Abwehr* files. Damn it, I should have known that you wouldn't leave them alone. I will have to report you to the RSHA."

Bauer leaned across the table and shook his finger at Karl-Heinz.

"Don't you threaten me, Dr Kramer!" Bauer warned. "We are only doing our jobs."

"Well, if you continue in this line of questioning, Herr Bauer, then you are writing your own ticket to the Russian front. This is top secret work and none of your business."

Red in the face, Bauer stood up and quickly grabbed his file before leaving the room. Karl-Heinz smiled at the back of the frightened man.

Peter had been driven to the Grand Hotel by Bernie in his newly acquired Opel car. He entered the lobby and saw a bespectacled man quietly reading a British newspaper who suddenly got up and disappeared through the door to the restaurant.

Peter followed the man and watched him go into the kitchen. Peter entered the kitchen and saw the man open the service door into the alley behind the hotel. Peter stepped outside and followed the man up the road to a local working man's bar.

The bar was full of painters, bricklayers and carpenters having their morning coffee and aquavit. Peter stepped up to a table at the back where the OSS station chief Wilho Tikander was sitting.

"Peter, it's good to see you," Wilho said, "sorry about the little detour."

The men shook hands and Peter sat down. Wilho signalled the waiter and ordered two coffees. He was a tall Finnish-American lawyer from Chicago. Bernie had received an anonymous card in the mail from the OSS chief, asking for an informal meeting with Peter and insisting that he follow him out of the Grand Hotel before actually making contact.

"I hope you didn't have any trouble recognizing me."

"No. Why the subterfuge, Wilho?"

"I am American but I'm also Finnish," Wilho said. "I have a family in Helsinki so I am a target of the NKVD."

"I'm sorry to hear it," Peter said. "As you know we have been warned off any collaboration with your organisation. Nothing personal, of course."

"I know. Our ambassador is not very keen on covert operations I'm afraid. Hershel Johnson thinks any kind of spying is the work of the devil."

"Well, he may be right but we all have jobs to do."

"Colonel Hallamaa sent me, Peter," Wilho said in a low voice. "It's not going well with Harold Nicolson and Anthony Eden. They have basically given Hallamaa the brush off."

"I'm sorry that it didn't work out."

"We Americans are using Colonel Hallamaa's code-breakers and helping finance their operations so we do owe them some favours. You know there are plans to move all the RTK staff in Helsinki to Stockholm and the government here recently approved it."

"I suppose they want to keep their operations out of the hands of the Soviets."

"Yes, that's the idea," Wilho said, "it's still in the planning stage of course. They need to find a ship to bring seven hundred Finnish code-breakers and their families to Sweden and then lodge them here in Stockholm. It's not going to be easy and it'll be very expensive."

"Yes, I can see that."

"Peter, the colonel considers you a very good friend, but he needs your help. He wants you to send a letter to Felix Cowgill, head of MI6's Counter-intelligence Section V."

"I will do whatever I can for Hallamaa, Wilho."

"Hallamaa will leave a letter for you at the British Legation," Wilho said. "He wants you to send it on to Cowgill by diplomatic courier as soon as possible. It's urgent."

"Of course, Wilho."

"Let's try to get together from time to time, unofficially of course. Your intelligence services need our help and we need yours," Wilho said as he dropped some Krona coins on the table and stood up. "I must be going. Please wait here for five minutes before leaving. Good-bye, Peter."

Peter nodded to Wilho and watched him leave the bar.

Hanne and Elsa stood at the door to the Kramer house and rang the doorbell. Eva opened the door.

"Hanne!" Eva exclaimed with surprise.

"I have come for my pay, Frau Kramer."

"Well, you better come in."

Hanne walked past Eva into the kitchen followed by Elsa.

A new girl was feeding little Heidi and looked up as Hanne entered the room. Eva went to a cupboard and handed Hanne an envelope with her pay.

"I'm so sorry, Hanne, I owe you an apology."

Hanne was astonished. Eva was not the kind of German woman who apologized easily. She led the women out of the kitchen into the hall.

"We discovered that it was Wilhelma who was stealing the toys," Eve said in a low voice. "They were for her sister's children."

"I accept your apology, Frau Kramer."

Elsa noticed the packed boxes lining the hallway.

"You are moving?" Elsa asked.

"The war is lost for Germany, some families have gone home. Others are applying for visas to stay in Sweden," Eva said with a pitiful air.

"Are you returning?" Hanne asked.

"No, we have decided to stay," Eva said and burst into tears.

"What's happened?" Hanne asked.

"They have Karl-Heinz, Hanne," Eva said, "the Gestapo has taken him. They took him on Monday and he hasn't come home."

Hanne smiled and felt the sweetness of retribution fill the air. She almost laughed when she realised that the Gestapo had seized the arrogant bastard who had delivered her to the selfsame torturers.

"I'm so sorry, Frau Kramer," Elsa exclaimed, frowning at Hanne's smirk.

"What will you do?" Hanne asked.

"I don't know. We're waiting for news," Eva said dabbing her tears with a handkerchief.

Peter headed back to the Grand Hotel along the quiet street. As he turned the corner, he noticed his friend Wilho dart out of a side street, followed by two large men who grabbed him by the arms hauling him back to their waiting car. A third man joined them, holding up a glass syringe which he quickly plunged into Wilho's neck.

Peter ran towards Wilho but saw that it was too late to stop the kidnappers. The car drove off at high speed leaving Peter standing in the road.

Fifty-two

Peter ran through the Grand Hotel to the front of the building where Bernie was reading a Swedish paper sitting in the car. He jumped into the passenger seat.

"Let's go, Bernie. The Russians just grabbed Wilho Tikander behind the hotel."

Bernie turned on the ignition and floored the accelerator. The car took off turning left into the narrow side streets behind the hotel.

"Hurry, Bernie."

"How many were there, Peter?"

"There were three of them and they drugged him. I saw a man with a hypodermic needle."

"Bloody hell. What have they got against Tikander?"

They drove through the narrow streets looking for the Russian car, but to no avail. The NKVD and their hostage were long gone.

"Show me where it happened, Peter."

"Pull up here."

They got out of the car and stood on the sidewalk.

"They were parked here. This is where they gave him the injection."

"Why'd they grab Tikander?"

"I think it has to do with his Finnish connections," Peter said, "he's an American, but he's close to Colonel Hallamaa."

Bernie stepped to the curb and looked up and down the empty street.

"Well, we're not going to find him here. Let's go."

Bernie drove Peter back to the Legation. They sat in the car parked behind the Legation building smoking cigarettes.

"I better go up and make the call to our US contact," Peter said.

"What do you think they'll do?" Bernie asked. "Wilho has no backup at the legation. He's on his own."

"Well, we need to tell them what's going on, Bernie."

"Peter, the ambassador is an arsehole. He won't lift a finger for Wilho. You remember the story of Sedov, the Russian defector in Paris."

"You mean Lev Sedov, the son of Trotsky?"

"Yeah, the NKVD did an appendectomy on him at a private clinic," Bernie said. "Tennant is always talking about it."

"I remember the story, Bernie."

It had been in the papers before the war. Sedov had been suffering from appendicitis in Paris in 1938. A friend advised him to go to the Clinique Mirabeau, a private clinic run by Russian emigrés instead of a Paris hospital. He didn't know that the friend, whose code name was Etienne in the Trotsky organisation, was an NKVD plant and had tipped off his handlers to the operation.

"I love the way those commie tossers are all workin' for the NKVD. We had them in Spain."

"If I remember correctly, the operation went well and everything appeared normal for several days. Then Sedov fell ill. They say he was poisoned by a Russian doctor."

"The perfect crime, the poor bugger died of an infection after the operation. No one was the wiser."

"So where would the NKVD take Wilho?" Peter asked. "A safe house in the city?"

"The question is what do they want from him?"

"They want to sabotage Hallamaa's Finnish operations."

"They snatched him on short notice, Peter. They couldn't plan the operation for long, so they only have their own local resources."

"What about the injection? They put him down in no time."

"Yeah, I'm thinking spur of the moment. They do the snatch and then load him up with sodium amytal to get him talking. A private clinic would be the best place for it."

Peter thought about it for a moment and then stubbed out his cigarette.

"They would need a doctor to administer the drugs. I think you may be on to something, Bernie."

"The other way is to beat him half to death, but it takes a professional to do it right."

Peter raised an eyebrow at this comment.

"You need a professional to know when enough is enough. It is too easy to kill someone and not get a word out of them."

"How many private clinics are there in Stockholm?"

"Half a dozen at most, Peter," Bernie said, "but I'm thinking of one in particular. I took Sabrina to a private clinic on Karlavägen last year. There was a Russian doctor there with a funny name."

Ten minutes later, Peter and Bernie pulled up in front of the private clinic and stopped the car.

"You better stay with the car," Bernie said, "they might recognize you."

Peter nodded as Bernie got out of the car.

"Give me ten minutes," he said, crossing the road to the clinic and entering the building.

Peter was annoyed that the NKVD would dare attack a diplomat and a colleague of his. Of course, they had done the same thing to him, hauling him off the street for a meeting with Ambassador Kollontai. He looked at his watch and stepped out of the car. He glanced up at the building, when Bernie appeared at the front door and returned to the car.

"Well. Did you find him?" Peter asked.

"Yeah, he's in there, Peter."

"Thank God you found him."

"He's in a private room on the fourth floor," Bernie said, getting into the car. "There's that damn Petrov woman watching the door. I didn't hang around."

"What do we do? We have to get him out of there."

"I agree, but we better not hang around here for long or they will spot us."

Bernie started the car and they drove away.

"He's gonna be out of it for a couple of hours,"Bernie said.

"We need to go in tonight before some butcher gets to him."

Peter remembered the grisly aftermath of the Lev Sedov murder. After the death of his son, Trotsky sent his trusted aide Rudolf Klement to investigate the murder in Paris. He was lured to an apartment on the Left Bank by the NKVD agent Ale Taubman where he was killed. Two agents cut off his head and legs, and stuffed his body parts into a trunk which was later discovered floating in the Seine. Several days later, the Trotsky organisation received a typewritten letter from Klement accusing Trotsky of collaboration with Adolf Hitler.

Etienne then became the leader of the beheaded Trotskyist organisation in Paris. It was Etienne who later introduced the American Trotskyist and interpreter, Sylvia Ageloff, to Ramon

Mercader. In love with Mercader, she blindly followed him to Mexico and helped him infiltrate into Trotsky's household where he murdered the man with an ice-axe in August 1940.

Bernie and Peter pulled into the British Legation car park and climbed out of the car.

"Give me a couple of hours to set this up, Peter?"

"Okay, I'll be in my office," Peter said, leaving Bernie at the entrance.

Fifty-three

"You won't believe this," Bridget said as Peter came into the Consular Services office.

"What?"

"Elsa called. She went with Hanne to collect her pay at the Kramer house this morning. Frau Kramer is worried about her husband who has been arrested by the Gestapo."

Peter looked astonished.

"Kramer has been arrested?"

"It appears so."

"I better get a word to London."

"Sir Victor wants a meeting."

"Bloody hell, I don't have time for the angry rabbit this morning," Peter said. "What is this about?"

"No idea, Peter," Bridget said getting up. "His secretary called."

She came around the desk and fixed Peter's tie brushing some dandruff from his suit.

"Really, Peter, you need to take better care of your appearance. Sir Victor is a diplomat and looks count."

"That's the last thing on my mind, Bridget. The NKVD just snatched Wilho Tikander. They've drugged him and taken him to a private clinic."

"Tikander is OSS," Bridget said alarmed, "we're not to have any contact with them."

"I know the rules, but I also have a job to do in this town. Look, I better go down and see what Sir Victor wants."

"Don't say a word about Tikander or they'll have you on the next plane out to London."

"Of course not. Wish me well, darling."

Bridget kissed Peter briefly on the lips, then looked at him and giggled.

"We can't have the angry rabbit see you like that," she said, taking out a tissue and wiping the trace of lipstick away. "Off you go, now."

At the Swedish Red Cross office, a teleprinter was printing out a message for Count Bernadotte. His secretary waited by the machine and then brought it to her boss.

"A telex from Berlin, sir."

"Thanks, Rose."

Bernadotte read the telex and frowned.

"It's a message from Colonel Björck. The buses from Dachau arrived at Neuengamme an hour ago," he said.

"That's good news, sir," Rose said, puzzled by her boss' reaction, "isn't it?"

"Not entirely, I'm afraid. Four hundred and fifty prisoners were transported, but some are in bad shape. Fifty were too sick to travel and had to be left behind."

"Even so, it's a good start."

"I suppose it is," Bernadotte conceded, smiling to show he appreciated her effort to encourage him, "but we still need permission to get them out of Germany."

"I'm sure you will succeed, sir," Rose said.

Bernadotte reflected on the chances of success of their operation. It was all very fine to move around the Scandinavian prisoners on a German chessboard, but if he couldn't get them out of the country in time, it would all be for naught.

"Get Felix Kersten on the line? He seems to be the only one who has Himmler's ear."

"Right away, sir."

Rose left the office to make the call. In the bizarre world of the Third Reich, the only man - other than Hitler - that Himmler listened to actually lived in Stockholm and held no formal position in the Nazi hierarchy. Felix Kersten was Himmler's personal masseur.

"I don't appreciate," Mallet said, sitting imperiously behind his Louis XIV desk in his ornate office, "our resident spook meddling in Ewan Butler's affairs. Butler is off limits."

"Of course, sir," Peter said, standing before the desk like a truant schoolboy.

"In the diplomatic service we have our priorities just like you do in MI6, Faye."

"I'm sure you do, sir."

"Sit down," Mallet motioned him to a chair, "let me explain a few things which will help you understand our delicate position here in Sweden. The war will be over in a few months and Britain will be a bankrupt nation, heavily indebted to the United States. As the war winds down, our nation may have the opportunity to reap some financial rewards that will help us keep our heads above water. Do you understand what I mean?"

"Of course, sir."

"Last year Himmler met with German industrialists at the Maison Rouge Hotel in Strasburg. Their aim was to secure the assets of Germany's largest industrial firms: IG Farben, Kruppe, Siemens, Volkswagenwerk, Rheinmetall, Conti Oil, Messerschmitt and others. With the end of the war looming, Himmler demanded that these companies transfer their assets and cash abroad, where they would be protected from seizure by the Allied powers and the Soviets."

"That's quite amazing, sir."

"The SS has been methodically stripping the wealth of the Reich right under the nose of the Führer. They have been moving industrial equipment, manpower and cash. Their plan is to reconstitute German power abroad under SS control at the end of the war."

Peter's mind wandered as he admired Mallet's ornate furniture.

"The Fourth Reich, sir?"

"Yes, that is their plan. We have been instructed by the Foreign Secretary to buy up as many of those assets as we can and we are not alone. The Swedes, the Americans, the Swiss, and many other countries are doing deals to acquire the foreign-owned assets of these companies."

"But if the British government is bankrupt, how can we acquire these assets, sir?" Peter asked.

"Through our banks, Faye."

"Private funds?"

"Yes, this is an opportunity to buy up German assets at deeply depressed prices."

"I see."

"I can't tell you anymore," Mallet said, "except that this is a top priority for our government. The negotiations are long and arduous, but with a bit of luck I think we will succeed."

On his way back to Consular Services, Peter knocked on Michael Tennant's door and found him packing boxes.

"You're off to Paris?"

"Yes, Peter," Michael said. "Just a few things to collect and then I'm flying home later today. I'm looking forward to my new job in the French capital."

"Do you have a moment, it's urgent?" Peter asked.

"Of course, come in and find yourself a seat."

"Wilho Tikander has been kidnapped by the NKVD."

"Pardon me, you say he's been kidnapped?"

"Yes, I had a coffee with him not an hour ago and he was jumped by the NKVD on the street behind the Grand Hotel."

"Peter, are you mad? We're not allowed to have any contact with Donovan's OSS, that includes MI6 and SOE together. You could be recalled if London hears about it."

"I know, but he contacted me unofficially. It seemed urgent. I like Tikander. He's a good chap."

"Where is he now?"

"He was taken to a private clinic on Karlavägen after they drugged him," Peter said.

"Let me call the Americans, maybe the Stockholm police can do a search for him."

Michael picked up the phone and dialled the US Legation.

Karl-Heinz stepped out of the German Legation on Hovslagargatan street. His driver spotted him at the entrance and started up the car. He pulled up near Karl-Heinz who got in the back next to Herr Golcher.

"How is business, Herr Golcher?"

"Very good, sir. Are you all right?" Golcher asked, looking concerned.

"You were worried about me, were you Herr Golcher?"

"Yes, of course, sir. Word was going around town that you had been arrested by the Gestapo."

"No need to worry. The Berlin office called. They had to let me go. Bloody fools. They think we have nothing better to do here in Stockholm."

"Good to see you again, sir."

"How's Herr Akerson?"

"Akerson has lots of buyers: Spain, America, Mexico, Argentina."

"Good. Keep up with it."

"How long do you think Berlin will be shipping us its art treasures?" Golcher asked.

"Good question. I wouldn't know, but as long as they do, we'll be selling the stuff. The SD needs hard currency, Golcher."

Fifty-four

Michael Tennant hung up the phone as Peter watched him sitting on a chair in his office.

"Bloody Yanks. I don't think they believed a word of it, but they're going to put in a call to the police."

"He'll be dead by the time they get around to it," Peter said.

"I know how you feel, Peter, but there is not much more we can do."

Michael moved a box from a chair behind his desk and sat down with a sigh.

"I don't like the sound of this," Michael said in a weary voice. "You remember the Sedov case in Paris. It was at a private clinic."

"Bernie mentioned it."

"The NKVD use private clinics to murder people, Peter."

"Yes, I've heard. Do you think they want to kill Tikander?"

"I can't think of any other reason," Michael said. "Tikander is Finnish American and anti-Soviet. By eliminating Tikander, they reduce the risk of the American Legation in Stockholm siding with Finland as they try to force a peace settlement on the government in Helsinki."

"Bernie is talking about going in there tonight."

"Bernie is a good man. Do whatever you have to do to save Wilho from those bastards. Just don't tell me anymore. I don't want to know."

"Of course, Michael."

"A word of advice. You have done very well here, just don't blow it with Mallet. Try to keep your nose clean."

"Thanks, Michael. Best of luck in Paris," Peter said as he left him to his packing.

Hamburg, Germany

At the German telephone exchange, Anders paid the clerk and went to a phone cubicle. He waited for the connection and then picked up the phone when it rang.

"Hello, Britta, it's me."

Anders listened and then laughed.

"I just got back from our trip to Dachau and Mauthausen. There's no sign of Rolf anywhere, Britta. He's not on any of the lists. There are plans to go to Ravensbrück, Theresienstadt, and other camps. All I can do is to keep at it."

In the Berger flat Britta watched young Nils, playing on the floor with a toy Red Cross ambulance.

"He cannot have just disappeared, Anders," Britta said in frustration. "He must be somewhere."

Tears flowed down her cheeks as she tried to maintain her self control.

"Don't give up, Anders. Please don't give up."

Young Nils looked at his mother and became alarmed.

"Mamma, don't cry."

"Sorry, Nils is here. He says hello to his pappa."

In the telephone exchange Anders thought about his lovely little boy and felt buoyed by the sentiment.

"Tell him I love him, Britta darling. I won't give up. I'll find your brother. I must go. Love you, bye now."

Anders looked physically sick as he stepped out of the cubicle.

Stockholm

It was after midnight when Peter and Bernie pulled up outside the private clinic in Bernie's stolen Opel. Mads and Hendrik were in the back seat. They got out of the car and Bernie opened the boot.

"I brought along some white lab coats," Peter said. "Let's kit up as doctors."

"Good idea," Mads said.

Each man took a white lab coat and put it on.

"Mads and Hendrik will go in first," Bernie said. "Don't worry about the night watchman. I've already had a word with him. The door should be unlocked."

Peter checked his Webley revolver. Bernie handed two silenced Welrod pistols with long barrels to Mads and Hendrik and then put the Thompson into a canvas bag.

"The plan is that we go in one at a time and regroup on the fourth floor."

Mads nodded to Bernie and set off across the street. He opened the door to the clinic without incident. Two minutes later, Peter tapped Hendrik on the shoulder and sent him on his way. There was no sign of trouble, so Peter followed two minutes later. He got inside the door and froze in his tracks when the night watchman walked into the lobby. The man merely nodded at him and motioned him away from the door. They waited in silence until Bernie came in a couple of minutes later. Bernie glanced at Peter and then went directly to the night watchman and slipped him some money. The night watchman then waved them up the stairs.

It was dark on the fourth floor as Peter and Bernie exited the stairs and looked down the long silent hallway. They checked the nearby rooms looking for Mads and Hendrik, when suddenly Mads appeared pushing a gurney with Hendrik lying under a sheet. Hendrik winked at Bernie and Peter in their lab coats.

"We go first, follow us but keep your distance," Mads said.

Peter nodded as Mads started down the hall pushing the gurney.

Fifty-five

In a surgery half way down the hall a medical doctor was preparing his surgical instruments as a nurse appeared in the doorway. The doctor spoke in Russian to the nurse.

"Everything ready, Elena?" Grigori asked.

"Yes."

"Good, bring him in. Let's get on with it."

The nurse left the surgery just as Mads appeared at the end of the hall pushing a gurney with Hendrik masquerading as a sleeping patient. It was easy to see which room was Wilho's. An NKVD guard was sitting outside the door of the room watching the nurse as she approached and then went inside.

In the surgery Grigori pulled a flask from his pocket and drank from it before putting on his blue scrubs. He had done this kind of thing many times in the past for his NKVD masters. It was a simple operation. The patient would recover or not depending on the information supplied to his superiors. The operation was a smoke screen and allowed them to pump the patient with sodium amytal at their leisure in a hospital environment.

Grigori looked up and noticed a strange man in a lab coat pushing a gurney down the hall. It was unusual to see activity so late at night, so he stepped towards the door to have a look.

The guard paid little attention to Mads as he swung the gurney around so he could back it into the room next door to Wilho's. He was just starting to back up when Hendrik turned on his side and shot the guard twice from beneath the blanket. The popping sounds from the Welrod were muted and sounded like the gurney had banged into a door.

Hendrik jumped off the bed and rushed into Wilho's room leaving Mads to watch for movement in the hall. He stood in the shadows watching Elena with her back to him move the bed away from the wall. He pointed his gun at her.

"Stop, stay where you are."

The nurse turned to look at Hendrik and seemed unimpressed by his gun.

"I have to take this man to surgery, sir."

"Stay where you are, don't move," Hendrik ordered her.

Down the hall Grigori ran back into the surgery and pulled a Tokarev pistol from his bag. He left the room.

Peter and Bernie had been moving from one room to the next to avoid being seen walking in the hall. As they left the room next door to the surgery, they noticed the doctor creeping up on Mads with the Tokarev in his hand.

Bernie pulled a wire garrote from his pocket and made a sign for Peter to stay out of sight. He kicked off his shoes and ran quickly in his socks down the hall towards the doctor. Just as Grigori surprised Mads with the pistol, Bernie yanked the doctor off his feet with the garrote. The Tokarev clattered to the floor as he struggled in vain.

Peter ran down the hall to lend a hand and took Mads' place at the door as he went in to assist Hendrik. As he entered the room, Elena lunged at Hendrik with a scalpel nearly cutting his throat. He instinctively raised his arm to ward her off and the blade cut deeply into his forearm. Mads didn't hesitate for a moment and shot the nurse in the chest. As she slumped to the floor, Hendrik looked down at his arm which was leaking blood all over his clothes.

"That damn bitch cut me."

"Put a compress on it," Mads said. "We need to stop the bleeding."

As Hendrik went out looking for bandages, Mads noticed that Wilho was starting to wake up.

"How are you feeling, Wilho?" Mads asked.

"What are you doing here, Mads?" Wilho asked, coughing loudly. "Where am I?"

"You're in a private hospital. We're taking you home."

Peter entered the room.

"How is he?" Peter asked.

"Just a bit woozy I think," Mads said. "Let's get him out of here."

Half an hour later, Mads and Bernie pushed a gurney out the delivery door in the basement towards a waiting car. They dumped the dead doctor in the boot on top of the NKVD guard. Peter and Hendrik arrived with Wilho in a wheelchair and helped him into the car.

"We'll take him home first," Peter said.

"Good idea. He needs to sleep it off," Hendrik remarked, looking down at his bandaged arm.

"One more to go," Bernie said as he returned with Mads to collect the dead nurse.

It was almost dawn when Bernie and Mads threw the last Russian into the canal with a resounding splash. They were parked in a secluded spot away from traffic on the road.

"Where'd you learn to use the garrote, Bernie?" Mads asked.

"A long time ago in the Spanish war. I was with the bloody International Brigade. We had to kill silently when we launched night attacks."

"Peter, do you want a drink?" Hendrik asked, standing nearby.

"I'd love a drink" Peter said. "Thanks."

Hendrik handed him a bottle of whisky that he had taken from Bernie's car.

"Everything tickety-boo, Peter?" Bernie asked, returning with Mads.

"Fine, Bernie."

"Blimey, they're drinking my scotch!" he exclaimed. "Gimme that bottle, will you Hendrik?"

Hendrik passed the bottle over to Bernie.

"We had a good night," Mads said.

"You fellahs were first class," Bernie said. "Bloody hell, did you see how Hendrik shot that NKVD tosser from the hip?"

"He's a talented chap," Mads said with a smile.

Bernie took a swig and passed the bottle around.

Fifty-six

April 1945

Count Bernadotte followed Gustav Lundquist into his large office at the Stockholms-Tidningen newspaper.

"So Folke, when do you return to Germany?" Lundquist asked as he sat down opposite his old friend.

"Tomorrow," Bernadotte said with a sigh.

He was under tremendous pressure to bring the Scandinavian prisoners home. Time was running out. The war was coming to an end in Western Europe. The Red Army had crossed the Oder river in late January and had gained ground rapidly in February and March putting them now at a distance of only fifty miles from Berlin. The Allies had slowed their advance from the West to allow the Red Army to take Berlin. The Americans had taken Frankfurt and had pushed east as the Soviets entered Austria.

German forces were retreating on all fronts and their concentration camps across Europe were in total chaos. Some had simply been abandoned by the SS who opened the gates and walked away. At others they had murdered the prisoners and burned their bodies to cover up war crimes.

"My journalist Anders Berger is over there," Lundquist said.

"Anders is a very nice young man. He's looking for his wife's brother."

"When do you think I can have him back?"

"I really don't know. Anders won't give up easily."

"How bad are things in Germany?"

"Terrible. The camps are in an awful state now with the war winding down, but we still don't have permission to move our prisoners out of the country. Gustav, I must reiterate the need to keep quiet about all this."

"Don't worry, Folke, we won't do anything to upset your negotiations. We're still under the publication ban so we'll wait before we publish anything."

"We are in a race against time to save all the prisoners we can. Himmler will allow it only if nothing is heard in the press. We're negotiating everything piecemeal on the spot. We hope to release as many women as possible out of Ravensbrück. This includes a lot of French, Dutch, Polish and Belgian nationals."

"So it's not just Scandinavians that you're helping to release?"

"Yes, that's true. We're doing whatever we can for all the prisoners, but it's become very frustrating."

Friedrichsruh, Germany

At Friedrichsruh Castle, a white bus with Bjorn Heger and several nurses pulled up at the front gate where Wanda, Anders and the Gestapo agent Schultz were waiting. Bjorn descended to help load the remaining baggage while the passengers climbed on board. Then the bus with 'Schweden' emblazoned on its side drove away heading for the autobahn. During the first hour the bus made good time on its way south. Afterwards progress slowed considerably as the bus had to thread its way through broken down traffic on the road.

The bus drove by an open truck full of wounded German soldiers, many of them very young.

"Pull over," Bjorn yelled to the driver.

"*Nein, Herr Doktor.* We don't have time to stop," Schultz said.

Bjorn ran to the front of the bus.

"Pull over, just do it," Bjorn said to the driver. "He can't stop us."

The driver pulled over and opened the door. Bjorn rushed off the bus followed by Anders and the enraged Schultz. Near the truck there were half a dozen bleeding young men with broken bones and head injuries. Wanda Hjort led the nursing staff off the bus.

Bjorn approached a young man and was joined by the nursing staff.

"This man needs a splint for his leg and we need to stop the bleeding on this other one," Bjorn ordered his staff.

Bjorn hurried along to another young soldier who was astonished by the arrival of nursing staff out of nowhere.

'Head wound, clean him up and bandage him."

Charmed by the presence of the young nurses, the young soldiers asked repeatedly who they were and where they were coming from.

"*Wer sind Sie? Wer kommen Sie her?*"

"*Wir sind Schwedisch.*"

"*Schwedische Krankenschwestern!*" exclaimed one young German officer in admiration.

Bjorn moved on to the next wounded man. Suddenly, out of a perfectly blue sky an Allied bomber appeared on the horizon and made a low pass over the autobahn. Everyone rushed off the bus and threw themselves into the ditch, but the plane didn't drop any bombs.

Bjorn and the nurses returned to their work, splinting broken legs and applying bandages. As soon as Bjorn felt they had done enough, he consulted with Wanda and they called the nursing staff back to the bus. Bjorn checked to see that everyone was on board and realised that they had lost their Gestapo man who was off in the woods relieving himself.

"Kommen Sie zuruck, Herr Schultz. We're leaving."

Schultz buttoned up his fly and ran back to the bus.

"Vielen Dank, Herr Doktor. Vielen Dank."

"Herr Schultz. We are not going without you."

"They are just youngsters, Hitler Youth recruits, *Herr Doktor.* You are a good man, you and your nurses."

Bjorn smiled at Schultz and took his place next to Anders.

"Sorry for the delay, Anders. Those boys shouldn't even be in uniform."

"Well done, Bjorn," Anders said. "They may be boys but they will never forget our Swedish nurses for as long as they live."

Bjorn and Wanda laughed.

"I hope your Rolf Lagerman is there," Bjorn said.

"That is my hope too."

Vaihingen-an-der-Enz, Germany

The light was failing as the bus drove along the country road approaching the camp at Vaihingen-an-der-Enz. Several peasant families were on the road, walking east with their farm animals, hauling mattresses, pots and pans to avoid the French forces attacking from the West. Trucks lined the road having run out of gas. The bus pulled up at the abandoned camp in the woods. The gates were wide open as Bjorn, Anders and Schultz descended from the bus and entered the camp on foot.

"The guards are gone," Bjorn remarked.

Bjorn and Anders walked ahead through the empty buildings. They stopped to look inside several wooden huts, but there was no one around.

"Do you think they took the prisoners east?" Anders asked.

"Listen, Anders," Bjorn said.

For a moment they stopped moving and listened to the faint rumble of tanks off to the west.

"Tanks," Bjorn said. "We're very close to the French lines. I doubt they would bother moving the prisoners."

Bjorn and Anders searched the buildings, fearful to find massacred prisoners within the walls. In a building near the barbed wire perimeter, a man in striped pyjamas appeared on the doorstep.

"*Sind Sie Französisch?*" he asked.

"*Schwedisch,*" Anders replied.

The man's eyes lit up.

"*Ich bin Norwegisch.* We are in here. Please, come."

Anders and Bjorn followed the man into barracks with bunk beds stacked in twos. The prisoners watched from the shadows. The smell was absolutely repulsive.

"We've not eaten anything in three days since the guards left. Do you have any food?" the prisoner asked in Norwegian.

"Of course, we do," Bjorn said. "We're going to feed all of you. How many are you?"

"We're sixteen remaining. My name is Trygve Bratteli."

Anders looked around at the faces of the men.

"I was told there were thirty Scandinavian prisoners in this camp," Bjorn said.

"Many have died in the last few days. We put the bodies in the building next door," Bratteli said.

"Do you have a Rolf Lagerman with you?" Anders asked with trepidation.

Bratteli smiled at Anders.

"Rolf. You have a visitor."

A head stuck up from behind a bunk and slipped on spectacles to look at the visitors. Rolf spotted Anders.

"Are you Anders? Britta's husband?" Rolf asked as he got to his feet.

"Yes, I'm Anders. I've come all the way from Sweden to find you. Britta sends her love."

Anders rushed over to hug his brother-in-law, who was nothing but skin and bones dressed in dirty striped pyjamas.

Fifty-seven

Stockholm

It was early evening and a warm day as Peter entered a bar in the Gamla Stan quarter of Stockholm. He found Saarson sitting at a table having a coffee. He walked over and sat down.

"I heard from Mads that you and your friend helped to save Wilho," Saarson said. "He's a good friend for us Estonians. He has helped us in the past. Thank you, Mr Faye."

"He's a good chap. So what will you do at the end of the war, Mr Saarson?"

"The war will be over for Germany, but not for us. The Red Army invaded our country in 1940 and sent thousands of our people to gulags in the Soviet Union. Then in 1941, the Germans pushed the Soviet forces out of our country; but now they are back. I don't know who were worse, the Germans or the Soviets. We are again mounting a resistance movement against the Soviet occupation."

The waiter brought a coffee for Peter and returned to the kitchen.

"I called you here because I want you to meet General Onodera. He has some information for you."

"When is he coming?"

"He will meet us here at the restaurant."

Peter drank his coffee as a Japanese manservant with a large torso appeared in the doorway. He exchanged a look with Saarson and then disappeared. Peter dropped some Krona coins on the table and they stood up.

A black sedan was parked opposite the restaurant. Saarson and Peter headed towards the vehicle as the manservant checked for surveillance. The Japanese driver opened the door for Peter who looked in at a small man smiling at him from the backseat.

"Hello, Mr Faye."

"Hello, General Onodera."

"Please, Mr Faye, climb in. We go for a drive."

Peter stepped into the car.

"Thank you, Mr Saarson. I see you later perhaps," General Onodera said as Saarson nodded and walked away.

The manservant joined the driver in front and the car pulled out into the medieval streets.

Vaihingen-an-der-Enz, Germany

The prisoners were installed in the only clean building, the SS officer's dining room. A soup had been prepared and the ravenous men were finishing their meal. Several nurses helped the worst cases who lay on stretchers and had to be spoon fed. Rolf ate hungrily dipping his bread in the soup.

"How are Britta and the child?"

"She is fine and so is little Nils. He's three years old now."

Rolf seized Anders' hand and squeezed it.

"Mother and father?"

"Yes, they are well. They are very worried about you."

Rolf hid his face in shame as he wept openly. Anders patted him on the back.

In the doorway Bjorn clapped his hands to make an announcement.

"Can I have your attention please? We are leaving in an hour. We are taking you north to Neuengamme and then on to Sweden. Be ready everyone."

The men were silent, hardly capable of believing the news of their liberation.

"We will be eating regular meals from now on, small portions. You need to eat slowly to pass the food. Don't worry, we have enough food for everyone."

"Bjorn, what do we do with the men who cannot sit up?" Wanda asked. "The ones that are too weak."

"We will fix it for them in the back of the bus. Any other questions?" Bjorn asked the group.

"How long will it take?" Bratteli asked.

"We hope to get there by dawn, so be prepared for a long night on the road."

Stockholm

It was just getting dark as General Onodera and Peter sat on a park bench watching ships heading out to the open sea.

"The war is over for Germany, Mr Faye. I have had good relations with them over the years. I provided them with intelligence from my sources and they have provided me with similar information. Germany was our ally in Europe. Now we turn the page I think."

"What do you want from me, General?" Peter asked. "My country is still at war with your country. There is a great deal of animosity in Britain against Japan."

"As you may know, I have had several meetings with your Victor Mallet during this last year. In neutral Sweden we talk to everyone, friends and enemies, that is the rule. I have called you here to discuss some very important secret intelligence that comes from our sources in the Soviet Union. You know the Soviets have sources everywhere in SIS, the FBI, the State Department, the Foreign Office, and the scientific community. Of course, American and British intelligence is fair game for us, but we can share a lot of it."

"If I understand correctly, you want to sell us a load of Soviet documents?"

"We give you everything we have from Soviet agents in Britain, in the US, Canada, Australia. The Soviet Union is an enemy of Japan and we expect them to declare war against us after the defeat of Germany. Stalin promised to do this at the Yalta Conference."

"What about the documents you have been providing the Germans?"

"Yes, I have them too. This is one-time offer."

"I will need to confer with London."

"No problem. I have a little gift for you. It will whet your appetite as they say. It comes from our German friends."

Onodera handed Peter an envelope which Peter folded into his suit pocket.

"Think of it this way. With this intelligence, you can root out all those Soviet spies who are compromising your government."

Lauffen am Neckar, Germany

Night had fallen and the bus with its heavy load of prisoners and nursing staff was on the road heading north.

Bjorn sat with Wanda near the front of the bus, while Anders shared a seat with Rolf in the back. Both men were soon fast asleep as were most of the prisoners.

They were driving on secondary roads near the Neckar river, hoping to get back on the autobahn for the long drive north. The driver slowed at a fork in the road and Bjorn told him to go left. The driver obeyed and the bus continued along the road for several minutes before he slammed on the brakes almost throwing Bjorn and Wanda from their seats.

"What the hell!" Bjorn said.

There was a *Wehrmacht* staff car in the middle of the road blocking traffic.

"Damn, it's a German army vehicle," Wanda said turning to look at the Scandinavian prisoners, many of them scrambling to get back into their seats.

A soldier banged on the door and the driver opened it. Schultz was already on his way to the front of the bus when he came face to face with a young officer brandishing a Schmeisser machine gun accompanied by a soldier.

"*Kommen Sie aus. Aussteigen, bitte!*" the officer shouted.

"*Herr Obergefreiter,*" Schultz addressed the officer. "They are Swedish prisoners."

"*Wer sind Sie?*" the man demanded.

Schultz drew himself up to his full height.

"*Hauptman Schultz der Gestapo, Herr Obergefreiter.*"

The officer's reaction was sudden and unexpected. He seized Schultz by the lapels and swung him around towards the door.

"*Scheiße. Gestapo. Aussteigen!*" he barked, shoving Schultz off the bus at gunpoint. He followed Schultz and ordered two soldiers to take him away.

Near the staff car, there were half a dozen *Wehrmacht* soldiers sitting in the tall grass with several wounded men among them. The *Obergefreiter* returned to the bus.

"*Schwedisch Gefangene*, we are taking over this bus," he said to the prisoners. "I have wounded men, you have nurses. Get the prisoners off the bus."

Nearby several shots were fired. The *Obergefreiter* grinned with pleasure seeing the fearful looks on the prisoners' faces.

"*Gestapo.* We kill Gestapo bastards," he yelled. "Get the prisoners off the bus. Now!"

Bjorn stood up, turning to the prisoners and the nursing staff.

"We have to go. Please move our people off the bus as fast as you can."

Anders and Bjorn stood to one side as the able-bodied prisoners filed out. The *Obergefreiter* stood at the front and watched as Bjorn and the others helped those too sick or weak to move on their own.

The Swedish prisoners collapsed in the tall grass. As soon as the last prisoner was off the bus, the *Obergefreiter* ordered his men to get the German wounded aboard. Torch lights came on inside the bus, as Bjorn and the Swedish nurses attended to the German wounded. Wanda sat next to Anders on the grass.

"It's going to be a long night," Wanda said, "but at dawn we'll walk east and catch a train to the north."

Anders looked at Wanda in disbelief. There was something very naive about Wanda. Nothing disturbed her. She was stoic about everything and nothing could diminish the flame within her.

"But Wanda, these men can't walk that far."

"We don't have a choice, Anders. We don't have a bus anymore. We'll be fine, you'll see."

Fifty-eight

The German soldiers on the bus had been into the food supplies, but the *Obergefreiter* – his name was Hoffman - had put a stop to it once he had seen how Bjorn and the nurses had cared for his men. Now he lit the stub of a cigarette and stood beside Bjorn as they watched one of the nurses change a soldier's bandage.

Two young soldiers Hans and Fritz climbed on the bus and gestured to Hoffman to come with them.

"We are having engine problems with the staff car," Hoffman said. "Do you have a mechanic among your prisoners?"

"I don't know about the prisoners," Bjorn said, "but our driver might be able to help."

Hoffman left the bus, followed by Bjorn who called to Anders sitting on the grass nearby.

"Anders, find the driver and ask him to take a look at their car. They are having a problem with the engine."

Anders stood up and went looking for the driver as young Hans sat down near Bjorn.

"I am sorry for your troubles, *Herr Doktor*," Hans said.

"It's not so bad," Bjorn shrugged, careful not to say too much.

"You took a wrong turn, you should have gone east."

"Where are we?"

"The French First Army is about ten kilometres to the west. Tomorrow we go east."

As the dawn light came up, Wanda started a small fire to make coffee for the prisoners. In the tall grass Bjorn, Anders and the Swedish driver were fast asleep wrapped in their coats against the morning chill. The prisoners were spread out across the grass wrapped in woolen Red Cross blankets.

On the bus the German wounded were sound asleep along with *Obergefreiter* Hoffmann and several able-bodied soldiers. Wanda was boiling water for the coffee, when suddenly out of nowhere the road was buzzed by an Allied fighter plane whose job was to clear the front for a French attack.

Wanda hit the ground as the plane strafed the bus and the staff car with 50-calibre bullets and then pulled up and away heading north.

Bjorn and Anders ran towards the bus. The German soldiers were dead where they lay with their blood sprayed over the seats. Hoffmann was unconscious after a bullet grazed his head. The entire roof was perforated with bullet holes.

"Let's move the dead outside. We need to help the *Obergefreiter*," Bjorn said.

Hans and Fritz, who had slept in the tall grass with the Swedes, entered the bus to look for their comrades.

"*Hilf mir, bitte*," Bjorn said to Hans, who was looking at his commanding officer and crying.

"*Herr Obergefreiter*, please don't die."

"We will look after him," Bjorn said to the distraught young man. "Please help us move the bodies."

Wanda appeared with a nurse after Hans and Fritz started to carry out the dead. They examined Hoffmann's head wound, which was bleeding profusely, and applied a disinfectant before wrapping his head in gauze.

Suddenly, Hoffmann jerked awake and struggled to stand up. He stumbled to his feet and grabbed his Schmeisser machine gun before running off the bus. Once outside he looked up at the blue sky and remembered the Allied attack. He glanced in astonishment at the Swedish prisoners sitting quietly on the grass and the two young soldiers Hans and Fritz laying a dead soldier down away from the group. In a wild fury he pointed his gun at the prisoners.

"*Tod allen Verrätern!* (Death to all the traitors)" he screamed at the prisoners and fired off several shots with the Schmeisser into the air.

Bjorn looked at the crazy man waving his gun around.

"*Herr Obergefreiter*, it was an Allied fighter plane," Bjorn said. "It just happened. We are not responsible."

"You're lying. Your men signalled to the plane. You planned to kill me and my men."

Wanda stepped off the bus with the nurse and moved away into the tall grass.

"*Er ist kein Verräter*," Wanda said in a loud voice. "He's not a traitor, he's a doctor who saves lives."

"*Herr Doktor*, you gave us the bus and then you signalled to the Allies," Hoffmann said, "you're coming with me."

Hoffmann grabbed Bjorn and, before he could protest, slammed him in the face with the Schmeisser bloodying his nose. He hauled the doctor away.

"*Kommen Sie hier, bitte*," Hoffmann signalled to Hans and Fritz to follow him.

The two young soldiers picked up their guns and followed

their superior officer some fifty yards away from the group. Then Hoffmann ordered Bjorn to kneel.

"*Auf die Knie!*"

The *Obergefreiter* gave Hans his Luger pistol as the doctor went down on his knees.

"*Schießen.* That is an order."

The boy's arm trembled as he pointed the gun at the doctor's head.

"*Schießen,*" Hoffmann yelled.

Wanda ran towards the soldiers.

"*Nicht Schießen, bitte, nicht Schießen,*" she yelled.

Hans broke down in tears and dropped the pistol. Hoffmann picked it up and was about to fire the gun into the back of Bjorn's head, when Rolf suddenly appeared behind him with a Schmeisser machine gun. He didn't hesitate for a moment before opening fire on Hoffman. He emptied the clip at the mad *Obergefreiter* whose body was torn to threads.

"*Der Scheisskerl*, Nazi bastard," Rolf whispered.

Fritz immediately dropped his gun as Hans cried out.

"I'm hit. Don't shoot, please," he said trembling with fear. His lower arm was bloody, hit by a stray bullet.

Wanda rushed over to embrace Bjorn as Anders arrived on the scene. They looked down at the dead *Obergefreiter*.

"Thank you, Rolf," Bjorn said as Wanda helped him to his feet. She had to support the doctor as his legs were shaking and he couldn't walk.

"You saved Bjorn," Anders exclaimed. "You saved us all."

Bjorn and Wanda returned to the bus as Anders took the Schmeisser away from Rolf.

"Where did you learn to shoot?" Anders asked Rolf.

"Swedish military service."

"You did very well, he was going to kill Bjorn."

The prisoners and nurses gathered around Rolf embracing him. Bjorn sat on the grass in silence near the bus, still shaken by his near execution. Wanda returned to examine Hans' bloody arm.

"The bullet went right through," she said, "missing the bone. Can you move your fingers?"

"Yes, I can move them. See."

"You're lucky, young man. We can't leave it like that, let's get you cleaned up."

"I didn't want to kill the doctor," Hans said in a quiet voice.

"The *Obergefreiter* was crazy," Fritz added.

"Patch him up, Wanda," Bjorn said, "and then let's get some food going."

The nurses and volunteers climbed back into the empty bus and hauled the remains of the food into the tall grass to make breakfast. Wanda and a nurse looked after Hans' arm, as the driver slipped under the engine looking for leaks in the gas line. He soon reappeared and gave Bjorn a thumbs-up. The doctor stood up and spoke to his people.

"Good morning, everyone. I know we are disturbed by recent events, myself in particular. No one could have predicted an Allied air attack, but we now have our bus back. We are going to continue with our mission and bring our people north. We will provide food for all of you. Everyone must eat something and then in one hour we will be on our way."

Fifty-nine

Berlin

Count Bernadotte sat naked on a bench wrapped in a towel. He watched as Felix Kersten gave Reichsführer-SS Himmler a massage in a Berlin bath house.

"The springtime in Sweden, Felix. How is it this year?" Himmler asked.

"*Herr Reichsführer*, the spring is early this year," Kersten replied.

"The gardens are in flower," Bernadotte added. "You must come to Sweden after the war is over, Heinrich."

"Yes, I would like that," Himmler said. "I need a favour of you, Folke. I want you to contact General Eisenhower for me. We want to make a separate peace with the Western Allies."

"You want to surrender to the Allies?" Bernadotte croaked in astonishment.

"The Führer is finished. It is time to make peace so we can fight the Soviets together. We will surrender to the Western Allies, but under no condition will we surrender to the Red Army."

"Give me the proposal and I will get it to Eisenhower, Heinrich, but first you must help me with my little problem. I need permission to transport the Scandinavian prisoners to Sweden."

A long silence followed.

"Folke, I have given you the old and sick, the mothers and the children," Himmler said. "You can also have those Danish policemen at Neuengamme. You can send them on to Copenhagen where they will be interned, but that is all I can do at the moment."

Kersten looked at Bernadotte and shrugged his shoulders.

"The camps are costing you a lot of money, Heinrich. You don't need to feed all those prisoners."

"Without prisoners, who will work in our factories?" Himmler said. "We need their labour for the war effort. The Führer will never give them up. I agree to help you, Folke, but we must go slowly."

Lauffen am Neckar, Germany

The bus with its perforated roof headed back the way it had come. This time it took the other fork in the road and went east. The bus interior had been cleaned up and most of the blood had disappeared. Several broken windows had been taped over. The prisoners had been fed and many were already asleep in their seats.

"What will they say at Friedrichsruh when they see us arrive?" Wanda asked.

"They will give us an Iron Cross for our German war effort," Anders said, grinning at his friends.

Wanda and Bjorn laughed as did several of the prisoners who were still awake.

"What shall we do with Hans and Fritz?" Bjorn asked.

"I think we should leave them at Heilbronn," Wanda said.

Bjorn got up and went to the back of the bus to speak to the boys.

"Where shall we take you? We're going north."

"We want to go with you," Hans said.

"You leave us here, they will shoot us as deserters," Fritz said with a resigned expression.

"The war is over, we'll try to go home," Hans said.

"Where is your home?" Bjorn asked.

"Kassel, *Herr Doktor*. We are both from Kassel."

"Well then, we'll take you as close as possible," Bjorn said. "It is near our route. You should be home in a few hours."

"Thank you, *Herr Doktor*, thank you," Hans said. "You know I didn't want to kill you."

"I know," Bjorn replied, squeezing the boy's shoulder.

Young Hans cried openly as Bjorn returned to his seat.

Friedrichsruh, Germany

Count Bernadotte's car arrived at the Swedish Red Cross HQ. It had been a long drive from Berlin. He stepped out and headed towards the entrance. Several tough-looking Gestapo men lounged in the doorway smoking cigarettes. Their job was to keep an eye on the Swedish volunteers. Bernadotte nodded to them as he went inside.

The first thing he noticed was the glum look on the faces of his staff.

"I've just come from Berlin," Bernadotte asked. "What's going on, why the long faces?"

Colonel Björck's secretary got up from his desk and hurried over to Bernadotte.

"We just got a call from *Obersturmbannführer* Pauly at

Neuengamme," the young man said. "We are to stop all rescue operations. The order came from Schellenberg's office."

"But that's not possible!" Bernadotte said. "I've just come from seeing Himmler himself in Berlin."

"The order came in only a few minutes ago, sir."

"Well, that is a stupid order. We have buses all over Germany. I have no way to stop them, even if I wanted to."

"There is something else, sir. A Mr Norbert Masur is here for you from the World Jewish Congress."

"Yes, I know him, but he will have to wait. First, I must call Schellenberg and get this straightened out."

Bernadotte headed to his private office when one of the volunteers stood up from behind a desk.

"We're not going to rescue Jewish prisoners, are we, sir?"

Bernadotte glared at the young man, exasperated. He fought to keep his temper. The man was a volunteer, after all.

"Let me be perfectly clear," he said, raising his voice just enough so everyone in the room could hear, "this is a humanitarian exercise. The Swedish Red Cross is here to save every prisoner it can, whether they are Jewish, Christian or Muslim. No exceptions."

Kassel, Germany

The white bus stopped on a road near the Fulda river. From here the Kassel road went north to Göttingen. The boy soldiers Hans and Fritz shook hands with the prisoners and hugged the medical staff before descending from the bus.

"*Auf wiedersehen, Herr Doktor,*" Hans said.

"*Auf wiedersehen,*" Bjorn replied.

"*Viel Glück,*" Wanda and Anders said, wishing the two

young men good luck on their return to their hometown. Who knows what would await them in the chaos that was Germany.

They watched the two boys walk down to the riverbank in the afternoon sunshine. Hans picked up a flat stone and bounced it off the surface of the water. Then they headed west on a muddy track.

"They are good boys, those two," Wanda said.

"Yes, they are," Anders replied.

He thought for a moment that Germany might have a future after the war with young men like Hans and Fritz. They were good German boys, much like good Swedish boys. They had their whole lives before them and war was not going to be a part of it.

Sixty

"*Vielen Dank, Walter.* Goodbye now," Bernadotte hung up the phone and looked at the expectant faces of his volunteers.

"Schellenberg says he has just countermanded that order from Pauly at Neuengamme. We have permission to move all our prisoners to Denmark but we are to do it very discreetly."

The Swedish volunteers burst into smiles and a round of applause. Colonel Björck's secretary did not join in, waiting for the general excitement to die down before clearing his throat and stepping forward.

"This is excellent news, sir, but how do we move three thousand prisoners in white buses without attracting attention?"

He said it without a trace of irony, but there were pockets of nervous laughter in the room.

"Indeed," Bernadotte conceded, "that's a damn good question. We need to move them as quickly as possible before the Germans change their minds. We'll travel only at night to avoid the Allied bombing and to limit questions from inquisitive Nazis."

"We can do that, sir," the secretary said, "but it will take more time. It's almost 500 kilometres to Copenhagen."

"I agree, but we have no choice," Bernadotte said. "We

must start tonight with every bus we have. Ring Pauly and tell him we will be moving as many people as we can starting as soon as possible."

Stockholm

Major Vladimir Petrov stood in the window smoking a cigarette as he looked out at the flowers blooming in the garden of the Soviet Legation.

"Moscow is sending in a team, Evdokia."

He turned to look at his wife sitting in a chair near the desk applying red nail polish to her carefully manicured fingers.

"We can handle it, Vladimir," Evdokia said. "I don't see why they need to do this."

"They don't like failure. The loss of Grigori and Elena was too much for them. Doctors and nurses with their experience are hard to replace."

"It's not our fault. Perhaps they're in hiding some place or maybe they fled to the West. If they're in Sweden, we'll find them."

"What we know is that Tikander got away and the Swedish police found our bodyguard dead in the canal."

"Tikander got away, but we'll get him the next time."

"Moscow doesn't care about Tikander. They have a new target."

"Who is it?"

"They're not saying. It's top secret."

"They don't trust us."

"They trust no one," Vladimir said. "Let's find Grigori and Elena. If Grigori tipped off the Finns, then we can wash our hands of the Tikander affair."

"I'll find the doctor and nurse if they're still in Sweden,

Vladimir, but I'm worried about this new target. You know their methods. Moscow doesn't realize the damage they can do. We could all be kicked out of Sweden."

"I'm sure they will act with discretion, Evdokia."

Evdokia shook her head in disbelief. Her husband was such an optimist but maybe that was his main strength. He could always put on a good face to any failed operation, a rare ability among the hard men at the NKVD.

Peter entered the basement document room. Bernie was photographing several documents on the Minox copy table.

"Peter, how are you?" Bernie asked. "Your engagement ring isn't quite ready yet."

"That's okay, Bernie."

"When are you planning to pop the question, Peter?"

"I'm not sure, Bernie. I am not very good at this."

"You'll be fine, Peter. Magnus has been busy, but he promised to deliver next week. He's expecting a significant upsurge in diamond prices when peace is declared. The boys will be coming home and getting hitched. Sure you don't want to make an investment?"

Peter shook his head and showed him a three-page document in German.

"I need a microdot copy of this document, Bernie. It's urgent."

"Microdot. Yes, I can do it. Where do you want to put it?"

"Behind the stamp."

"Very good, Peter. I'll do it right now. How big do you want it?"

"I'll leave that up to you, Bernie."

"Let me see," Bernie said looking at the document. "I can reduce it to around 2-3mm in diameter."

Peter thought about Jane receiving an anonymous postcard from Sweden at her house in Walton-on-the-Naze and searching for the microdot behind the stamp. It all sounded quite surreal. Life in the English countryside and postcards with microdots from Sweden.

Sixty-one

It was Wednesday, May 2, 1945. The sun poured into the kitchen of Peter's flat where he was preparing breakfast for Bridget and himself. Peter poured water into the tea kettle and went to collect the paper at the front door. He opened the door and looked at the front page of a local Swedish newspaper. He hurried back inside.

"Bridget. Come out. You have to see this."

Bridget came out of the bathroom in Peter's robe with her wet hair wrapped in a towel.

"What is it, Peter?"

"Look at the headline. Hitler is dead."

Bridget glanced at the front page, emitted a joyful cry and embraced Peter.

"That's wonderful news, maybe the war will be over soon."

"It says that Admiral Donitz is forming a provisional government. What time do you have to be in?" Peter asked as he turned on the radio and played with the dial, trying to get the BBC.

"9 o'clock."

"I think I will go in with you and see what is happening."

"The Legation will be buzzing with all the excitement," Bridget said.

"Yes, it will. I want to get out and pick up the British papers," Peter said. "This is just incredible news."

A BBC news report came on the radio:

"This is London calling. Here is a news flash. The German radio has just announced that Hitler is dead. I will repeat that. The German radio has just announced that Hitler is dead."

Joanna entered the Press Office and ran into Ewan Butler.

"Ewan, what are you doing here?"

"I have to pick up a few things," Ewan said as he searched his desk drawers. "Mallet has got me working weekends, Joanna. It isn't fair."

"Hitler's dead. Have you seen the news?"

"Yes, I have. The war will be coming to an end shortly."

"I haven't seen you in quite a while. When are you coming back to work?"

"I'm not sure I am, Joanna."

Joanna went to her desk and sat down.

"How's Mary?"

"She's kicked me out of the flat. I'm staying at a hotel."

"My God, Ewan. What did you do?" Joanna asked and then thought the question was rather stupid.

Ewan ignored her and poured himself a slug of whisky from a silver flask.

"Anthony Blunt is here," Ewan said, downing the whisky.

"Is he now?"

"I want you to deliver a package to him. He's staying in Mallet's suite at the Grand Hotel. Room 416."

"All right."

"You must leave right away," Ewan insisted, "it's urgent that he get the package immediately. Can you do that?"

"Of course, Ewan."

At the Bromma airfield Anders and a group of Swedish Red Cross volunteers disembarked from a Luft Hansa Ju52. Family and friends awaited them on the tarmac. Among the crowd were Britta and Nils.

"Anders, over here!" Britta yelled over the noise of the crowd.

Anders rushed over to embrace his wife and child.

"Britta my love."

"We missed you terribly," Britta said, weeping with joy. "Give your daddy a kiss, Nils."

Anders embraced young Nils.

"Rolf has left Neuengamme for Copenhagen. He'll be in Malmo in a few days."

"That's wonderful news, Anders. Mamma and Pappa will be so thrilled."

"We were lucky to get out in time, Britta. The air field was in very bad shape. We're waiting on news of a train that left Ravensbrück with some four thousand women prisoners. It was supposed to arrive in Lübeck three days ago. Our ship, the *Magdalena*, is waiting in the harbour to transport them to Sweden. The situation is very desperate now with prisoners from camps all over Germany trying to get out."

Joanna arrived at the Grand Hotel and went upstairs. She knocked quietly at room 416. Anthony Blunt opened the door and took the package from her.

"Thank you, Miss Dunn. Please come in a moment."

"Of course, sir."

Joanna stepped into the luxurious suite and Blunt closed the door. In the living room there was a breakfast tray with two cups and a coffee thermos.

"Please sit down," Blunt gestured towards a chair. "Would you like some coffee, Joanna?"

"No thank you, sir."

Blunt poured himself a coffee and then sat down.

"Tell me about your brother."

Sixty-two

Karl-Heinz Kramer was talking on the phone in his office as Peter Faye appeared at the front door of the German Press Office.

"I know the market is getting nervous, Herr Golcher. How much are they offering?"

Karl-Heinz stood up and looked at the new arrival.

"That's a ridiculous offer for a Degas," Karl-Heinz said. "I will have to call you back."

Karl-Heinz hung up and went to the front desk.

"*Guten morgen*," Karl-Heinz said. "We're closed. I'm sorry, sir."

Peter approached and Karl-Heinz finally recognized him.

"Mr Faye. What a pleasant surprise!"

"So what are your plans for the peace, Dr Kramer?" Peter said. "Your Führer is dead."

"Yes, he is. Berlin has fallen and we have a new government."

"The Dönitz government is doomed to fail, sooner or later. The Americans are mopping up any resistance."

"Admiral Dönitz is in Flensburg. He's a good man and doing the best he can to surrender our forces to the Western Allies. There is great fear among our people of Soviet

314

reprisals."

"Yes, I am sure there is."

"You haven't come here to lord over us poor Germans the loss of the war," Karl-Heinz said with a laugh.

"Of course, not. The war has been lost for quite some time."

"Yes, I agree. The Führer made one disastrous decision after another. It was inevitable. Can I offer you some coffee or a schnapps, perhaps?"

"Please, schnapps."

Karl-Heinz pulled a bottle from his desk drawer and two glasses. He poured the schnapps and lifted his glass.

"*Prosit.*"

"Cheers. To the peace."

"To the peace. I'm afraid I no longer have a job," Karl-Heinz said. "Our people are staying at home, listening to the news reports. No one wants to return to Germany."

"I believe your boss Walter Schellenberg is still at it, working in the shadows," Peter said.

"He likes his job, Mr Faye. He wants to remain at the helm until the peace is signed. He has a lot of secrets for sale. Perhaps the Americans or you British will make a deal with him."

Peter downed the schnapps.

"How about we go for a walk or a drive?"

"That's a wonderful idea. It's very depressing working in an empty office."

"Do you still have that wonderful DKW?"

"Of course, Mr Faye. We can go for a drive in it if you like."

At the newspaper Anders entered Lundquist's office.

"Anders, you're back. Have you seen the news?"

"Yes, I have. The war should be over soon."

"How's your brother-in-law?" Lundquist asked.

"Rolf will be in Malmo in a few days."

"Wonderful news. Have you started working on your report?"

"Yes, I've written a good deal of it, my adventures in Germany," Anders said. "It may be a too long. How do you want to go with the story?"

"I sent Stefan to Malmo. He called me an hour ago to tell me he had pictures of the Ravensbrück women on the ferry. We shall have them here by tonight. We need to put something together for tomorrow's publication if you're ready."

"No problem, sir. I will lead with the story about the Ravensbrück women and how they were released."

"Excellent. It's good to have you back, Anders. We were all very worried about you tramping around Germany with the war on."

Karl-Heinz and Peter drove along the canal road in the white DKW. They pulled off the road into a lovely park running along the canal. They climbed out and walked slowly on a footpath towards the water.

"An *Abwehr* document has come into my hands, Dr Kramer," Peter said. "You remember a Soviet agent by the code-name of Otto?"

Karl-Heinz raised his eyebrows. He had been hoping that MI6 might require his services and make him an offer. He wouldn't mind working for the British secret services. He reminded himself not to appear too eager.

"Perhaps."

"Arnold Deutsch. He was an Austrian who was arrested by

the German police in 1933, but was later released. A PhD in chemistry, I believe, from the University of Vienna."

"I think I remember seeing something to that effect," Karl-Heinz said. "This Otto, didn't he have a woman companion? Her name was Edith I think."

"You have a very good memory, Dr Kramer," Peter said. "Yes, Edith Suschitzky, the photographer. She had a very good friend in Vienna, Litzi Friedman, born Alice Kohlmann."

"This is old history I think, Mr Faye."

"Yes, it is. The *Abwehr* under Canaris was very active in Spain during the Civil War. The report I have mentions a certain correspondent of *The Times* attached to General Franco's forces."

"Now, I know who you are talking about. Kim Philby. He was decorated by Franco."

"Yes, he was, after he survived a bombing that killed three other journalists. According to the report, Philby married Litzi Friedman in 1934 in Vienna and was recruited by Litzi and Edith as a Soviet agent. Otto and Edith were recruiting agents in London throughout the 1930s."

"You know Canaris loved Spain, perhaps more than he did Germany," Karl-Heinz said. "He spoke excellent Spanish and was very active in Spain. I remember this Philby had a friend in the *Abwehr*: a man by the name of Von der Osten, Ulrich. His code-name was Don Julio. I think it's Don Julio who filed that report."

"So you think the report is genuine?"

"Absolutely, I remember it."

"I heard that Canaris was executed at Flossenburg about a month ago," Peter said.

"A very big loss for Germany," Karl-Heinz said. "Not just for Germany, but for the Western Allies. Admiral Canaris was a very great man, a courageous man who stood up to Hitler."

"Yes, he was. It's unfortunate he was linked to the July bomb plot against Hitler."

"He had nothing to do with it. I know that for a fact. It was guilt by association."

"I'm sorry to hear it."

"This Philby is now an important man at MI5 I think. Section IX and perhaps a Soviet spy?"

"The evidence seems to suggest it," Peter said. "Krivitsky, after he defected to the US, told us that Moscow had an agent, an Englishman who was sent to Spain as a journalist."

Karl-Heinz smiled at Peter.

"Sounds like a match to me with the wife a communist sympathizer. I think you British need a good German intelligence officer to help you sort out your Soviet spies."

"We better get back, Dr Kramer."

The two men turned around and walked back to the car.

"You remember Hanne Gabor, Mr Faye, my cleaning woman. She talked under sodium pentothal. I thought it was curious that a Hietzinger Jew from Vienna chose to work for my family."

Peter remained silent.

"She called herself 'Mata Hanne' as a joke. It didn't take long for the Gestapo to discover her treachery, but I must say I was against sending her back to Germany. I'm happy your people managed to save her. She would surely have been executed in Berlin."

Sixty-three

In the evening Peter and Bridget were playing Crazy Eights at the kitchen table when they heard a knock at the door.

"I'll get it," Peter said, putting down his cards and going to open the door to the flat.

A small man stood on the threshold in the uniform of a BOAC airlines pilot.

"Can I help you?" Peter asked.

"Hello there. You speak English. Very good. I am a friend of Jane Archer. I have a letter here for Peter Faye. Is that you?"

"Yes, thank you."

"Can I see your identification papers?" the pilot asked.

Peter went to get his passport and showed it to the man who glanced briefly at it before handing the letter to Peter.

"Are you a pilot?"

"Yes, I am. I'm with BOAC. I fly into Stockholm quite often. Jane is my aunt, Mr Faye. She asked me to wait for your reply. I can come back in an hour or two if you like. I am with some American blokes having a few drinks on the town celebrating Hitler's demise."

"Of course. Yes, I will reply to Jane, give me an hour."

"See you later, then."

The BOAC pilot left and Peter closed the door. He put on

his reading glasses and sat down to read the letter.

"Any news?" Bridget asked.

Peter stood up and put Mozart on the gramophone, turning up the sound as a precaution.

"The *Abwehr* report has confirmed Jane's suspicions about Philby. She worked for several months for the man in Section IX, the Anti-Soviet Section. Philby put her on radio traffic analysis and then she was eased out of her job."

"So she suspects Philby?" Bridget asked.

"Yes, she does. She says she mentioned her suspicions to Guy Liddell and then put out a feeler very discreetly to the Foreign Office, but they are not in the mind to heed any warnings about Soviet agents, not with the VE day celebrations around the corner. She suggests that I take the Onodera offer to the Americans, to Wilho Tikander."

"Tikander owes you, Peter," Bridget said from the kitchen as she made tea.

"Tikander can get the *Abwehr* report to Allen Dulles in Bern. Then maybe the Americans can put some pressure on our intelligence services."

Peter read the letter a second time and then struck a match, holding it to the bottom of the letter, before dropping it into the ashtray. He picked up his fountain pen and started to write a reply to Jane on a piece of stationery.

On May 5, 1945 a Swedish official limousine drove through the streets of the old city with the flag on its bonnet, followed by two motorcycle outriders and preceded by a security car. Ordinary Swedish people gathered on the street to watch the procession.

In the crowd Anders and Stefan raced along near the car. A

window came down and Himmler's *Sonderbevollmächtigter* and head of SD foreign intelligence Walter Schellenberg, now a minister in Dönitz's provisional government, waved at the crowd gathered in the road. Stefan snapped pictures of Schellenberg in the moving car.

"I got him, Anders."

"What's Schellenberg doing in Sweden?" Anders asked.

"He must be a guest of the government."

Anders and Stefan headed back to their car.

"I wonder what he's up to meeting with our government," Anders said. "Maybe he's seeking asylum here in Sweden."

"He's a war criminal," Stefan said. "They'll never allow it."

The limousine and its entourage turned the corner and headed south towards Trosa. After about an hour they turned into the main gate at Tullgarn, the eighteenth century summer palace of the Swedish royal family. Schellenberg descended from the limousine to a formal welcome by Folke Bernadotte, the Swedish minister Von Post and the Foreign Secretary Eric Bohemann. Various porters handled the German's baggage and the men headed towards the main entrance surrounded by flowers in full bloom.

Schellenberg had long been accustomed to the trappings of power in his senior position in the RSHA, but as the Swedes ushered him into the palace he realised that his new ministerial position had taken him to an entirely different level. He could only hope it would last for a while.

Peter walked along a footpath near the canal. It was a quiet morning and there were few people about. A black sedan followed him on the road, stopping a hundred yards away. Conscious of the surveillance, Peter surmised that the Säpo car had been tailing him for quite some time.

He started to walk faster, looking down into the canal where there were several work boats with private docks running parallel to the shore. A few old men were out and about mopping the decks of their boats. He maintained a quick pace, checking the vehicle behind him from time to time. There were three men in the car. He kept walking until he heard the sound of an engine accelerating. He turned just in time to see the black sedan jumping the curb and heading straight for him. With a fraction of a second to spare, he threw himself off the footpath into the canal and landed in the murky water near the dock. The car quickly swung back onto the road and continued on its way.

The cold water and the adrenaline rush shocked him into action. He grabbed hold of a ladder and quickly pulled himself dripping wet up onto the private dock. He stood up, fumbling for his revolver as an old gent saluted him for his morning dip.

"God Morgon," the old man said with a grin.

Peter ignored the friendly Swede and started up the boat ramp. Somehow the Webley had remained in his pocket and he pulled it out as he got to the top of the ramp. He looked around but the car had disappeared.

Ten minutes later Peter limped into a popular dockside restaurant looking for Bridget. She was seated near several young Americans who were drinking beer on the terrace. Her eyes widened in alarm as she saw his sodden clothes.

"Lovely morning," Peter said as he sat down.

"What happened to you?" Bridget asked.

"I fell into the canal."

"Just like that?"

"Well, not just like that. I had to jump into the canal to avoid being hit by a car," Peter signalled for the waiter, "I'm actually quite lucky to be alive."

Bridget started to say something but stopped herself when the waiter appeared at their table. Peter was dripping water on the terrace, but the man pretended not to notice.

"A double Macallan and a coffee, please."

Bridget waited for the man to leave and then put a hand on Peter's arm.

"Peter, that's what happened to Keith in London."

"I know."

"Are you sure you're all right?"

"I sprained an ankle," Peter shrugged, "and my pride is hopelessly damaged, but other than that I'm fine."

"Peter, you can't just be walking around like that. Bernie's right, you need protection."

Peter smiled at Bridget and remembered the engagement ring burning a hole in his pocket. He pulled out the small box and put it on the table.

"What's that?" Bridget asked.

"Open it."

"Oh, Peter!"

The waiter arrived with the whisky and coffee. Peter shivered in his wet clothes and drank some whisky. He then picked up the box and opened it for Bridget.

"I want to marry you, Bridget," Peter announced with a determined air.

"Are you sure you are all right?"

Peter's heart sank as he saw her frown.

"Somebody just tried to kill you and you fell into the canal and you're soaking wet and..."

"I'm fine, Bridget."

Peter slowly removed the engagement ring, admiring Bernie's diamond and Magnus' fine work setting it in a gold ring. He took a moment to dump the remaining water in the box on the floor as Bridget laughed.

He looked her in the eyes, then took her left hand and slipped the ring on her finger. It fit perfectly.

"What a lovely ring, Peter!" Bridget said. "Are you sure?"

"Of course, I'm sure. I love you. I want to marry you."

Sixty-four

The Stockholms-Tidningen and Aftonbladet newspapers both featured front page photographs of Schellenberg waving from a Swedish government car.

"Look at the Aftonbladet," Bridget said indignantly, "it used to be pro-German and now it's criticizing the government for working with a Nazi war criminal. It says that the government is offering him Swedish citizenship."

Peter had just come into the office with the newspapers and dumped them unceremoniously on Bridget's desk.

"Well, Schellenberg did help Bernadotte save thousands of Scandinavian prisoners from German concentration camps," Peter said. "That's a strong argument in his favour."

Bernie knocked on the door and entered.

"Hello Peter, Bridget."

"Hello, Bernie," Bridget said, removing the newspapers from her desk.

"Is that an engagement ring I see on your finger, Bridget?"

"Yes, it is. Peter and I are planning to get married."

"Congratulations to you both. When do you think you will tie the knot?"

"We don't know yet," Bridget said, "but you will be the first to know."

"Thanks for coming," Peter said. "I called you because we have a bit of a security problem."

"A bit of a problem!" Bridget exclaimed. "Peter was almost run over on the weekend."

Bernie dropped into the nearest chair.

"You better tell me the whole story."

"Cup of tea, Bernie?" Bridget asked.

"Please."

Bridget went to fetch the tea as Peter sat down in Bridget's chair.

"I was in London recently to see my boss at MI6. He's an old friend of mine, Major Keith Linwood. He was struck from behind by a car at the corner of Broadway and Victoria Street. The car jumped the curb and crushed his legs. He's now in a wheelchair. He could have been killed."

"So you think the same people are after you?" Bernie asked.

"I was walking on the footpath near the canal when a car jumped the curb. I was lucky. I threw myself into the canal at the last moment."

"You jumped into the bleedin' canal? Were you hurt?"

"No, I fell into the water and was able to pull myself out."

"Did you recognize any of your attackers?"

"No, all I remember is that there were three men in the car."

"Were they German?"

"It happened so fast, they'd scarpered before I got out of the water."

Bridget handed Bernie a cup of tea.

"I think someone is trying to get a message to you, Peter."

"A message?" Bridget exclaimed. "Someone is trying to kill him."

"I rather agree with Bernie," Peter said. "If they wanted to kill me, they would have stayed to finish the job."

"For an ordinary bloke working at a desk job," Bernie said,

"you seem to be attracting a lot of attention."

Peter shrugged.

"I know you met with that Saarson chap and that Jap general recently, but who have you really teed off, Peter? Outside of the NKVD, the 'Svestapo', and the Germans?"

"The war is over, Bernie," Bridget said. "It's got to be the Russians."

"Bridget, please," Peter said.

"This might not be the local boys," Bernie said, "but a hit squad. Same MO as in London."

"A hit squad? Peter!" Bridget exclaimed.

Peter frowned at Bernie.

"They want to make it look like an accident. You remember the Sedov case."

"Yes, Bernie. Yes, I do."

"Who is Sedov?" Bridget asked.

Peter decided that Bernie had said enough. He glared a warning at him before turning to Bridget.

"Just a Russian chap in Paris," he said dismissively, "an old story Tennant likes to tell."

The waterfront bar was popular with foreign journalists and military personnel. It was very crowded, and it took Peter a few moments to locate the man he was looking for and push his way to the bar.

"Ewan, how are you?"

Ewan looked lost and miserable, alone among the lunchtime crowd, and his eyes lit up with the prospect of company.

"Well, well. You got my message, Peter. It's a pleasure to see you old chap."

"It's been quite some time," Peter said. "How is the angry

rabbit treating you?"

"That bastard can go to hell. What can I get you, Peter?"

"A whisky, please."

"Bring a Macallan for my friend," Ewan told the bartender in a loud voice slurring his words.

"So what is Schellenberg doing at Tullgarn?"

"I can't talk about it, Peter."

"They're saying he's looking for Swedish citizenship."

"I wouldn't know about that. Officially he's here to negotiate the surrender of 400,000 German soldiers in Norway. He sent the German ambassador to the border to talk to General Boehme who has refused to recognize the Dönitz government."

The waiter brought the whisky for Peter.

"Cheers, Peter," Ewan said.

"Cheers, Ewan."

They clinked their glasses.

"Let's drink to a speedy end to the war," Peter said.

The two men sipped their whisky as lively conversations sprang up around them.

"Schellenberg is a nasty piece of work," Peter said.

"Not for us, he isn't," Ewan insisted. "He's going to be a big man in intelligence circles, mark my words. His secret files will be worth a bloody fortune in the West."

"You still working with Anthony Blunt?"

"I can't talk about that, Peter," Ewan said, "but I can tell you that Mr Blunt has taken an interest in our Joanna."

"Joanna?"

"Yes, I sent Joanna to deliver some papers to Blunt the other day at the Grand Hotel and he's requested that she provide him with assistance in whatever he is doing."

"Joanna is SOE. She shouldn't be working with Blunt."

"I agree, Peter. I thought you might be interested."

"Joanna doesn't have the clearance to work with Blunt."

"Agreed, Peter."

"Have you asked her about the meeting?"

"I haven't seen her."

A huge party was underway at the British Legation celebrating the 'Victory in Europe' day. The German High Command in the person of General Alfred Jodl had signed an unconditional surrender on May 7 of all German forces. The war in Europe was officially over. Victor Mallet had pulled out all the stops for the celebration with an open bar and party decorations. Numerous Americans were in attendance, including Wilho Tikander and Ambassador Hershel Johnson, who was chatting with Mallet and his wife. Peter and Bridget joined Bernie and Wilho.

"Bridget, this is Wilho Tikander from the American Legation," Bernie said.

"Good evening, Bridget, Peter," Wilho said.

"You were looking just a little bit pale the last time I saw you, Wilho," Peter said with a laugh.

"Yes, I remember very well," Wilho said.

"Hello, Bridget," Sabrina said as she arrived with a glass of white wine for herself and a whisky for Bernie.

"Sabrina. It's so good to see you."

"I heard about your engagement. Bernie tried to keep it a secret, but I pestered him long enough that he let it slip."

"I'm sorry, Peter," Bernie said. "I only told Sabrina."

"Bridget, I never got around to thanking you for Aksell's award. He's preparing his acceptance speech and so looking forward to travelling to Britain. Bernie and I are trying to diminish the importance of the award, but it doesn't seem to be working."

"Well, well. You know Peter and I never thought about the long term consequences of handing out a bogus award."

Sabrina and Bridget laughed as a blonde woman in a tight dress picked up a microphone and started to sing *Boogie Woogie Bugle Boy* accompanied by three black musicians. Peter and Bridget joined the crowd on the dance floor.

Outside the hall with its VE Day balloons and decorations, Peter was on his way to the men's room when he bumped into Anthony Blunt.

"Mr Blunt. I didn't expect to see you here?"

"Well, well. I do try to get around. How are you by the way?" Blunt asked with genuine curiosity.

"I'm fine, sir. A wonderful night."

"Yes, it is. I'm here consulting with your colleague Ewan Butler. Top secret work, I'm afraid," Blunt said.

"Yes, I heard, sir," Peter said. "Major Linwood chewed me out about it, so I have kept my distance."

"Good advice. Poor Linwood, he had that terrible traffic accident not so long ago. Someone ran over him and now he's in a wheelchair."

"Yes, I know, sir."

"The poor man's gotten into his head all kinds of conspiracy theories, quite ridiculous assertions if you don't mind me saying so. We had to get rid of him. He took early retirement."

"Early retirement?" Peter asked, stunned by the news. "I thought he was still away on sick leave. I've known Keith from prep school, sir. He's not one to exaggerate or to make ridiculous assertions."

"How's Jane?" Blunt asked.

"Jane, sir?"

"Jane Archer. We got a report about your visit to her home from security. She has quite a lovely cottage in Essex, Walton-on-the-Naze, I think the town is called. She's a very valuable member of the intelligence community."

Peter was stunned and could only stare.

"Well, it's been a pleasure, Faye. Keep up the good work."

"Good-bye, sir."

Peter returned to the party in a state of shock and joined Bridget, Sabrina and Bernie. The blonde singer and band were playing *There'll Be Bluebirds over the White Cliffs of Dover* and the dance floor was packed with couples. Many a tear flowed from the cheeks of the British staff hearing Vera Lynn's sentimental song.

Peter pulled Bridget aside.

"I just ran into Anthony Blunt," Peter said. "He said that Keith was forced to take early retirement. He knows about my visit to Jane Archer."

"What's he doing in Stockholm?" Bridget asked.

"I've heard that he's involved in the discussions with Schellenberg. The Swedish government has kicked him out of Tullgarn so he's staying with Folke Bernadotte at his summer cottage."

"Well, he doesn't suspect you of anything, does he?"

"He knows of my concerns, Bridget. He knows I've been talking to Jane and Keith."

"Well, you better keep out of it or you could lose your job."

Sixty-five

It was late as Peter and Bridget packed their bags. Bridget put some shirts in a suitcase as Peter entered the bedroom with his dirty laundry bag. They had decided to move out of the flat temporarily as a safety precaution.

"Which suit are you taking with you, Peter?"

"The new one."

Bridget took the suit off the hanger and folded it into his suitcase.

"Have you got everything?" Bridget asked, as she closed the case.

"Yes, I think so."

"Bernie said to leave a light on."

Across the street on the roof of an old warehouse, an NKVD watcher observed Peter's flat and saw Bridget standing in the living room window before she turned away. He signalled to a second agent with white hair who started across the street towards Peter's building.

At the door Peter held Bridget's coat for her and then put on his own. They left the flat and started down the stairs.

The NKVD agent waited near the entrance, listening to the sounds coming from the building. He could hear a radio on the first floor and footsteps on the stairs. He started up and soon ran into Peter and Bridget on their way down, carrying their bags. He nodded politely to them and continued on his way up.

Peter whispered in Bridget's ear.

"Who's that?"

"Perhaps a neighbour, Peter."

"I don't think so. I've never seen him before," Peter said as they hurried down the stairs.

The agent had decided to give their target a head start, to avoid panicking them inside the building. He let them get ahead of him and then turned, following the noise of their footsteps on the stairs, as he descended to the entrance. He ran out into the street, looking around for his colleague. A man was parked near the curb and stuck his head out of a car door. With his hands raised, he indicated that he hadn't seen anyone exit the building.

Meanwhile Peter and Bridget had slipped out the back door and ran down the alley to the Legation car parked out of sight.

"Everything all right?" Bernie asked.

"There was a man on the stairs," Peter said. "I had never seen him before."

"I couldn't see anyone watching your flat, but I would assume they are."

"They?" Bridget asked.

"These NKVD blokes don't work alone, Bridget, there will be at least three of them."

Bridget exchanged a look with Peter and then got into the back of the car. Peter closed the door and got in next to Bernie in the front seat. They drove away and after a short ride pulled up in front of a hotel in Gamla Stan. Peter and Bridget went to the front desk to check in, while Bernie brought in their bags.

The following morning Peter was led down the hall by a

secretary at the US Legation and entered a spacious office.

"Nice to see you again, Peter," Wilho said, shaking hands.

"How are things?"

"Busy. Americans are flocking to Sweden to get in on the reconstruction planned for Germany."

"Isn't it a bit early to rebuild?" Peter asked. "There's a humanitarian catastrophe going on."

"Of course, but you know how Americans are."

"So what will you do, Wilho, now that the war is over?"

"I don't know, Peter, but a lot is happening. I heard from a Swedish colleague that a Luft Hansa Ju52 arrived this morning at Bromma. You know what they found on board?"

"No, I'm afraid not."

"Six zinc-lined trunks with the warning '*streng geheim*' and the SS insignia stamped on them. They are believed to be Schellenberg's top secret files."

"It sounds to me like there is going to be a lot of horse trading going on," Peter remarked.

"Yes, US Army intelligence in Frankfurt wants it all and they don't care who they deal with," Wilho said with a sly grin.

"London will surely be in on the bidding."

Wilho nodded as his secretary brought in a carafe of coffee and cups. She poured the coffee and left. Peter took a sip and grimaced.

"Sorry about the coffee, Peter. American coffee is pretty bad, but our ambassador refuses to find a good Swedish supplier and has this stuff shipped in from the US."

"I hear that our Finnish friends have moved all their radio intelligence personnel and cryptography materiel to Sweden," Peter said.

"Yes, the Stella Polaris operation."

Peter remembered that Colonel Hallamaa had described

the plan to evacuate all Finnish radio intelligence personnel and equipment in the case of a Soviet occupation of the country. After the Soviets had signed an armistice with the new president Mannerheim in Helsinki, Colonel Hallamaa activated the plan and brought over some 750 people including intelligence officers and their families on four ships. They were now working for the Swedish government and any other clients they could find.

"A brilliant coup," Peter said.

"Yes, it was," Wilho said. "The RTK is selling a treasure trove of keys for deciphering Soviet army and NKVD codes to the Swedes and the Japanese."

Peter sipped his coffee.

"I need your help, Wilho."

"Sure, what can I do for you?"

"You know Jane Archer, I believe," Peter said with a serious air. "She was brought in to interrogate the Soviet defector Krivitsky."

"Of course, Peter. Jane is a legend at MI5."

"I need a favour."

Peter pulled out an envelope containing a copy of the *Abwehr* document he had received from Onodera and laid it on the desk.

"This envelope contains a secret document that I need you to send to Allen Dulles in Bern, Switzerland, by diplomatic courier. You are not to look at it for your own safety, Wilho."

"For my own safety, Peter?" Wilho said wide-eyed.

"Let me just say that this is rather sensitive material and that there are certain people who might want to suppress its distribution. I mean it when I say for your own safety."

"Why don't you send it yourself, Peter? You could send it in your own diplomatic bag."

"I'm afraid I can't. It would raise too many red flags. You'll have to trust Jane and me on this. It won't harm your career, nothing in the document will have any effect on the US mission in Sweden. That's all I can say."

Wilho looked down at the envelope as if it were suddenly red hot.

"OK, Peter. I owe you, but don't ask me to do this again."

"Thank you."

Sixty-six

Count Bernadotte's car pulled up outside the British Legation office. The driver opened the door to Folke Bernadotte and Walter Schellenberg who climbed the stone stairway to the entrance. Schellenberg had lost his official role and was now a private citizen and also a war criminal. A crowd had gathered at the gate and was held back by several guards. Jostled by the crowd, Anders and Stefan managed to find a decent vantage point and Stefan took pictures of the two men as they turned to look briefly at the crowd from the doorway.

In the hall leading to the conference room, Bernadotte and Schellenberg shook hands with the Legation staff who had been lined up in the hallway and put on their best behaviour at the request of their chief.

"This is Bridget Potter and Peter Faye of our Consular Services office," Mallet said.

"Good day," Peter said, shaking hands.

"A pleasure, sir," Bridget said.

"Ah, Mr Faye," Schellenberg smiled. "I have heard about you from some of my colleagues. I am happy to meet you at last."

"Yes, sir," Peter mumbled.

The remaining staff shook Bernadotte's hand, but were

rather hesitant to shake the hand of the famous Nazi so greetings were short and subdued. Mallet hustled his guests into the first floor conference room. As soon as they were seated, he pulled the door closed as Ewan Butler snuck in at the last moment with a heavy briefcase.

Peter and Bridget took the stairs to Consular Services when a secretary called.

"Mr Faye. I have a call for you."

Peter descended to the lobby to take the call, leaving Bridget on the stairs on her way to the office.

"Who is it?" Peter asked.

"A policeman, sir."

Peter frowned and picked up the phone.

Peter entered his apartment building and ran into a Swedish fire inspector in a yellow tunic, boots and a fireman's hat coming out.

"What happened?"

"Are you the lodger on the top floor?" the fireman asked in accented English.

"Yes, I am."

"There's been a fire in your flat, sir. What's your name?"

"Peter Faye. I work at the British Legation."

"The fire started sometime last night, a slow burning fire."

"I left the flat at around 11 p.m. and stayed the night in a hotel, so I don't know anything about a fire."

"Let's go up."

Peter and the fireman climbed the stairs. Near the landing Peter could see the blackened walls from the smoke. He followed the fireman through the fire-damaged flat. His precious record collection was a melted ruin near the wrecked gramophone. There was nothing left to save. Peter looked around in shock.

"You see the intense charring on the walls. This was a slow, smouldering fire, probably started with a lighter and fed with paper and the curtains," the fireman said with a suspicious air.

"You think someone deliberately set fire to my flat?"

"The door was unlocked and a window was open to create a draft. Did you leave the door unlocked, Mr Faye?"

"No, the door was locked and the window was shut."

"This is clearly a case of arson. I have already reported it to the police. They will be calling on you."

Peter left the building and headed back to the Legation office. As he crossed a side street, he felt a sudden biting pain in his shoulder. He discovered a tranquillizer dart stuck in his shoulder and looked around for the assailant. There was no one around. He started walking fast, trying to get away from the area, but soon two NKVD thugs took up the chase. Across the street he saw a man with white hair put a long box into the backseat of his car.

Peter felt nauseous and faint. A woman approached and noticed his unsteady gait, thinking that he was just another drunk Swede. The two Russians easily caught up with Peter and grabbed his arms. They turned him around and headed back towards their car. Suddenly, they were interrupted by a voice from across the street.

"Peter! What happened?" Anders asked, crossing the street.

"Anders," Peter murmured, slurring his speech.

The two Russians stepped away as Anders arrived.

"I heard someone set fire to your flat."

Anders watched the two Russians reluctantly return to their car as Stefan arrived.

"Careful, Anders. I think he's going to be sick."

"Peter, are you all right?"

Peter collapsed onto the pavement just as Anders grabbed his arm.

"He's out cold. Is he drunk? We better find him a doctor."

"Let's take him to your place, Anders. It's closest."

Young Nils played with a toy airplane in the living room near Peter in shirt sleeves and unconscious under a blanket on the chesterfield. The boy made airplane noises as he buzzed Peter's face. Anders and Britta entered the room and noticed that their friend was coming around.

"We were worried about you, Peter," Anders said. "I had a doctor come in to take look. We saw blood on your shirt. We think you were shot with a tranquillizer dart."

Peter sat up suffering from a terrible headache.

"You brought me here?" Peter asked.

"Yes," Anders replied.

"I will get you some tea," Britta said. "You need to drink a lot, doctor's orders."

Britta left for the kitchen.

"You are going to be okay," Anders said, "but you need to rest up a bit. I think somebody doesn't like you, Peter. They torched your flat and then shot you with a dart."

Britta returned with a mug of tea and handed it to Peter who took a sip.

"I talked to a policeman at the site. The fireman said it was arson," Peter said. "Bridget and I saw a strange man with white hair, climbing the stairs when we left the flat last night."

"Who would want to torch your flat?" Anders asked.

"I really don't know."

340

Sixty-seven

Anders drove Peter back to the Legation.

"I heard you were able to find your wife's brother in the camps in Germany, Anders."

"Yes, Rolf is arriving by ferry to Malmo tonight."

"That's wonderful," Peter said. "Bernadotte and his white buses have achieved the impossible."

"It was quite an adventure, Peter. Look I need your help with something. We have a photograph of Walter Schellenberg entering the British Legation. The paper wants me to write a report on what is going on with the British. Can you tell me anything at all?"

"There is some kind of deal going down with Mallet but I can't tell you much. I would imagine that Schellenberg is looking for immunity from prosecution for war crimes for Himmler and for himself, but that is just a guess."

"I met Schellenberg in Germany with Bernadotte on my first visit. He was very helpful. Without him, I doubt we would ever have succeeded in bringing out our people."

"So you think Sweden should give him a visa to live in this country?"

"No, he's a war criminal. Public opinion is strongly against keeping him here."

"Schellenberg was Himmler's right hand man, Anders," Peter said. "He knows where all the bodies are buried. That's why the Brits and the Americans are after him."

"I think you may be right."

They drove into the Legation car park and Anders helped Peter stumble through the main entrance into the lobby. He collapsed on a chair in the waiting area as Anders approached the receptionist.

"Miss, can you have Bridget Potter called? Tell her Peter Faye is downstairs and is feeling poorly."

"Of course."

The receptionist called Bridget on the interior line and then got up to fetch a glass of water for Peter.

"Drink some water, Mr Faye. Bridget is on her way down."

Peter took the glass and drank as Bridget arrived.

"Peter, are you all right?" Bridget asked. "I heard about the fire. What happened?"

"Someone torched his flat," Anders said.

"The door was unlocked and a window was open," Peter said. "The fireman thinks it was arson."

"But we locked the door last night."

"I know."

"Someone shot Peter with a tranquillizer dart, Bridget."

Bridget looked alarmed.

"I was on the street, coming back here when I was struck by a dart. I couldn't believe it," Peter said. "It was lucky Anders and Stefan were there to help me."

After work Bridget and Peter went to their hotel and were packing, when Bernie knocked on the door.

"Sorry about your flat, Peter," Bernie said as Peter opened the door.

"Thanks, Bernie," Peter replied.

"I heard they tried to take you out with a tranquillizer dart. These NKVD blighters aren't messing around."

"What can we do?" Bridget asked as she emerged from the bathroom.

"If they can't grab you off the street, they will try to destroy your life here. Flush you out of Stockholm where you will be easy prey."

"Is there any way to call them off?" Peter asked.

"I doubt it, they probably get their orders from Moscow."

"Why don't we go to the police?" Bridget asked. "We can ask for their protection."

"I think the police suspect Peter of arson, Bridget," Bernie said. "They aren't going to move very fast to protect him."

"Are you sure we need to change hotels?" Bridget asked.

"These bastards mean business, Bridget," Bernie replied. "We can't take the chance that they are checking hotel registers."

"We better get going," Peter said, picking up his suitcase and passing Bridget's valise to Bernie.

"We'll go out the back," Bernie said. "My car is parked on the side street."

"A Polish submarine captain is asked: 'Suppose you see a German and a Soviet cruiser in your periscope. Which one do you attack first?'"

Federmann smiled as he told the story, sitting in his booth at the nightclub, puffing on a cigar.

"'Of course the German one, duty always comes before pleasure.'"

Peter and Bridget laughed at the joke as they sat opposite

Der Grosse watching the floorshow. A waiter served him a cognac and champagne for Peter and Bridget. It was a relatively quiet night and most of the customers were American GIs celebrating the victory in Europe. Even the scantily clad chorus girls seemed to put on a lacklustre performance. It was as if the war was at an end and so was the cabaret floorshow.

"The war was good for business, Mr Faye, but now with the peace, we don't know anything."

"Yes, sir."

"Bernie called me about your little problem," Federmann gestured towards his bodyguard, "Karl here will take you upstairs. You should be safe here for a couple of days."

"Thank you."

"And who is this lovely lady with you?"

"Her name is Bridget, sir. She works at the Legation."

"Have you ever done any dancing, miss? We're missing a girl."

"No, I am afraid not. Sorry," Bridget said with a laugh.

Bernie arrived with their bags and signalled them from the entrance.

"Well, off you go then," Federmann said.

Peter and Bridget stood up and thanked the man again, before joining Bernie at the entrance.

"Karl here will look after you," Bernie said. "You're in safe hands."

"Thanks, Bernie," Peter said. "You better get on home now, Sabrina will be worried."

"Cheerio, see you in the morning."

Karl led Peter and Bridget upstairs, past a large dressing room, a carpentry shop and storage rooms for stage flats and decorations, before entering a small flat on the third floor at the back of the building.

"We're open until 3 a.m.," Karl told them, checking the windows, "so there will be some noise in the hallway. Good night."

"Good night, Karl. Thank you," Peter said.

Bridget stood in the living room of the spartan flat, glumly taking in her surroundings. In addition to the living room, the flat had a tiny kitchen, bathroom and small bedroom with two single beds that were little more than cots.

"It's only until we get sorted out, Bridget."

She gave him a wan smile.

"We'll be safe here, Peter, that's all I care about."

Bernie headed home. He pulled the Opel to the curb near the entrance to his flat and stepped out. He crossed the narrow cobblestone street to a three-storey building. Nearby an NKVD watcher in a black sedan noted his arrival and stepped into a phone booth to make a call.

Bernie opened the door to his flat and stepped quietly inside. He went to the kitchen and poured himself a glass of milk, before sitting down at the kitchen table and looking at the newspaper.

Sabrina appeared in her nightdress from the bedroom.

"So did you find a place for Peter and Bridget?"

"Yeah, they're at Federmann's. Karl is looking after them."

"Good."

"I think they'll be safe there for a few days," Bernie said. "It's quite convenient being so close to the office."

"How are they taking it? The flat? The attempts on Peter's life?"

"I think poor Bridget has had enough, darling. She's not cut out for this kind of thing."

"No, I imagine she isn't."

It was a few minutes after closing time at the nightclub, as Federmann counted the nightly receipts in the office. The band and the showgirls had gone for the night. Josef, the barman, deposited the cashbox on the desk near Federmann and left.

Karl was drinking a glass of aquavit with his boss when there was a fierce knocking on the backdoor.

Karl went to the entrance.

"Who is it?"

"It's Josef," said the voice.

Karl unlocked the door and was just pulling it open, when it burst inward. Two NKVD thugs slammed Josef into Karl and sent both of them sprawling. Karl was still trying to get out from under Josef when a third man with striking white hair stepped inside the door and calmly shot them with a Tokarev pistol. He rushed down the hall to the office where Federmann sat wide-eyed and frozen behind his desk.

"I have money," Federmann said.

"Of course, you do," the white-haired man said as he shot *Der Grosse* between the eyes.

Sixty-eight

The noise from the nightclub entrance awakened Peter who sat up in bed. Bridget was having trouble sleeping and was already awake.

"What was that?" Peter asked.

"I don't know," Bridget said with alarm. "It sounded like an explosion."

"Get dressed, Bridget. I'll go take a look."

Peter slipped on a shirt and pants and left the bedroom. He looked through the peephole but could see nothing in the hall. He opened the door and heard the tramping of feet coming from the stairs. He locked the door and ran back to the bedroom.

"We need to get away," Peter said, stuffing his clothes in his suitcase. "There's someone coming up the stairs."

Bridget was already dressed and putting on her shoes. Peter grabbed Bridget's suitcase and his own, and headed for the door. He removed the Webley revolver from his pocket and glanced through the peephole again. In the hall he could see two large men coming out of the storage rooms on the same floor and heading his way.

Peter joined Bridget in the living room and opened a window to the street. He noticed a ledge running the length of the building.

"Come along, Bridget," Peter said, "we can get to the fire escape."

"Peter, I don't think..."

A loud banging sound came from the front door and startled them.

"Come on, Bridget," Peter ordered as he casually tossed their bags out the window and stepped out onto the ledge.

"You threw my bag out the window?"

"Don't worry about your bloody valise, Bridget, it's only three storeys. I can see it on the pavement. Let's hurry."

Bridget looks stunned by the harsh words but followed Peter out the window. They scrambled along the ledge to the fire escape at the corner of the building. Inside the flat, the banging continued as Peter and Bridget started down the fire escape. A moment later, they had collected their bags and were walking quickly down the alley towards the Legation offices.

Peter was standing near the window in the Consular Services office in his undershirt, shaving in front of a tiny mirror. He looked up and noticed an ambulance racing through the streets in the early dawn light.

"Bridget, have a look at this."

Bridget joined him at the window and they saw the ambulance disappear into a street near the nightclub.

"Those were gunshots. Someone was hurt." Bridget said, pouring water into the tea pot.

Peter finished shaving and washed his face, before putting on his shirt. He went to the phone and rang Bernie at home.

"He's not replying. I better go take a look at the nightclub."

"No, you don't," Bridget replied. "The police will be all over that building. You don't want to get mixed up in a sordid gang shootout, not after what we went through with the fire and the bloody NKVD."

"What an awful night," Peter said, "having to climb out the window like a cat burglar to get to the fire escape."

"We were lucky to get away."

"Are you hungry?"

"I'm starving," Bridget replied.

"After our tea, let's go for breakfast. I have an early meeting."

On their return to the Legation, Peter and Bridget joined the crowd of onlookers on the pavement outside the nightclub. The Stockholm police were busy removing a body from the building to a waiting ambulance.

"What happened?" Peter asked an old man standing on the perimeter of the police cordon.

"Looks like a revenge killing, sir."

"How many were killed?"

"That's the third body they've brought out," the man said. "They shot *Der Grosse* and two of his men."

Peter and Bridget were shocked by the news. This was madness, a gang shootout in peaceful Stockholm. Federmann was a wealthy man and worked with criminals, so it must have been a revenge killing. Surely nobody knew they were hiding out at the nightclub. Obviously they had been in the wrong place at the wrong time. Poor Federmann. He had generously offered them protection and now he was a victim of a violent crime.

They walked away, returning to the Legation offices. As Bridget went up the stairs to Consular Services, Peter stopped by the main reception desk.

"Has Bernie Dixon come in?"

"No, sir, not yet," the receptionist said.

"If he calls, can you put him through to my office?"

"Of course, Mr Faye. There are several people looking for him this morning."

Peter's attention was aroused.

"We have two new employees this morning. They were scheduled to have their picture taken, but Mr Dixon didn't show up. We had to give them temporary passes."

"Thank you."

"By the way, sir. There's a police officer waiting for you upstairs."

Peter took the stairs up to Consular Services. Sigge was busy with a client and Bridget was at her desk while a police detective hovered near the door. He approached Peter.

"Mr Faye, I am Inspector Dahl with the Stockholm police department. I have a few questions about that fire in your flat."

"Hello, Inspector," Peter said. "I need to look for someone. Can we step outside to talk?"

"Of course, sir."

"I'll be back shortly, Bridget."

Peter smiled at Bridget and left with the inspector.

Dahl drove Peter over to Bernie's flat, after he mentioned to the inspector that Bernie might have a few ideas about the fire. They left Dahl's car on the narrow street and climbed the stairs. Peter knocked on the door, but there was no reply.

"Bernie, it's Peter," he said in a loud voice.

Peter knocked again and tried the doorhandle. He noticed that it was unlocked. He opened the door very slowly.

"Bernie, it's Peter."

There was only silence as Peter stepped inside followed by

Inspector Dahl. He immediately noticed the books spread out across the floor in the living room and the pungent metallic smell in the flat. He then saw Bernie's lifeless body lying on his back behind the coffee table with a bloody gash across the throat. His eyes were open and his bruised and battered mouth had a sock sticking out of it.

Peter stepped back in shock as Dahl signalled for Peter to keep his distance from the body.

"Mr Faye, stay back please."

The inspector continued on through the flat going to the bedroom. He went in to take a look and suddenly ran to the bathroom to throw up.

Peter entered the bedroom to see Sabrina tied to the four corners of the bed and tortured with a knife before her throat was cut. The killers had cut off her nose and hacked her ears away. The violence was so extreme that Peter stepped away as quickly as he could. He saw Dahl, wiping his mouth with a handkerchief, as he went to the telephone to call in backup.

Peter sat alone on a wicker chair on the verandah with its potted plants at the back of the flat. He felt numb and miserable as he considered himself to be partially responsible for Bernie's death. Dahl reappeared and sat down next to him.

"My colleagues are on their way. Can you tell me anything about Mr Dixon and his wife?"

"Bernie was a good man, a very good man, Inspector Dahl. He survived the trenches in France and the war in Spain, only to be murdered in Stockholm. His wife Sabrina is Swedish. They're very fine people."

"So you think these are same people who torched your flat?" Dahl asked.

"I would think so, sir."

Sixty-nine

Bridget and Joanna were chatting over tea in the Consular Services office when Peter entered the room looking very pale.

"What happened, Peter?" Bridget asked.

"The Russians killed Bernie and Sabrina."

"Bernie? Sabrina? How?"

"They were tortured, it was not a pretty sight."

Bridget and Joanna looked aghast as Peter collapsed at his desk.

"But why, Peter?" Joanna asked. "Bernie and Sabrina, why would anybody want to kill them?"

"I don't know, Joanna," Peter said. "These people torched my flat, shot me with a tranquillizer dart, and last night I think they killed Federmann. These people are mad and very dangerous."

Peter stood up and embraced Bridget and Joanna.

"The police believe theft is the motive. Sabrina's brother told them that Bernie had a fine collection of diamonds and gold, which appears to be missing. But we know otherwise, don't we Bridget?"

"We have to get out of Stockholm," Bridget said horrified. "We can't stay here any longer."

Bridget was crying and wiping her nose, as Joanna quietly

left the room and returned to her office.

At the end of the day, Peter and Bridget got Allan to drive them over to the Grand Hotel in the Legation car. Bridget was crushed by the death of their friends and needed to rest. Allan was distraught, having worked with Bernie for several years.

"Peter, I don't understand why anyone would kill Bernie."

"Neither do we," Peter replied.

"We need to find these bastards," Allan said. "We can't let them go around killing people, can we?"

Allan couldn't stop himself from questioning them about the murder. Peter and Bridget were relieved when he left them at the hotel entrance. They felt safe walking into a public place like the lobby of the old hotel. Diplomatic staff gathered there and the hotel was immune to the violence of the street. Their plan was to leave the city in the morning and get as far away as possible.

The dining room was empty when Peter and Bridget came down at the crack of dawn. A waiter arrived bringing in tea and a plate of fresh bread rolls. They sat down with their cups of tea and ate a quick breakfast before returning to their room.

"I'll leave you to pack, Bridget. I'm going to call Anders from the lobby. Be back in a minute."

Bridget nodded and started to pack as Peter left the room. On his way down he noticed the maid service cart in the hallway. He nodded at the maid who appeared with a pile of dirty sheets.

In the lobby Peter sat in a phone booth with a glass door near the front desk. There were not many people around due to the early hour. He was talking to Anders when he glanced at the front desk and saw the Russian agent with white hair talking to the clerk. Two thickset NKVD men stood near the entrance, looking around the lobby.

"See you later, Anders. I have to go."

Peter hung up and snuck out of the phone booth heading for the elevator, holding up a hand to hide his face. The white-haired man was busy at the front desk and didn't see Peter standing near the elevator.

On the fourth floor Peter knocked on the door of room 321 and rushed inside as soon as Bridget opened the door.

"Let's go," Peter said as he grabbed their bags.

"What's going on?" Bridget said in alarm.

"They're downstairs."

Peter hustled Bridget out of the room.

Down in the lobby the agent with white hair headed towards the stairs accompanied by one of his men. At the front desk an NKVD man stood near a very nervous clerk, watching the traffic in the hall.

Peter and Bridget raced down the hallway to the elevators. They passed the maid service cart and then heard the door to the stairs opening near the elevators.

"Go back," Peter whispered to Bridget who collided with him. They ran back towards the maid service cart and stepped into the room being cleaned.

"Quick, get into the bathroom," Peter said.

The maid, who was vacuuming the room, turned to watch them as Peter put a finger to his lips demanding silence. She continued her work as they slipped into the bathroom.

"I think they may have spotted us," Peter said. "Quiet now."

From the bathroom door, they saw the Russians pass by their room and head down towards room 321. Peter pulled out the Webley revolver and waited. In the hall the white-haired agent knocked on the door and waited with a Tokarev pistol in his hand. He fumbled with a skeleton key and managed to open the door. The two men quickly searched the empty room and headed back down the hall. The man with white hair hesitated a moment at the maid service cart and looked in at the maid vacuuming the room.

Huddled together near the bathroom door, Peter and Bridget listened to the man's footsteps as he followed his colleague down the hall.

"I think they've gone, Peter," Bridget said with a sigh of relief. She was having a panic attack, trembling and breathing with difficulty.

Peter looked at Bridget with concern and shut the door.

"We'll give them five minutes," Peter said, "then we'll go out the back."

He slipped his arm around her kissing her on the mouth. She started to relax and to breathe normally. She stopped shaking and started to cry silently.

As Peter watched her struggling with her nerves, a calm resolve came over him. He thought about how much he admired her and how she represented everything that was good in the world. He loved her mouth, her hair and her fine features. They were alive and he intended to keep them alive.

He thought about Bernie, such an ordinary man but with such strength and courage in the face of adversity. Maybe it was his war experience that had hardened him. He owed it to his friend and to Bridget to be just as strong in the face of this new threat. Luck had been on their side, but it would run out soon enough. He needed to be ready to act.

Seventy

"I have the immense regret to announce that Bernie Dixon and his wife Sabrina were murdered in their flat yesterday morning," Victor Mallet said in a grave voice.

The chief had convened all the staff in the Legation boardroom.

"As you know, Bernie Dixon was a model employee here at the Legation. He had been with us for over ten years and he will be missed by everyone. He was a mainstay along with his lovely wife Sabrina, a wonderful woman. The police will be interviewing our staff over the next few days, as they attempt to find the perpetrators of this horrible crime."

Several employees looked anxiously at their chief. Peter stood next to Bridget and Joanna at the conference room door. They had come in to collect a few things before leaving town.

"Sir, are we in any danger?" a secretary asked.

"Certainly not," Mallet said. "The police seem to think it was a theft with violence. Bernie was dealing in diamonds, according to his brother-in-law. This may have attracted the criminals. At the moment we know very little."

"Bernie was a good chap," Allan said, "he was perfectly harmless. The diamonds were a hobby. He worked in the documents division in the basement. Why would anyone want to kill him?"

"I heard they were tortured, sir. Why torture Bernie and Sabrina?" asked a Swedish accountant in a heavily accented English.

"It doesn't make sense," said another woman, "everyone liked Bernie and Sabrina."

"We really have no idea," Mallet replied. "The police have offered no explanation. I will keep you informed as to plans for the funeral, but the police have still not released the bodies. I hope all of you can attend. We must stand together in these difficult times."

The meeting broke up with Joanna fleeing the room in tears. Peter and Bridget watched her go.

In Consular Services Peter poured a glass of brandy for Joanna as Bridget sat down opposite her. They had sent Sigge home and locked the door.

"What about Tikander, Joanna?" Bridget asked.

"I tipped them off. That's all I did. They wanted to know where Peter was meeting him," Joanna said with tears in her eyes.

"They tried to kill Tikander,"Bridget said, her voice rising. "Didn't you bloody well know that? Did you tip them off about Bernie too?"

"No, of course not."

"They slaughtered Bernie and Sabrina, Joanna. They tortured and killed them..."

"...to send me a message," Peter finished the sentence for her.

Joanna drank her brandy and looked at Peter.

"I know about your brother, Joanna. I was told he was a scientist on a list of communist sympathizers, but I never would have thought his sister would betray her country."

Joanna was stunned by this revelation. First Anthony Blunt had mentioned her brother, now Peter Faye. It must be in her file.

"You were tagged by the security services," Bridget said. "That's why you had only limited clearance, just enough to work for SOE."

"I never knew anything about this," Joanna said.

"What are you doing for Anthony Blunt?" Peter asked. "I know he asked for you."

"I can't tell you, Peter. Blunt swore me to secrecy."

"So it was your brother who put you up to this?"

"I won't say anymore."

Peter was frustrated by Joanna's denials and was trying to maintain some self control, but he could tell that Bridget was starting to lose it. She had been deeply shaken by the deaths of Bernie and Sabrina and her anger had fused into a blind rage.

"You bitch!" Bridget exploded, lunging for Joanna and pummelling her with her fists.

Joanna raised her hands to protect her face as Peter tried to restrain Bridget. He managed to get his arms around her and pull her away.

"You got Bernie and Sabrina killed!" Bridget shouted as Joanna cowered in her chair. "Your tears aren't worth tuppence."

Peter was amazed at how strong Bridget was. He had to pin her arms tightly against her sides until he felt her body relax.

"She's an accomplice to murder, we should have her arrested."

Peter held Bridget's gaze for a moment and then turned to Joanna.

"How do you contact them?" he asked softly.

"Tell us, you sodding bitch," Bridget yelled.

Joanna's mouth began to move.

"A woman," Joanna whispered, "she meets me after I call a number."

Peter and Bridget looked at each other as they realised that Joanna had just given them something of real value.

Anders and Stefan drove over to Bernie's flat. They climbed the stairs and stopped as the front door with its yellow police tape barring their way. While Stefan took pictures for the newspaper of the police tape on the front door, Anders returned to the street to look for Bernie's Opel. He found it a short distance from the flat. It was unlocked. He opened the door and looked for a key under the mat. The key was exactly where Peter had told him it would be. He called to Stefan who was standing in the street photographing the building.

"I'll leave it to you, Stefan. See you later."

Stefan waved and Anders got into the Opel and started the engine.

Peter trained his binoculars on the Swedish employees leaving the Soviet Legation at the end of the working day. He was sitting next to Anders in Bernie's Opel parked up the street from the front gate. In the back seat Bridget kept a lookout for nosy policemen.

"Peter, are you sure she will stop for me?" Anders asked.

"Of course she will, she'll be curious," Peter said as he looked at his watch. "She should be on her way to her meeting with Joanna about now."

Anders pulled a photograph from his briefcase.

"I borrowed this picture from a contact in Säpo. You know who that man is?"

Peter looked at a surveillance photograph of Anthony Blunt

at Tullgarn Palace.

"Nicked it, did you?"

"I prefer the term 'borrowed', Peter."

"Yes, I know who it is. He works for MI5. His name is Anthony Blunt. He works with Ewan Butler and Victor Mallet."

"I saw him again at Bernadotte's cottage in Trosa. He's out there every few days with Bernadotte and Schellenberg."

"I'm not privy to what is going on, Anders, but I surmise that Blunt's interest is the man's secret files. You know that a load of secret RSHA files recently arrived at Bromma. Schellenberg thinks he can hire out to the British or the Americans in post-war Germany."

"This is extraordinary."

"The Foreign Office wants first dibs on those files to avoid any embarrassment with our American allies when the contents are revealed. You didn't hear this from me, Anders. There's still a chance I might have a job when this is all over."

Bridget sat up suddenly.

"She's coming this way."

Peter looked up and saw Evdokia Petrov leaving the gate in a grey raincoat and scarf.

"Now, Anders," Peter said.

Anders nodded and stepped out of the car.

"Get ready, Bridget."

Bridget pulled a bottle and a rag from her handbag and slipped out of the car on the driver's side.

Anders started along the footpath towards Evdokia who didn't seem to be unduly alarmed by his presence. She had obviously seen him before at press conferences and probably recognized him as a journalist. She frowned as he approached, but made no effort to avoid him. He stopped in front of her.

"Hello, Madam Petrov. We've heard that the NKVD has been running illegal operations on Swedish soil. I am with the

Stockholms-Tidningen newspaper. Do you have a comment for the paper?"

She appeared shocked, but quickly recovered.

"No comment, please. No comment."

She started to walk away, but Anders hustled after her.

"We hear you and your husband Vladimir Petrov have been involved in serious violations of Swedish law. Your people firebombed the flat of a member of the British Legation, murdered three respectable Swedish citizens and murdered a British citizen and his Swedish wife. It's going to be in all the papers tomorrow."

In a panic Evdokia hurried away along the footpath towards Anders' car. She was so upset by his allegations that she was focussed solely on getting away from him and didn't notice Peter and Bridget until it was too late. Peter stuck a Brownie Hawkeye camera equipped with a flashbulb out the window of the car and took a picture blinding Evdokia. Bridget quickly came up behind her and slapped a rag dipped in a chloroform solution over her nose. The woman struggled briefly against Bridget but soon lost consciousness.

Peter and Bridget dragged Evdokia to the back of the car and dumped her body in the boot. Peter slammed it shut and joined Anders at the front of the car.

"Good luck, Peter, Bridget," Anders said as he gave Peter the keys to Bernie's Opel and collected the camera.

"Thanks, Anders."

Peter and Bridget then climbed into the car and waved as they drove away.

Seventy-one

Peter and Bridget drove along an isolated road near a canal, where several old freighters were tied up. It was a desolate area, wind-swept and near the open sea.

"How are you feeling?" Peter asked Bridget.

"I'm feeling elated. It felt so good to bring down that bitch."

"I am too. Let's see what we can make of it."

They drove on until Peter spotted a phone box on the road.

"Are you sure we'll be safe?" Bridget asked.

"Once we're on the boat, they'll never find us."

"I'll miss Stockholm."

"I'm sure you will."

Peter stepped out of the car and opened the boot. Evdokia started to scream.

"*Svoloch*, you bastard," Evdokia yelled.

"Hello, Mrs Petrov, I wonder what happened to you?"

"*Svoloch*."

"Now calm down, Mrs Petrov. We're stopping here so you can ring your husband."

"*Svoloch*."

"I have a very nice photograph of you with our journalist friend on the street. I am sure that your Russian colleagues in Moscow will understand perfectly, when it is published on the front page of the newspaper with the title: 'NKVD agent linked to assassination of British Legation employee'."

"Why you do this?"

"The NKVD killed my friend Bernie Dixon and his wife Sabrina. A particularly gruesome murder."

"That is not us, Mr Faye, that is Moscow," Evdokia pleaded. "They send an assassination squad."

"Who are they? I want their names."

Evdokia remained silent, refusing to comply.

"We can call your husband to have you picked up, Mrs Petrov, or we can leave you locked in the boot of the car for a few days until the journal publishes your criminal activity."

Evdokia struggled to sit up.

"There's a man with white hair. His name is Sasha. That's all I know."

"What about the kidnapping of Wilho Tikander? That was Moscow too?"

Evdokia remained silent as Peter bound her hands behind her back with wire, before pulling her roughly out of the boot.

"Come with me, we're going to talk to your husband."

Bridget remained in the car as Peter slammed the boot closed and dragged Evdokia over to the phone booth. He kept a firm grip on Evdokia's arm as he dialled the number.

"Hello, I would like to talk to Vladimir Petrov, please," Peter said into the phone.

A black car pulled up near them. Mads and Hendrik got out and went over to talk to Bridget.

" Hello, Mr Petrov. Peter Faye here. I have your lovely wife with me."

In the failing light Peter and Bridget returned to the city in the Opel, followed by Mads and Hendrik in the second car with Evdokia in the back seat.

"Let's just leave, Peter," Bridget said, "we don't have to do this."

"This man Sasha, he will not give up. The NKVD will hunt us down wherever we go," Peter said.

"If we go home, we can hide. You can return to teaching."

"I'm not going to hide, darling. I want my life back and I want them to pay for what they did to Bernie and Sabrina."

Bridget looked at Peter with a curious look.

"These people are animals," he said. "Bernie would have wanted us to do something, to strike back at them. That's the least we can do. We may not win this war but we will still have our self-esteem. And if we fail, well we might still have the option to run for it."

Bridget listened silently. She took Peter's hand in hers.

"OK, Peter. Let's do it."

Bridget thought her decision was insane. I'm the daughter of a diplomat. I don't do revenge. I don't do violence. I don't strike back against NKVD assassins. It was absurd but she felt lighthearted and at peace as she chose to help Peter accomplish his plan.

He pulled over near a restaurant in a side street off Stortorget Square in old Gamla Stan. Mads stopped his car and came over to Bridget's window.

"Hello, Peter, Bridget," Mads said. "Hendrik and I want to offer you our condolences for the loss of Bernie and his wife."

"Thank you," Peter replied.

"Bernie was a good person and a fighter."

Peter nodded his thanks at Mads.

"I'm worried about one thing, Peter," Bridget said. "How do you know they won't shoot at you?"

"Not with Evdokia next to me," Peter said. "Vladimir certainly wouldn't allow it."

"I'll be watching," Mads said.

"Listen to me, Bridget," Peter said. "We have a good plan. Mads will take good care of you. They won't dare shoot at us in the middle of a square in neutral Sweden."

Bridget embraced Peter and reluctantly got out of the car. She joined Mads who was carrying a long wooden box under his arm. Peter quickly drove away followed by Hendrik in the second car.

In a side street off the famous square, Peter waited near the car with Evdokia dressed in a grey raincoat. Her head was covered with a black cloth bag. The street lights had come on and a car came to a stop on the opposite side of the square. Two men left the vehicle.

Peter recognized one of the men as the NKVD head of station, Major Vladimir Petrov, in a business suit and a fedora. He led the way into the square followed by a second man wearing a workman's cap over his white hair. They advanced towards Peter and Evdokia who approached from a side street. Hendrik was nowhere to be seen.

The hand-off was to happen in the middle of the square. Evdokia stumbled badly on the cobblestones in her heels and grabbed Peter's arm to support herself as they stopped in the middle of the square. Peter brought up his Webley revolver to show the Russians he was taking no chances with Evdokia.

"Mr Faye. Thank you so much for bringing my wife," Vladimir said. "Why have you put a bag on her head?"

"To shut the bitch up, Mr Petrov."

"Ha, ha. You have a sense of humour, I think. You don't intend to shoot her, do you?"

"Maybe I will, Mr Petrov. The woman is a lot of trouble."

"Please don't, Mr Faye. Evdokia is very dear to me."

"Is this your man Sasha?"

"Yes, this is Sasha from Moscow."

"Tell him to hold up his arms while you search him."

Vladimir searched Sasha who grinned at Peter as he put his hands on his head.

"He's unarmed, Mr Faye. We take no risk with my wife's safety. We're good."

"You will not live long, Mr Faye," Sasha said. "You remember your friend Bernie Dixon. He screamed like a pig. We do the same to you."

"*Zatknis, Sasha.* Shut up, he has my wife," Vladimir said.

"Send him over, Petrov."

Vladimir pushed Sasha forward. The man grinned, stumbling forward like the whole thing was a joke showing his empty hands. All of a sudden, he pulled a stiletto from his sleeve and put the knife very close to Peter's ashen face.

"Don't move, Mr Faye," Sasha said. "Give me your gun. My men have you covered."

On the second floor of the darkened restaurant overlooking the square, Bridget was seized by fright. Peter's prisoner exchange was unravelling before her eyes.

"He's got a knife, Mads," Bridget said.

She could clearly see Sasha holding a knife on Peter.

"Shoot the bastard, Mads."

Bridget and Mads had watched the events unfold from a table where Mads has installed his Soviet M/91-30 sniper rifle with a scope. At this distance Mads could easily take out Sasha with a head shot.

Seventy-two

In the square Peter glanced briefly at Mads and Bridget on the second floor of the restaurant. He was unarmed and Sasha was holding a knife to his throat.

"You have white hair like an old man," Peter said, taunting the Russian.

"The white hair," Sasha said. "You like it? It's in the genes, Mr Faye."

"Let's get this over, Sasha," Vladimir said.

"How many innocent people have you killed?" Peter asked with feigned interest.

"No one is innocent," Sasha said. "They all deserved to die."

"Why did you kill Federmann and his men?"

"You mean that fat Nazi and his friends."

"They didn't deserve to die."

"Enough time wasting, Mr Faye," Sasha said. "Let's get this over with. Remove the head covering from the woman."

"Of course."

On the second floor of the restaurant Bridget was terrified.

"I can't make the shot," Mads said with his finger on the trigger. "The Russian is standing too close to Peter."

"Shoot him, Mads, please."

Bridget could hardly bear to see the denouement of the confrontation, her fear was so great.

"He's lifting his hand, Bridget, Peter is lifting his hand."

Bridget stared at Peter in the square as he raised his hand to touch the top of Evdokia's head.

Peter started to pull the black bag from Evdokia's head. Sasha had stepped back to observe the woman as Peter gave a sharp tug to the bag. The surprise was total. Sasha and Vladimir were looking at a man in Evdokia's grey coat, wearing women's stockings and shoes. From behind his back Hendrik brought up a Suomi submachine gun and fired into Sasha's chest on full automatic blasting him clear off his feet like a rag doll. He turned the gun on Vladimir who ran for his car.

Peter quickly recovered his Webley from the dead Russian and pulled Hendrik over to the monument in the middle of the square as gunshots pinged off the cobblestones. Hendrik turned his gun on Sasha's henchmen, wounding one of the men firing from the shadows. The second man escaped as Vladimir raced his car out of the square into the narrow streets.

From the second floor of the restaurant, Bridget ran downstairs and out into the square, followed by Mads with his long rifle. Bridget joined Peter and Hendrik at the monument.

"Are you all right?" Bridget asked.

"We're fine," Peter said, embracing Bridget.

Mads crossed the square with the sniper rifle safely back in its box. Together they hurried out of the square. They stopped at Mads' car and opened the boot where Evdokia waited with a rag stuffed in her mouth. Hendrik pulled out the rag and helped Evdokia out, untying her hands.

"Where's my husband?" Evdokia asked and then looked at Hendrik in her raincoat.

"That's my coat, you bastard."

Hendrik struggled to remove Evdokia's raincoat which was tight around the shoulders. Peter helped him out of the coat.

"He took off after the shooting, I'm afraid," Peter said.

"You killed Sasha?" Evdokia asked as she collected her coat.

"Yes, he's dead."

"Very good, that man is the devil."

"We've got to go now," Mads said, "the police are on their way."

"Tell your husband when you see him that I kept my part of the bargain," Peter said. "Now go."

Evdokia nodded and ran off into the night as Peter and Bridget climbed into the Opel. Mads and Hendrik jumped into the second vehicle and the two cars drove away.

At the main dock in Nynäshamn, Peter and Bridget climbed aboard a Swedish fishing vessel with their bags and waved to Mads and Hendrik on the dock. Captain Ludvig was in a hurry to be off and the boat started to pull away from the dock.

"Peter, Bridget. The captain will take you as far as Karlskrona where you will catch another boat to Copenhagen. Have a nice trip. Remember to visit us in Finland."

Hendrik tried to pass a bottle of Swedish aquavit to Peter, but finally had to toss it over the gunwale. Peter struggled to catch the bottle.

"A present for you, Peter," Mads said.

"For my nerves?" Peter asked.

Mads nodded.

"Aquavit cures every ill."

HISTORICAL NOTES

A large part of this story is true. A few names have been changed, but the fiction has followed the facts quite closely. To facilitate the telling of this story, I have folded the events between August 1943 and May 1945 into a single year and have given myself some liberty with the dates.

The story of the surveillance of Dr Karl-Heinz Kramer by British SIS intelligence officer Peter Falk (name changed to Peter Faye) and his secretary Bridget Pope (name changed to Bridget Potter) is true. The Kramer maid (Hanne) really existed and went by the name '*Frau H12*' (agent 36704) and her Austrian friend (Elsa) by the name '*Frau E*'. The stories of Ewan Butler, Peter Tennant (name changed to Michael Tennant), Legation Chief Victor Mallet (the 'angry rabbit' was his nickname), *S.D. Brigadeführer* Walter Schellenberg and Anthony Blunt have been described in the history books of the period.

The same goes for the 'White Buses' adventure involving Count Folke Bernadotte, Colonel Gottfrid Björck and the Neuengamme concentration camp. The Norwegian doctor Bjorn Heger and the social worker Wanda Maria Hjort Heger were real characters. The stories of Colonel Hallamaa of the Finnish RTK, the Japanese General Onodera, the Soviet Ambassador Alexandra Kollontai, the NKVD agents Vladimir and Evdokia Petrov (who later defected to Australia) and the Estonian Saarson are mostly based on fact. Of course, the Swedish journalist Anders Berger, his wife Britta, Rolf Lagerman, the Finns Mads and Hendrik, the British Documents Officer Bernie Dixon, his wife Sabrina and father-in-law Aksell are entirely fictional.

It is hard to imagine how British intelligence could remain unaware of the Soviet penetration of their agencies during the last years of the war. The Soviet counter-intelligence expert, Elena Modrzhinskaya, who was in charge of assessing intelligence material produced by the 'Cambridge Five' - Kim Philby, Donald Maclean, Guy Burgess, Anthony Blunt and John Cairncross - actually doubted the veracity of the information provided by the British spies. She felt that the SIS had to be complete fools not to notice the suitcases full of documents leaving their offices. She couldn't believe that the SIS had overlooked Philby's communist wife, Litzi Friedman. She thought that they were all double agents working for the British.

Clearly there was sufficient evidence to suspect that Philby and Blunt were spies, that they had been recruited by Arnold Deutsch (code-name Otto) and Edith Suschitzky during the 1930s. Philby and Blunt were particularly agitated to learn that British negotiations with Schellenberg might provide the SIS with an immense treasure trove of German intelligence on Soviet spies working in Britain.

During those early post-war days in Stockholm, the British and Americans became bitter rivals for the secret Nazi files under SS control. Unfortunately for the British, Schellenberg decided at the last moment to deal with the Americans and was flown to the US Army Intelligence Centre in Frankfurt on June 17, 1945, in an American Dakota with six zinc-lined trunks filled with files. He was well received by the Americans, but feared that the British might renege on their secret offer of immunity from prosecution. The British were very upset to lose Schellenberg and Anthony Blunt sent Kim Philby to Frankfurt to interrogate him. In early July Philby was allowed two days of talks with the prisoner, after having refused to permit an FBI officer to sit in on their discussions. It is believed that Philby learned enough to establish what the Americans had gotten from Schellenberg and to reconfirm the British understanding of their agreement.

The 'Sonia' in our story was Ursula Hamburger Beurton Kuczynski, a German communist, also known as Ruth Werner. She worked as a courier in 1943 for Klaus Fuchs and Melita Norwood and was responsible for providing Stalin with proof that Britain and the US were secretly working on a nuclear bomb. She was a housewife living in Oxford and mother of three children. She met secretly with the nuclear scientist Fuchs in and around Oxfordshire. Fuchs was given security clearance to work at the Los Alamos laboratories in the US and at Harwell in England. He was eventually arrested in 1949 and put on trial. Meanwhile Sonia fled to East Berlin in March 1950 to avoid arrest. The 'Elli' in our story was long suspected to be Sir Roger Hollis who was head of MI5 from 1956-65. Hollis was believed to have met with Sonia in Shanghai in the 1930s. It was Hollis who cleared Fuchs for work in nuclear research despite evidence of the scientist's political leanings and association with known communists.

It wasn't until 1961 that an official investigation of Philby was launched and 1963 in the case of Blunt. Philby eventually confessed to spying, but avoided arrest by escaping on a Soviet freighter from Beirut in January 1963. In a 1981 lecture to the Stasi in East Germany, Philby gave two reasons for the failure of the British Secret Service to unmask him: the first was the British class system which found it inconceivable that one 'born into the ruling class of the British Empire' would be a traitor; the second was the fact that so many in MI6 had so much to lose if he was proven to be a spy.

ACKNOWLEDGEMENTS

I would like to thank my wife Andrée Tousignant, son Thomas Kinsey, my editor Doug Sutherland and everyone else who believed in this adventure and provided assistance.